I0020353

Data Science for Malware Analysis

A comprehensive guide to using AI in detection, analysis, and compliance

Shane Molinari

BIRMINGHAM—MUMBAI

Data Science for Malware Analysis

Group Product Manager: Pavan Ramchandani

Publishing Product Manager: Neha Sharma

Senior Editors: Sujata Tripathi and Runcil Rebello

Technical Editor: Nithik Cheruvakodan

Copy Editor: Safis Editing

Project Coordinator: Uma Devi Lakshmikant

Proofreader: Safis Editing

Indexer: Manju Arasan

Production Designer: Alishon Mendonca

Marketing Coordinators: Marylou De Mello and Shruthi Shetty

First published: December 2023

Production reference: 2141124

Published by Packt Publishing Ltd.

Grosvenor House

11 St Paul's Square

Birmingham

B3 1RB

ISBN 978-1-80461-864-6

www.packtpub.com

This book is dedicated to the brave men and women in cybersecurity who work tirelessly behind the scenes, ensuring our digital worlds are safe and secure. To my mentors, who taught me the essence of threat management, and to all cybersecurity professionals and the next generation of cyber warriors who will stand guard in this evolving landscape.

– Shane Molinari

Foreword

As a privacy expert heavily involved in the intersection of law and technology, I found *Data Science for Malware Analysis: A comprehensive guide to detection, analysis, and compliance* to be a game-changing resource. The book offers an unparalleled deep dive into the intricacies of malware and data science, demystifying complex topics in a manner that is accessible yet substantive.

What sets this book apart is its multifaceted approach to cybersecurity, integrating legal, technological, and analytical perspectives. It goes beyond the typical fear-mongering around cyber threats to offer actionable insights and solutions, informed by data science. As someone who advises organizations on complying with GDPR and CCPA, I particularly appreciated the nuanced discussions around these regulations and their global impact on cybersecurity measures.

Shane Molinari's extensive experience in cyber risk and data protection is evident on every page. He manages to blend theoretical frameworks with practical applications seamlessly, making the book both an educational guide and a practical manual. It serves as a phenomenal reference tool for framing discussions with clients and colleagues and within the legal community.

In an age where privacy and security concerns are not just the purview of IT departments but also should be integrated into every aspect of business strategy and legal compliance, this book is a must-read. Whether you're a cybersecurity professional, a data science enthusiast, or a legal expert navigating the evolving landscape of cyber law, *Data Science for Malware Analysis* is an indispensable addition to your library.

Jim Packer, JD, MBA, CIPP, CISSP

Principal, Data Privacy & Governance

What the experts say

As a software quality engineer, I often see security measures being sidelined. *Data Science for Malware Analysis* is a game-changer, blending cybersecurity with data science in a digestible format. Shane Molinari's deep experience in cyber risk is evident, offering practical insights perfect for integrating into QA-testing paradigms. The book's discussions on GDPR and CCPA compliance are also invaluable. Clear, concise, and technically sound, this guide is a must-read for anyone looking to enhance their cybersecurity know-how while maintaining software quality. Highly recommended!

Ganna Makarkina

Software Quality Engineer

Find out what you have been missing! I don't claim to be a cybersecurity expert, but as a marketing professional, the nexus between cybersecurity and data analytics has never been clearer thanks to *Data Science for Malware Analysis*. Shane Molinari provides an indispensable roadmap for understanding the cybersecurity landscape in an increasingly data-driven world. I have personally known Shane for many years and his authority and command of knowledge and expertise in this area is evident. His integrity is beyond reproach. His discussions on GDPR and CCPA are especially helpful, providing a robust framework for risk management in marketing strategies. The book's clear and actionable insights make it an essential read for anyone tasked with safeguarding brand integrity in the digital age. You don't want to miss out on Shane's unique expertise.

Ezio Sabatino, CCP, CEIP

Sabatino Marketing

Chief Influence Officer – Ethical Influence & Persuasion

Contributors

About the author

Shane Molinari is a cyber-threat management veteran with over 20 years of experience in the military, Department of Defense, and civilian sectors. As an authority in the cyber-risk industry, he brings a nuanced understanding of data science's role in combating malware. Shane holds degrees focusing on engineering and systems design, respectively. A **Certified Information Systems Security Professional** (**CISSP**), he's penned thought leadership articles and has been a featured speaker on cybersecurity podcasts. His diverse experience spans from implementing business continuity programs to advising Fortune 500 companies on navigating data privacy regulations such as GDPR and CCPA. This book is an amalgamation of Shane's in-depth knowledge of data science applications and malware defense techniques, designed to serve as a practical manual for bolstering day-to-day cyber resilience.

About the reviewers

Zhassulan Zhussupov is a professional wearing many hats – a software developer, a cybersecurity enthusiast, and a mathematician. He has been developing products for law enforcement agencies for more than nine years. Professionally, Zhassulan lends his expertise as a cybersecurity researcher to Websec B.V. in the Netherlands and Cyber 5w in the USA. He is also an active contributor to the Malpedia project. Zhassulan's literary achievements include authoring the *MD MZ* e-book, the details of which can be found on his personal GitHub page. He is also the proud founder of MSSP Lab. He has been a speaker at various international conferences (Black Hat and many more). His love for his family reflects in his roles as a loving husband and a doting father.

I'd like to thank my family and friends who understand the time and commitment it takes to research. Working in this field would not be possible without the supportive malware analyst and threat hunter community that has developed over the last several years. Thank you to all of the trailblazers who make this field an exciting place to work in each and every day. We are grateful for everything you do!

Reginald Wong has worked as a malware reverse engineer for more than 20 years. He has performed and taught malware analysis in top companies such as Trend Micro, ThreatTrack, and IBM Security. He received a BSc in electronics and communications engineering from Saint Louis University. He is currently employed by Halcyon, a fast-growing cybersecurity company that develops tools to protect clients from ransomware. He is the author of the *Mastering Reverse Engineering* book, which teaches readers how to start reverse-engineering software.

Terrence Williams has successfully navigated the cybersecurity world through the lenses of the U.S. Marine Corps, Amazon, Meta, and Google, with more than 10 years of experience in the field. Terrence obtained a Bachelor of Science in computer science from Saint Leo University and is pursuing a master's in computer science at Vanderbilt University. He learned the arts of data science during multiple investigations for several large-scale companies. Terrence has a passion for working at the intersection of data science, digital forensics, and incident response.

Table of Contents

Part 1– Introduction

1

Malware Science Life Cycle Overview   3

2

An Overview of the International History of Cyber Malware Impacts 19

Part 2 – The Current State of Key Malware Science AI Technologies

3

Topological Data Analysis for Malware Detection and Analysis   49

4

Artificial Intelligence for Malware Data Analysis and Detection   73

5

Behavior-Based Malware Data Analysis and Detection   105

Part 3 – The Future State of AI's Use for Malware Science

6

The Future State of Malware Data Analysis and Detection   137

7

The Future State of Key International Compliance Requirements   159

8

Epilogue – A Harmonious Overture to the Future of Malware Science and Cybersecurity   179

Preface

In an age where our digital lives are expanding at an unprecedented pace, cybersecurity is a growing concern. Malware is more than a fleeting nuisance; it's a complex field requiring a nuanced, multi-layered defense strategy.

This book sits at the intersection of cybersecurity and data science, offering a comprehensive guide to understanding and combating malware. Drawing from my 20+ years of experience in military and civilian cyber-threat management, I aim to make this complex subject matter accessible to cybersecurity professionals and data science enthusiasts alike.

The book comprises seven focused chapters and an epilogue, each contributing to a multi-faceted understanding of malware.

The examples and case studies peppered throughout are designed for real-world application, aiming to arm you with the knowledge and tools to enhance your cyber resilience.

I owe a debt of gratitude to my industry peers and the many researchers whose work forms the foundation of this book. Their critiques and encouragement have been invaluable.

Whether you are a seasoned cybersecurity expert, a student of data science, or someone who is keen to understand modern digital threats, this book aims to serve as a practical guide.

Thank you for investing your time in reading *Data Science for Malware Analysis*. Together, let's build a safer digital future.

Who this book is for

Targeted at a range of professionals and enthusiasts, *Data Science for Malware Analysis* is essential for cybersecurity experts keen on adopting data-driven defense methods. Data scientists will find value in applying their skill set to this pressing security issue. Compliance officers navigating global regulations such as GDPR and CCPA will gain indispensable insights. Academic researchers exploring the intersection of data science and cybersecurity, IT decision-makers overseeing organizational strategy, and tech enthusiasts eager to understand modern cybersecurity can all benefit.

What this book covers

Chapter 1, *Malware Science Life Cycle Overview*, is an introduction to malware's life cycle stages, challenges, and applicable data science techniques.

Chapter 2, *An Overview of the International History of Cyber Malware Impacts*, gives a look at the evolving landscape of cyber threats and global countermeasures, emphasizing data science's role.

Chapter 3, *Topological Data Analysis for Malware Detection and Analysis*, is an exploration of how topology data analysis can unearth patterns in malware behavior.

Chapter 4, *Artificial Intelligence for Malware Data Analysis and Detection*, is a discussion on AI's capabilities for automating malware analysis and detection.

Chapter 5, *Behavior-Based Malware Data Analysis and Detection*, is an insight into behavior-based analysis techniques for identifying malicious activities.

Chapter 6, *The Future State of Malware Data Analysis and Detection*, is an examination of upcoming trends and challenges in malware analysis.

Chapter 7, *The Future State of Key International Compliance Requirements*, is a review of the regulatory landscape and organizational compliance steps for GDPR and CCPA.

Chapter 8, *Epilogue – A Harmonious Overture to the Future of Malware Science and Cybersecurity*, metaphorically compares the evolving field of malware science to a symphony, emphasizing its role as a proactive and dynamic defense against the ever-changing landscape of cybersecurity threats.

Get in touch

Feedback from our readers is always welcome.

General feedback: If you have questions about any aspect of this book, email us at `customercare@packtpub.com` and mention the book title in the subject of your message.

Errata: Although we have taken every care to ensure the accuracy of our content, mistakes do happen. If you have found a mistake in this book, we would be grateful if you would report this to us. Please visit `www.packtpub.com/support/errata` and fill in the form.

Piracy: If you come across any illegal copies of our works in any form on the internet, we would be grateful if you would provide us with the location address or website name. Please contact us at `copyright@packt.com` with a link to the material.

If you are interested in becoming an author: If there is a topic that you have expertise in and you are interested in either writing or contributing to a book, please visit `authors.packtpub.com`.

Share Your Thoughts

Once you've read *Data Science for Malware Analysis*, we'd love to hear your thoughts! Scan the QR code below to go straight to the Amazon review page for this book and share your feedback.

`https://packt.link/r/1804618640`

Your review is important to us and the tech community and will help us make sure we're delivering excellent quality content.

Download a free PDF copy of this book

Thanks for purchasing this book!

Do you like to read on the go but are unable to carry your print books everywhere?

Is your eBook purchase not compatible with the device of your choice?

Don't worry, now with every Packt book you get a DRM-free PDF version of that book at no cost.

Read anywhere, any place, on any device. Search, copy, and paste code from your favorite technical books directly into your application.

The perks don't stop there, you can get exclusive access to discounts, newsletters, and great free content in your inbox daily

Follow these simple steps to get the benefits:

1. Scan the QR code or visit the link below

https://packt.link/free-ebook/9781804618646

2. Submit your proof of purchase
3. That's it! We'll send your free PDF and other benefits to your email directly

Part 1– Introduction

To understand the technologies used today and what is expected in the future, we will cover an overview of malware science and key international drivers for leveraging AI to better manage the cyber-threat landscape.

This part has the following chapters:

- *Chapter 1, Malware Science Life Cycle Overview*
- *Chapter 2, An Overview of the International History of Cyber Malware Impacts*

1
Malware Science Life Cycle Overview

Malicious software (**malware**) is a type of software that is designed to harm, exploit, or gain unauthorized access to computer systems, networks, and mobile devices. Malware can take many different forms and can be spread through various means, such as email attachments, infected websites, and infected software downloads:

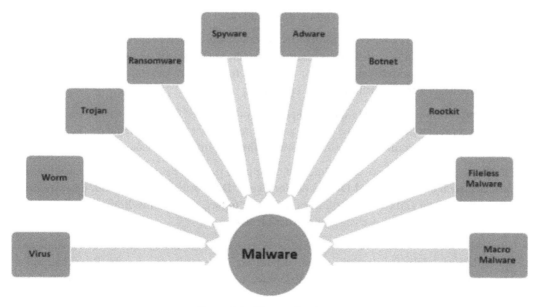

Figure 1.1 – Types of malware

These include viruses, worms, Trojans, ransomware, spyware, adware, botnets, rootkits, fileless malware, and macro malware. Let's take a closer look:

- **Viruses**: A computer virus is a type of malware that is capable of replicating itself and infecting other programs on a computer. Once a virus has infected a system, it can cause damage by deleting or corrupting files, stealing data, or disrupting system operations. A virus typically requires user action, such as opening an infected email attachment or downloading a malicious file, to spread to other systems.

- **Worms**: A computer worm is a type of malware that can spread itself over networks and the internet without requiring user action. Worms can quickly infect large numbers of systems and can cause significant damage by consuming network bandwidth, deleting files, and spreading other types of malware.

- **Trojans**: A Trojan is a type of malware that appears to be legitimate software but contains malicious code that can be used to gain unauthorized access to a system or steal sensitive data. Trojans can be spread through email attachments, infected websites, and other means.

- **Ransomware**: Ransomware is a type of malware that encrypts a victim's files and demands payment in exchange for the decryption key. Ransomware can be extremely damaging as it can cause the loss of important data and disrupt business operations. Ransomware can be spread through email attachments, infected websites, and other means.

- **Spyware**: Spyware is a type of malware that is designed to gather information about a victim's computer usage and transmit it to a remote server. Spyware can be used to steal sensitive data, track online activity, and monitor user behavior. Spyware can be spread through email attachments, infected websites, and other means.

- **Adware**: Adware is a type of malware that displays unwanted advertisements or popups on a victim's computer. Adware can be used to generate revenue for the attacker and can be extremely annoying for the victim. Adware can be spread through infected websites and other means.

- **Botnets**: A botnet is a network of infected computers that can be used to launch coordinated attacks, such as **Distributed Denial-of-Service (DDoS)** attacks. Botnets can be extremely difficult to detect and can cause significant damage to targeted systems. Botnets can be spread through infected emails, websites, and other means.

- **Rootkits**: A rootkit is a type of malware that is designed to hide its presence on a system and provide a backdoor for attackers to gain unauthorized access to the system. Rootkits can be extremely difficult to detect and can be used to steal sensitive data, modify system configurations, and execute other types of malware.

- **Fileless malware**: Fileless malware is a type of malware that is designed to run in memory and avoid detection by traditional antivirus and anti-malware software. Fileless malware can be used to steal sensitive data, modify system configurations, and execute other types of malware.

- **Macro malware**: Macro malware is a type of malware that is embedded in macros within Microsoft Office documents. Macro malware can be spread through email attachments and infected documents and can be used to steal sensitive data and execute other types of malware.

Each type of malware has characteristics and effects, and attackers may use a combination of different types of malware in their attacks. As malware attacks become more sophisticated and complex, individuals and organizations need to remain vigilant and adopt best practices for protecting against malware infections.

In this chapter, we will cover the following topics:

- Combining malware
- Managing malware

Combining malware

Cyber attackers have become increasingly sophisticated in their approach to infiltrating computer systems, and one tactic that has become increasingly popular is combining different types of malware in their attacks. This technique enables attackers to launch complex and coordinated attacks that can be difficult to detect and block. The following diagram depicts a simplistic example of combining separate malware:

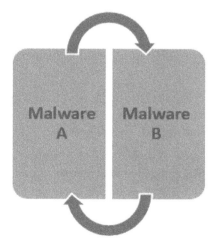

Figure 1.2 – Malware combinations

By using multiple types of malware, attackers can exploit different vulnerabilities in a target's defenses, making it more difficult for security controls to detect and block the attack.

Let's dive deeper and review some typical malware combinations that can be used by bad actors.

Worms and Trojans combination

Worms are a type of malware that is designed to spread over networks and the internet without requiring any user interaction. Once a worm infects a system, it can replicate itself and spread to other systems on the network. Trojans, on the other hand, are a type of malware that appears to be legitimate software but contains malicious code. Once a Trojan infects a system, it can be used to gain unauthorized access to the system or steal sensitive data.

An attacker might use a worm to gain initial access to a network because it can spread quickly and easily. Once the worm has infected one system, it can quickly spread to others, giving the attacker access to multiple systems. The attacker can then use a Trojan to create a backdoor for future access to the network. A backdoor is a hidden entry point into a system that allows an attacker to bypass security controls and gain unauthorized access to the system.

The use of a worm and a Trojan in combination can be very effective for an attacker because it allows them to gain access to a network quickly and create a backdoor for future access. Once the attacker has access to the network, they can use spyware to gather information about the network and its users. This information can be used to launch a targeted ransomware attack, which can be very profitable for the attacker.

Once the attacker has gained access to the network, they may use spyware to gather sensitive information about the network and its users.

Ransomware and spyware combination

Ransomware and spyware are two types of malware that attackers often use in combination to maximize the damage they can inflict on a target.

Ransomware encrypts a victim's files and the attacker places demands for payment in exchange for the decryption key. Ransomware attacks have become commonplace recently as attackers have realized the potential for financial gain by holding victim's files hostage.

Attackers use ransomware for a variety of reasons. One common use of ransomware is to extort money from victims by encrypting their files and demanding payment in exchange for the decryption key. The attackers may threaten to delete the victim's files if they do not pay the ransom, creating a sense of urgency and fear that can motivate victims to pay.

Another use of ransomware is to disrupt the operations of a target, such as a business or government agency. By encrypting the victim's files, attackers can cause significant disruption and damage to the victim's operations, potentially causing financial loss or reputational damage.

Ransomware can also be used to steal sensitive information from the victim. Some types of ransomware are designed to exfiltrate data from the victim's system before encrypting it, allowing attackers to steal sensitive information and use it for nefarious purposes.

There are several different types of ransomware, each with its characteristics and methods of operation. One common type of ransomware is **locker** ransomware, which locks the victim out of their system or specific files, such as a web browser or desktop. Another type of ransomware is **crypto** ransomware, which encrypts the victim's files and demands payment in exchange for the decryption key. Other types of ransomware may use different methods of attack, such as exploiting vulnerabilities in software or tricking victims into downloading and installing malware.

Ransomware attacks can be very disruptive and costly for victims. In addition to the direct financial cost of paying the ransom, victims may also incur indirect costs, such as lost productivity, reputational damage, and legal fees. Ransomware attacks can also result in the loss of sensitive data, which can have serious consequences for individuals as well as organizations.

Spyware, on the other hand, is a type of malware that is designed to gather information about a victim's computer usage and transmit it to a remote server. Spyware can be used for a variety of purposes, such as stealing passwords, monitoring web browsing activity, or recording keystrokes. Attackers use spyware to gain access to sensitive information about a victim, such as financial information, passwords, or personal data.

One common use of spyware is to steal passwords and other sensitive information. Spyware can be used to record keystrokes or capture screenshots of a victim's computer activity, allowing attackers to steal passwords, credit card numbers, and other sensitive data. This information can be used by attackers to commit identity theft or financial fraud.

Another use of spyware is to monitor a victim's web browsing activity. Spyware can be used to track the websites that a victim visits, the searches that they perform, and the online purchases that they make. This information can be used by attackers to build a profile of the victim and target them with personalized phishing attacks.

Spyware can also be used to record audio and video from a victim's computer system. This type of spyware can be used to monitor a victim's conversations, record video of their computer screen, or capture images from their webcam. This information can be used by attackers for blackmail or other nefarious purposes.

There are several different types of spyware, each with its characteristics and methods of operation. One common type of spyware is a **keylogger**, which is used to record keystrokes on a victim's system. Another type of spyware is a **screen capture** tool, which is used to capture screenshots of a victim's computer activity. Other types of spyware can be used to monitor web browsing activity, record audio and video, or perform other types of surveillance.

Spyware can be very difficult to detect and remove as it often operates in the background and does not display any visible symptoms. However, there are some signs that a system may be infected with spyware, such as unusual system behavior, unexplained network activity, or changes to system settings.

In addition to the direct financial cost of spyware attacks, victims may also incur indirect costs, such as lost productivity, reputational damage, and legal fees. Spyware attacks can also result in the loss of sensitive data, which can have serious consequences for individuals as well as organizations.

The combination of ransomware and spyware can be particularly devastating for a victim. Not only are their files encrypted and inaccessible, but the attacker also has access to sensitive information that can be used for further attacks or extortion. This tactic can be very effective because the attacker can threaten to release the sensitive data if the victim does not pay the ransom. The victim may feel compelled to pay the ransom to prevent the release of their sensitive information, even if they have backups of their data.

Botnets and DDoS attacks combination

A botnet is a network of computers that have been infected with malware and are under the control of a remote attacker. The term "botnet" is derived from the words "robot" and "network," as the infected computers are often referred to as "bots" or "zombies."

Once a computer has been infected with malware and becomes part of a botnet, it can be controlled remotely by the attacker. The attacker can use the botnet to carry out a variety of malicious activities, such as launching DDoS attacks, sending spam emails, and stealing sensitive information.

DDoS attacks are a type of cyber-attack in which an attacker attempts to overwhelm a target's website or network with a massive amount of traffic. By flooding the target with traffic, the attacker can make the website or network inaccessible to legitimate users. DDoS attacks can be very effective for attackers because they can cause significant damage with relatively little effort.

DDoS attacks are typically launched using a botnet, which is a network of computers that have been infected with malware and are under the control of a remote attacker. The attacker can use the botnet to generate a large amount of traffic and make it difficult for the target to mitigate the attack. The most common type of DDoS attack is the volumetric attack, in which the attacker floods the target's network with a massive amount of traffic. This traffic can be generated in a variety of ways, such as by using a botnet, or by using a network of compromised servers or other devices.

DDoS attacks can be used for a variety of reasons. Some attackers use DDoS attacks as a form of protest, such as to target websites of organizations they disagree with. Other attackers use DDoS attacks as a smokescreen to distract from other malicious activities, such as stealing data or installing malware. DDoS attacks can also be used to extort money from a target, by threatening to continue the attack unless a ransom is paid.

To launch a successful DDoS attack, the attacker must first identify vulnerabilities in the target's defenses. This can be done through a variety of methods, such as scanning the target's network for vulnerabilities or using social engineering techniques to gain access to the target's systems.

Once the attacker has identified vulnerabilities in the target's defenses, they can begin to launch the DDoS attack. This typically involves using a botnet to flood the target's website or network with traffic. The traffic generated by the botnet can be very difficult to distinguish from legitimate traffic, making it difficult for the target to mitigate the attack.

DDoS attacks can cause significant damage to a target, both in terms of financial loss and damage to reputation. If a website or network is inaccessible for an extended period, it can cause significant financial harm to the target. DDoS attacks can also damage a target's reputation as users may perceive the target as being unable to provide reliable services.

An attacker might use a botnet to launch a DDoS attack against a target's website or network. By overwhelming the target with traffic, the attacker can disrupt operations and cause significant damage.

Rootkits and fileless malware combination

A rootkit is a type of malware that is designed to hide its presence on a victim's computer system. Rootkits are often used by attackers to maintain long-term access to a system, steal sensitive information, or launch other types of attacks.

A rootkit can be thought of as a "cloaking device" for malware as it is designed to hide the malware's presence from the victim and security software. A rootkit can be installed on a system in a variety of ways, such as by exploiting a vulnerability in software or by tricking the victim into downloading and installing the malware.

Once a rootkit has been installed on a system, it can be very difficult to detect and remove. This is because the rootkit is designed to be invisible to the victim and security software. The rootkit can also be designed to have a very low profile, consuming very little system resources and avoiding activities that might trigger alerts from security software.

Attackers use rootkits for a variety of reasons. One common use of rootkits is to maintain long-term access to a victim's system. By hiding their presence on the system, attackers can continue to access the system, even if the victim installs security software or takes other measures to protect their system.

Another use of rootkits is to steal sensitive information from the victim. Rootkits can be used to log keystrokes, capture screenshots, or record audio and video from the victim's system. This information can be used by attackers to steal passwords, financial information, or other sensitive data.

Rootkits can also be used to launch other types of attacks, such as DDoS attacks or malware distribution. By using a rootkit to hide their presence on a system, attackers can launch attacks without being detected.

There are several different types of rootkits, each with its characteristics and methods of operation. User-level rootkits operate at the same level as the user's applications and are used to hide malware from the user and security software. Kernel-level rootkits operate at a lower level, within the operating system's kernel, and can be used to hide malware from security software that runs at a higher level. Bootkits are a type of rootkit that infects the boot process of a computer, making it very difficult to detect and remove.

Rootkits can be very difficult to detect and remove, but there are some signs that a system may be infected with a rootkit. These signs include unusual system behavior, such as slow performance or crashes, unexplained network activity, or unexplained changes to system settings. However, these signs can also be caused by other types of malware or by legitimate software, so it can be difficult to determine if a system is truly infected with a rootkit.

Fileless malware is a type of malware that is designed to operate entirely in memory, without leaving any files on the victim's computer system. Unlike traditional malware, which installs files on a victim's system that can be detected and removed, fileless malware can be very difficult to detect and remove.

Attackers use fileless malware for a variety of reasons. One common use of fileless malware is to maintain long-term access to a victim's system. By operating entirely in memory, fileless malware can be very difficult to detect and remove, allowing attackers to maintain access to the system even if the victim installs security software or takes other measures to protect their system.

Another use of fileless malware is to steal sensitive information from the victim. Fileless malware can be used to log keystrokes, capture screenshots, or record audio and video from the victim's system. This information can be used by attackers to steal passwords, financial information, or other sensitive data.

Fileless malware can also be used to launch other types of attacks, such as DDoS attacks or malware distribution. By operating entirely in memory, fileless malware can be used to launch attacks without leaving any trace on the victim's system.

There are several different types of fileless malware, each with its characteristics and methods of operation. In-memory malware is a type of fileless malware that operates entirely in memory and does not leave any files on the victim's system. Macros and scripts are another type of fileless malware that can be used to execute malicious code on a victim's system.

Fileless malware can be very difficult to detect and remove, but there are some signs that a system may be infected with fileless malware. These signs include unusual system behavior, such as slow performance or crashes, unexplained network activity, or unexplained changes to system settings. However, these signs can also be caused by other types of malware or by legitimate software, so it can be difficult to determine if a system is truly infected with fileless malware.

An attacker might use a rootkit to hide the presence of malware on a system while using fileless malware to avoid detection by traditional antivirus and anti-malware software. This type of attack can be particularly difficult to detect and block.

Macro malware and ransomware

Macro malware is a type of malware that is embedded in macros within documents, such as Microsoft Office documents. Macros are small scripts that automate tasks within a document. Macro malware is designed to exploit the functionality of macros to execute malicious code on a victim's computer system.

Attackers use macro malware for a variety of reasons. One common use of macro malware is to install additional malware on a victim's system. The macro malware can be used to download and install additional malware, such as ransomware or spyware. This can allow attackers to maintain long-term access to a victim's system and steal sensitive information.

Another use of macro malware is to steal sensitive information directly from the victim's computer system. Macro malware can be used to record keystrokes, capture screenshots, or access files on the victim's system. This information can be used by attackers to steal passwords, financial information, or other sensitive data.

Macro malware can also be used to launch other types of attacks, such as phishing attacks or DDoS attacks. By exploiting the functionality of macros within a document, attackers can create convincing phishing emails that appear to be from a trusted source. The macro malware can be used to launch a DDoS attack against a victim's website or network.

There are several different types of macro malware, each with its characteristics and methods of operation. One common type of macro malware is a **dropper**, which is used to download and install additional malware on a victim's system. Another type of macro malware is a **downloader**, which is used to download additional malware from a remote server. Other types of macro malware can be used to launch DDoS attacks, steal sensitive information, or perform other malicious activities.

Macro malware can be very difficult to detect and remove as it is often embedded in a legitimate document. Attackers may also use social engineering techniques to trick victims into enabling macros and executing the malware. However, there are some signs that a system may be infected with macro malware, such as unusual system behavior, unexplained network activity, or changes to system settings.

Ransomware, as we discussed previously, is a type of malware that encrypts a victim's files and demands payment in exchange for the decryption key.

An attacker might use macro malware to gain initial access to a system, and then use ransomware to encrypt the system's files and demand payment in exchange for the decryption key. This type of attack can be particularly effective against organizations that rely heavily on Microsoft Office documents for their day-to-day operations.

Managing malware

Each type of malware has its characteristics and effects, and attackers may use a combination of different types of malware in their attacks. Consequently, malware is one of the most significant threats to the security and privacy of computer systems and can cause extensive damage to both individuals and organizations.

Managing malware data involves analyzing, detecting, preventing, and mitigating malware attacks on computer systems. The following is an overview of the science of malware data and the respective management life cycle:

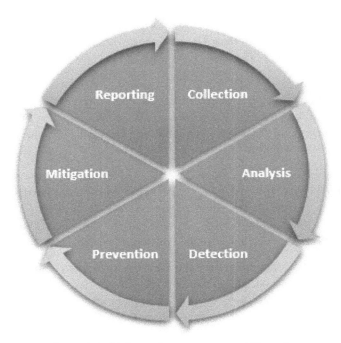

Figure 1.3 – Malware data management life cycle

Let's walk through the malware data management life cycle in more detail.

Collection

The first step in managing malware data is to collect and gather all the necessary data. This includes data about the malware itself, such as its code, behavior, and characteristics, as well as data about the affected system, such as its configuration, operating system, and software installed.

Collecting malware data involves gathering information from various sources to build a comprehensive understanding of the malware and its behavior. Several types of data can be collected during this process:

- **Malware samples**: Malware samples are the actual programs or files that contain malicious code. They can be obtained through various means, such as downloading them from the internet or extracting them from infected systems.

- **System data**: System data includes information about the computer or device that was infected by the malware, such as its configuration, installed software, and operating system version. This data can help in understanding how the malware operates and how it might be prevented in the future.

- **Network data**: Network data refers to the traffic flowing across a network, including data packets, protocols, and ports. Collecting network data can help in identifying the source and extent of the malware infection, as well as the targets of the attack.

- **User data**: User data includes information about the users who interacted with the infected system or network. This data can provide clues about how the malware was introduced, such as through a phishing email or a malicious website.

- **Contextual data**: Contextual data includes information about the broader context of the malware infection, such as the time and location of the attack, the target industry or organization, and the motivations of the attackers. This data can help in understanding the larger threat landscape and developing effective countermeasures.

Once the necessary data has been collected, it can be analyzed and used to inform the subsequent stages of the malware management life cycle, such as detection, prevention, and mitigation.

Analysis

The next step is to analyze the collected data to identify the type of malware, its behavior, and the extent of the damage caused. This analysis can be performed using a variety of techniques, including signature-based detection, behavior-based detection, and machine learning algorithms.

Malware analysis is a critical step in the malware management life cycle as it enables security professionals to understand the behavior and characteristics of the malware and develop effective countermeasures. There are several types of malware analysis:

- **Static analysis**: Static analysis involves examining the code and structure of the malware without executing it. This can be done by analyzing the file headers, examining the assembly code, and looking for patterns or signatures that are characteristic of known malware families.

- **Dynamic analysis**: Dynamic analysis involves running the malware in a controlled environment to observe its behavior. This can be done using virtual machines or sandboxes, which allow the malware to execute in an isolated environment without affecting the host system. Dynamic analysis can reveal how the malware communicates with command and control servers, what files it accesses or modifies, and what registry keys it creates or modifies.

- **Behavioral analysis**: Behavioral analysis involves observing the effects of the malware on the infected system. This can be done by monitoring system logs, network traffic, and other indicators of compromise. Behavioral analysis can reveal the ultimate goals of the malware, such as stealing data or conducting a **Denial-of-Service (DoS)** attack.

- **Reverse engineering**: Reverse engineering involves decompiling the malware code to understand its underlying logic and functionality. This can be a time-consuming and complex process, but it can provide valuable insights into the inner workings of the malware.

The type of analysis used depends on the nature of the malware and the available resources. In general, a combination of static, dynamic, and behavioral analysis is used to build a comprehensive understanding of the malware and its behavior. The results of the analysis can be used to develop signatures and rules for detecting and blocking the malware, as well as to develop effective mitigation strategies.

Detection

Once the malware has been identified, the next step is to detect its presence on other systems. This is typically done using antivirus software and intrusion detection systems, which monitor network traffic for signs of malware activity.

Detection is a critical step in the malware management life cycle as it enables security professionals to identify and isolate malware infections before they can cause further damage. Several techniques can be used to detect malware:

- **Signature-based detection**: Signature-based detection involves comparing the characteristics of a file or program to a database of known malware signatures. If a match is found, the file is flagged as malware and either deleted or quarantined.

- **Heuristic detection**: Heuristic detection involves using a set of rules or algorithms to identify files that exhibit suspicious behavior or characteristics. Heuristic detection can be effective at detecting new or unknown malware that has not yet been added to signature databases.

- **Behavioral detection**: Behavioral detection involves monitoring the behavior of programs and files for suspicious activity, such as accessing sensitive files or communicating with unknown servers. Behavioral detection can be effective at detecting malware that has been designed to evade traditional detection methods.

- **Sandboxing**: Sandboxing involves running programs and files in an isolated environment to observe their behavior. Sandboxing can be used to detect malware that would otherwise remain hidden as it allows security professionals to observe the malware in action without risking infection of the host system.

- **Machine learning**: Machine learning involves using algorithms to analyze large datasets and identify patterns or anomalies that may be indicative of malware activity. Machine learning can be effective at detecting new or unknown malware that may be missed by traditional detection methods.

The choice of detection technique depends on the nature of the malware and the available resources. In general, a combination of signature-based, heuristic, and behavioral detection, along with sandboxing and machine learning, can be used to detect and isolate malware infections before they can cause further damage. Once malware has been detected, it can be removed or quarantined to prevent it from spreading or causing further harm.

Prevention

To prevent malware from infecting systems, various measures can be taken, including implementing security policies, training employees on safe computing practices, and using antivirus and anti-malware software.

Prevention is a critical step in the malware management life cycle as it aims to stop malware infections from occurring in the first place. Several techniques can be used to prevent malware infections:

- **Employee education**: Employee education is a critical component of malware prevention. Employees should be trained to recognize phishing emails, suspicious websites, and other tactics used by cybercriminals to introduce malware into the network. They should also be educated on safe computing practices, such as not clicking on unknown links or downloading files from untrusted sources.

- **Access control**: Access control involves limiting the access of users and programs to sensitive systems and data. This can be done by implementing **role-based access control** (**RBAC**), which restricts access based on the user's job function, or by using firewalls and other network security controls to limit access to certain network segments.

- **Patch management**: Patch management involves keeping software and operating systems up to date with the latest security patches and updates. This can help prevent malware infections that exploit known vulnerabilities in software.

- **Anti-malware software**: Anti-malware software, such as antivirus and anti-spyware programs, can be used to detect and remove malware infections before they can cause harm. These programs should be kept up to date with the latest definitions and signatures to ensure maximum effectiveness.

- **Network security**: Network security involves using firewalls, intrusion detection and prevention systems, and other network security controls to prevent malware from entering the network. These controls can be configured to block traffic from known malicious IP addresses, as well as to detect and block suspicious traffic patterns.

The choice of prevention technique depends on the nature of the network and the available resources. In general, a combination of employee education, access control, patch management, anti-malware software, and network security controls can be used to prevent malware infections and protect against cyber threats.

Mitigation

If a malware infection does occur, the next step is to mitigate the damage caused. This may involve isolating infected systems from the network, restoring data from backups, and repairing or replacing affected hardware. The following figure depicts the integrated mitigation processes that support the malware management life cycle:

Figure 1.4 – Mitigation

Mitigation is a critical step in the malware management life cycle as it aims to minimize the damage caused by a malware infection. Several techniques can be used to mitigate the effects of malware:

- **Isolation**: Isolation involves disconnecting infected systems from the network to prevent the malware from spreading. This can be done by disabling network adapters, unplugging network cables, or powering off infected devices.

- **Restoration**: Restoration involves restoring systems and data from backups to remove the malware and return the system to a known good state. This can be a time-consuming process, but it is often the most effective way to remove malware and restore functionality to the affected systems.

- **Patching**: Patching involves applying security patches and updates to the affected systems to prevent further malware infections. This can be done after the malware has been removed and the system has been restored to a known good state.

- **Anti-malware software**: Anti-malware software can be used to remove malware infections and prevent future infections. This software should be kept up-to-date with the latest definitions and signatures to ensure maximum effectiveness.

- **Incident response**: Incident response involves following a formalized process to manage and respond to a malware incident. This process may include identifying the cause and extent of the infection, containing the infection, and restoring the affected systems and data.

The choice of mitigation technique depends on the nature and severity of the malware infection. In general, a combination of isolation, restoration, patching, anti-malware software, and incident response can be used to minimize the damage caused by a malware infection and restore affected systems and data to a known good state.

Reporting

Finally, it is important to report malware incidents to relevant authorities and stakeholders. This includes providing details about the type of malware, its behavior, and the extent of the damage caused, as well as any remediation steps taken. The following figure depicts the types of reporting processes involved in the malware management life cycle:

Figure 1.5 – Types of reporting mechanisms

Reporting is a critical step in the malware management life cycle as it enables security professionals to share information about malware incidents with relevant stakeholders and authorities. Several types of reporting may be necessary during and after a malware incident:

- **Internal reporting**: Internal reporting involves reporting the malware incident to internal stakeholders, such as IT and security teams, management, and legal and compliance departments. This may include providing details about the nature of the malware infection, the systems and data affected, and the steps taken to mitigate the damage.

- **External reporting**: External reporting involves reporting the malware incident to external stakeholders, such as customers, vendors, partners, and regulatory authorities. This may be required by law, regulation, or contractual obligation. External reporting may include providing details about the nature and extent of the malware infection, the impact on customers and other stakeholders, and the steps taken to mitigate the damage.

- **Incident response reporting**: Incident response reporting involves documenting the incident response process and providing a summary report of the incident to stakeholders. This report may include details about the cause and extent of the infection, the steps taken to contain and mitigate the damage, and recommendations for preventing future incidents.

- **Threat intelligence sharing**: Threat intelligence sharing involves sharing information about malware incidents with other organizations and security professionals to help prevent future incidents. This may involve sharing **indicators of compromise** (**IOCs**), such as IP addresses, domain names, and file hashes, as well as details about the behavior and characteristics of the malware.

The choice of reporting technique depends on the nature of the malware incident and the stakeholders involved. In general, timely and accurate reporting can help minimize the damage caused by a malware infection and prevent future incidents.

Summary

In the realm of cybersecurity, understanding the diverse landscape of malware and its applications is paramount. Malicious software, or malware, takes various forms, from ransomware, which holds data hostage, to rootkits, which stealthily gain control. Attackers ingeniously combine different types of malware to orchestrate complex, coordinated assaults. This fusion allows them to exploit diverse vulnerabilities, making detection and defense a formidable challenge.

The malware management life cycle, which encompasses collection, analysis, detection, prevention, mitigation, and reporting, forms a comprehensive strategy against these threats. Attackers strategically wield malware combinations such as swords, employing worms for initial access, Trojans for persistent control, and spyware for reconnaissance, all culminating in devastating ransomware attacks. The synergy of macro malware and spyware further bolsters their capabilities, infiltrating through documents and surreptitiously capturing user activity.

Understanding these mechanisms is vital to constructing effective defenses. As attackers adapt and innovate, cybersecurity professionals must stay ahead by developing robust strategies that encompass proactive measures, user education, and technological solutions. The battlefield between attackers and defenders continues to evolve, but by grasping the intricacies of malware and its amalgamations, the security landscape becomes more navigable, bolstering our ability to safeguard digital realms from these insidious threats.

2

An Overview of the International History of Cyber Malware Impacts

International history has witnessed the rapid evolution and integration of technology across a wide range of sectors. In parallel, the rise of cyber threats, particularly malware, has significantly impacted nations, economies, and societies worldwide. This broad impact has changed the dynamics of international relations, warfare, crime, and economic interactions.

In this chapter, we will cover the following topics:

- The evolution of cyber threats and malware
- The future of malware
- Key downstream impacts on key industries globally
- The use of **artificial intelligence** (**AI**) systems with malware
- Cybersecurity, malware, and the socio-economic fabric

The evolution of cyber threats and malware

To understand the impact of cyber malware on international history, we must first delve into its evolution. The emergence of malware traces back to the early days of computing. The term "malware" was coined around 1990, but its earliest instances predate the term. For example, the "Creeper" virus emerged in the early 1970s, infecting mainframe computers. The 1980s saw the rise of the PC, which was met with an increase in PC viruses.

The internet's birth in the 1990s facilitated the spread of malware, triggering a surge in its evolution and sophistication. The first major attack that brought the global threat of malware into the spotlight was the ILOVEYOU worm in 2000. It affected millions of computers globally, causing billions of dollars in damages and marking a turning point in international cyber threats.

In the 21st century, malware has morphed from a minor inconvenience into a potent tool for crime, espionage, and warfare. It's no longer just about rogue hackers; nation-states, terrorist organizations, and criminal syndicates have harnessed malware's destructive potential.

Impacts on international relations and security

The potential for states to use malware in offensive cyber operations has dramatically impacted international relations and security. Espionage, traditionally carried out by human agents, has been revolutionized by malware. Governments can now intrude into the confidential systems of rival nations to gather intelligence or cause disruption. A significant example was the Stuxnet worm, allegedly developed by the US and Israel, which targeted Iran's nuclear facilities in 2010.

Cyber warfare has emerged as a significant concern for national and international security. Malware can disrupt a nation's critical infrastructure, including power grids, transportation systems, and financial markets, affecting the economy and citizens' daily lives. For instance, the WannaCry ransomware attack in 2017 affected hundreds of thousands of systems worldwide, including the UK's **National Health Service (NHS)**. Notably, here are more recent examples of malware attacks with international relations and security implications:

- **May 2022**: A Russian-linked malware attack dubbed *HermeticWiper* was discovered on Ukrainian satellite systems, disrupting communications and navigation services. The attack was seen as a sign of Russia's escalation of its cyber warfare campaign against Ukraine.

- **February 2022**: A North Korean-linked malware attack dubbed *Cyclops Blink* was discovered on Lithuanian government networks. The attack was seen as a retaliation for Lithuania's decision to allow Taiwan to open a representative office in Vilnius.

- **January 2023**: A ransomware attack dubbed *LockBit 3.0* was launched against the UK postal service, the Royal Mail. The attack was attributed to a Russian-linked hacking group.

- **January 2023**: Iran-linked hackers executed ransomware attacks dubbed *TTP 5390* and *CVE-2022-22576* on US public infrastructure and private Australian organizations.

- **January 2023**: Hackers used ransomware dubbed *Conti* to encrypt 12 servers at Costa Rica's Ministry of Public Works, knocking all its servers offline. The attack was attributed to a Russian-linked hacking group.

Impacts on the economy and cybercrime

The international economic landscape has also been significantly impacted by malware. Cybercrime, driven largely by malware, costs the global economy billions of dollars annually. Companies face the threat of financial loss, reputational damage, and loss of customer trust following malware attacks.

Beyond direct financial impacts, malware also affects international trade and competition. Industrial espionage, aided by malware, allows unethical competitors to steal proprietary information and technology. Also, the threat of malware attacks can be a non-tariff barrier to trade in digital services.

The future of malware

In the future, malware will continue to have significant impacts internationally. The rise of the **Internet of Things (IoT)** and advancements in AI and **machine learning (ML)** provide new opportunities for malware deployment. This new era of cyber threats requires nations, businesses, and individuals to adopt a proactive and dynamic approach to cybersecurity.

Moreover, the role of international cooperation and regulation in tackling cyber threats is becoming increasingly important. Collaborative efforts such as the *Paris Call for Trust and Security in Cyberspace*, launched in 2018, are steps in the right direction, but more needs to be done.

Malware's role in international history cannot be understated. Its impact has been felt across the spectrum of international relations, security, economy, and crime. As technology continues to evolve and the world becomes more interconnected, malware's significance in shaping international history will undoubtedly continue to grow.

Expanded viewpoint on the impacts on international relations and security

International relations and security have been dramatically impacted by cyber threats, particularly malware. It's introduced new dimensions to state and non-state interactions, from diplomacy and espionage to conflict and warfare.

Cyber espionage

Malware has revolutionized the field of espionage. Unlike traditional espionage, which requires physical access and human agents, cyber espionage can be conducted remotely, covertly, and on a massive scale. Malware provides an avenue for governments to infiltrate the secure systems of adversaries, gather intelligence, steal technology, or create disruptive effects.

One of the most well-known examples of cyber espionage is the Stuxnet worm, which was allegedly developed by the US and Israel. Discovered in 2010, Stuxnet specifically targeted Iran's nuclear facilities, causing substantial damage and disruption. This demonstrated the potential of malware as a tool for sabotage and opened a new chapter in international cyber warfare.

Cyber warfare and malware

The potential for states to use malware in offensive cyber operations has added a new facet to international conflict. Traditional warfare involved physical attacks and visible damage, but cyber warfare can be conducted remotely, often without the attacker's identity being revealed.

For instance, in 2015, Ukraine experienced a power grid failure attributed to the BlackEnergy malware. This attack left around 230,000 people without electricity and highlighted the potential for malware to disrupt critical infrastructure. This was a stark example of how a nation's security could be undermined without a single bomb being dropped or a bullet fired.

Malware and terrorism

Non-state actors, particularly terrorist organizations, also leverage malware. They use it for various purposes, from disrupting services and spreading propaganda to funding their activities through cybercrime, notably ransomware attacks. This new form of terrorism – cyber terrorism – poses a significant challenge for international security.

Impacts on diplomacy and international cooperation

Malware and broader cyber threats have also changed the dynamics of diplomacy. Cyber diplomacy now forms a key part of international relations. Governments must negotiate complex issues related to cybercrime, cyber warfare, and digital espionage. Additionally, countries also have to collaborate to fight against common cyber threats, leading to increased international cooperation.

An example is the *Paris Call for Trust and Security in Cyberspace*, where nations and organizations pledge to work together to improve the security and stability of cyberspace. However, the effectiveness of such agreements is often limited by conflicting national interests and the challenge of attribution in cyberattacks.

In conclusion, malware's impact on international relations and security has been profound. It has changed the way states interact, leading to the emergence of cyber espionage and warfare, affecting diplomacy, and necessitating greater international cooperation. As the digital landscape continues to evolve, these issues will continue to be central to international relations and security.

Expansion on cybercrime impacts on the general economy

The economic implications of cyber threats, particularly malware, are vast, touching upon direct financial costs, reputational damages, innovation competitiveness, and international trade.

Direct financial impact

The financial impact of malware is staggering. According to a report by McAfee in collaboration with the **Center for Strategic and International Studies** (**CSIS**), cybercrime costs the global economy around $600 billion annually, which is approximately 0.8% of global **gross domestic product** (**GDP**). A significant portion of this cost is attributable to malware.

Reputational damage and loss of trust

When businesses suffer malware attacks, they often face significant reputational damage. Here are the findings of some studies on the subject:

- A study by the Ponemon Institute found that the average cost of lost business due to an erosion of customer trust was $1.44 million. This was the highest external cost faced by businesses after a data breach, accounting for 36% of the total cost.

- Another study, in 2022, by the IBM Security Institute found that 70% of consumers would stop doing business with a company after a data breach.

- A study by the Aite-Novarica Group found that the average cost of customer churn is $250 per customer.

- A study by the Aberdeen Group found that companies with high customer satisfaction scores have a 31% higher customer retention rate than companies with low customer satisfaction scores.

Further, IBM's *Cost of a Data Breach Report 2023* stated that the cost of lost business is the second highest cost associated with a data breach, after the cost of notification and remediation. It is reasonable to assume that some of the cost of lost business is due to loss of customer trust. When customers lose trust in a company, they are more likely to take their business elsewhere.

Impact on innovation and competitiveness

Malware can also affect a country's economic competitiveness. Malware-driven industrial espionage can lead to the theft of **intellectual property** (**IP**) and proprietary technology. According to a report by the Commission on the Theft of American Intellectual Property, the theft of trade secrets, much of it enabled by cyber means, costs the US economy between $180 billion and $540 billion annually.

Impact on international trade

Malware threats can also indirectly impact international trade. In today's digital economy, businesses are highly interconnected, and cross-border data flows are critical. The threat of malware can act as a non-tariff barrier, inhibiting the growth of the digital services trade. An **Organisation for Economic Co-operation and Development** (**OECD**) report highlighted that cybersecurity risks are a significant deterrent to firms looking to digitize, which in turn can impact the growth of international e-commerce.

The rise of cybercrime economies

In parallel to the legal economy, there's also been a rise in illegal cybercrime economies. Ransomware, a type of malware, has become a lucrative business model for cybercriminals. A report from Cybersecurity Ventures predicts that ransomware damages will cost the world $20 billion in 2021, up from $325 million in 2015.

Malware's impact on the global economy is significant, influencing direct and indirect costs, the pace of innovation, and the shape of international trade. It also fosters the growth of illicit economies, complicating the landscape of international cybercrime. As digital transformation accelerates globally, the economic implications of malware will likely continue to escalate.

Direct financial impacts of malware – a global overview

Malware, an overarching term encompassing various forms of malicious software, has become a pivotal aspect of the digital age. Its damaging effects permeate various facets of society, with its direct financial implications being particularly concerning. The global economy has been hit hard by the increasing proliferation and sophistication of malware, resulting in costs that amount to hundreds of billions of dollars annually.

Cybersecurity firm McAfee, in collaboration with the CSIS, published a comprehensive report on the economic impact of cybercrime. In this report, they estimated that cybercrime, a significant portion of which is attributable to malware, costs the global economy around $600 billion annually, or roughly 0.8% of global GDP.

The financial burden of malware is not solely the consequence of immediate cleanup or data recovery efforts. Additional costs can emerge from the necessity of implementing more robust cybersecurity measures and infrastructure in the aftermath of an attack. Further, data breaches can result in regulatory penalties, especially with an increasing global focus on data protection legislation, such as the **General Data Protection Regulation (GDPR)** in Europe.

Among the various forms of malware, ransomware has proven to be particularly damaging from a financial perspective. Ransomware is a type of malware that encrypts a victim's files, and the attacker then demands a ransom from the victim to restore access to the data upon payment. A report from Cybersecurity Ventures predicted that ransomware damages alone would cost the world $20 billion in 2021, increasing exponentially from $325 million in 2015. More recent reporting by Cybersecurity Ventures, reflects the global cost of ransomware is expected to exceed $30 billion in 2023. This is a significant increase from the $20 billion estimated in 2021. The report also found that the average ransom payment has increased to $1.5 million in 2023, up from $1.1 million in 2021. This suggests that ransomware attackers are becoming more sophisticated and demanding higher ransoms.

The burden of these financial losses is not evenly distributed. Businesses, particularly **small and medium-sized enterprises (SMEs)**, are often hit hardest. For instance, the *2019 Official Annual Cybercrime Report* from Cybersecurity Ventures predicted that businesses would fall victim to a ransomware attack every 11 seconds by 2021, up from every 40 seconds in 2016. More recent updates on the frequency of ransomware attacks against businesses in 2023—according to a report by Sophos, a cybersecurity firm, a ransomware attack is now launched every 2 seconds. This is a significant increase from the 11 seconds predicted by Cybersecurity Ventures in 2019.

The direct financial impact of malware is a serious concern for individuals, businesses, and governments worldwide. As we move forward, it's important to ensure that our expanding digital landscape is matched by the appropriate investments in cybersecurity.

Ransomware's global economic impact – a continental overview

Ransomware has emerged as one of the most disruptive forms of malware, inflicting significant economic damage worldwide. Cybersecurity Ventures predicted that ransomware damages would reach a staggering $20 billion globally in 2021, a dramatic rise from $325 million in 2015. Even more, Cybersecurity Ventures predicted that ransomware damages would exceed $30 billion globally in 2023, up from $20 billion in 2021.

North America

In North America, ransomware attacks have had a considerable economic impact, especially in the US. The US has been a prominent target due to its wealth and highly digitalized infrastructure. The *2021 State of the Phish* report by Proofpoint indicates a significant increase in ransomware attacks on US organizations. A study by Emsisoft suggested that in 2019 alone, ransomware incidents cost US governmental and healthcare entities over $7.5 billion. More recent examples include these:

- Ransomware damages in the US are expected to exceed $12 billion in 2023, up from $9 billion in 2022 – Cybersecurity Ventures, *2023 Ransomware Damages Report*

- The average ransom payment in the US has increased to $1.5 million in 2023, up from $1.1 million in 2022. – Sophos, *The State of Ransomware 2023*

- Healthcare and education are the two most targeted sectors in the US, accounting for over 50% of all ransomware attacks. – Emsisoft, *2023 Global Ransomware Report*

- **SMEs** are disproportionately affected by ransomware attacks. – Coveware, *Q2 2023 Ransomware Attack Trends Report*

Europe

Europe, too, has suffered from the economic impact of ransomware. The 2017 WannaCry ransomware attack severely hit the UK's NHS, causing an estimated loss of £92 million. Additionally, according to Europol's 2020 **Internet Organised Crime Threat Assessment** (**IOCTA**) report, ransomware remains the most reported cybercrime, causing significant economic damage across the **European Union** (**EU**). More recent examples include these:

- Ransomware damages in Europe are expected to exceed €14 billion in 2023, up from €12 billion in 2022, cited by Cybersecurity Ventures, *2023 Ransomware Damages Report*.

- The average ransom payment in Europe has increased to €1.2 million in 2023, up from €1 million in 2022 as reported by Sophos, *The State of Ransomware 2023*.

- The most targeted sectors in Europe are healthcare, manufacturing, and financial services, as reported by Emsisoft, *2023 Global Ransomware Report*.

Asia

Asian countries also face an increasing number of ransomware attacks. Japan and South Korea have been notable targets due to their advanced technological infrastructure. A report by SonicWall indicated a spike in ransomware attacks in Asia by 31% from 2019 to 2020.

Australia

Australia, part of the Oceania continent, has seen an uptick in ransomware incidents. According to a report by the **Australian Cyber Security Centre** (**ACSC**), ransomware was the highest reported cybercrime in 2020.

Africa

African countries, while not as frequently targeted as their more digitalized counterparts, have not been immune to ransomware attacks. The growing digitalization of services in the continent provides a new frontier for cybercriminals. Symantec's *2020 Internet Security Threat Report* indicated a rise in ransomware incidents in South Africa, making it the most targeted African country.

South America

South American countries have also experienced a surge in ransomware attacks. A 2020 report from Kaspersky indicated that Brazil faced the highest number of ransomware attacks in the region.

The economic impact of ransomware is a global issue, causing significant losses across all continents. As the digitalization of services continues to grow worldwide, so does the potential threat of ransomware. Therefore, continuous investment in cybersecurity measures is critical to minimize potential economic damages caused by these threats.

Ransomware's economic impact in North America – a deeper look

The threat and consequential economic impact of ransomware in North America, particularly the US, has grown substantially in recent years. The prominence of the region, combined with its wealth and digital infrastructure, has made it a prime target for cybercriminals.

Scope of the problem

According to the *2021 State of the Phish* report by Proofpoint, US organizations saw a significant increase in ransomware attacks. This rise impacted a range of sectors, from healthcare and education to local government and private industry, leading to a significant economic toll.

In 2019, the US was hit by a wave of ransomware attacks targeting city and state governments. Attackers locked down computer systems in Atlanta, Georgia; Baltimore, Maryland; and more than 20 municipalities in Texas. While these attacks resulted in significant direct financial damage due to ransom demands and recovery costs, indirect costs, including lost productivity and business disruption, were much higher.

Healthcare sector impact

The healthcare sector is another crucial area of ransomware vulnerability. According to an Emsisoft study, in 2019, ransomware incidents cost US governmental and healthcare entities over $7.5 billion. The healthcare industry is particularly susceptible because of its dependence on digital systems for patient care and the critical nature of its services, which may drive organizations to pay ransoms to quickly restore operations.

Increasing costs

Notably, the ransoms demanded by cybercriminals have been rising. Coveware's *Q4 2020 Ransomware Marketplace* report indicated that the average ransom payment climbed to $154,108, a 34.4% increase compared to Q3 2020. These increasing ransom demands underscore the escalating financial threat facing North American organizations.

Regulatory impact and GDPR

Furthermore, the introduction of more stringent data protection regulations, such as the GDPR in Europe, has implications for North American businesses operating internationally. These regulations can result in hefty fines for data breaches, adding to the financial impact of ransomware attacks.

The economic impact of ransomware in North America is a growing concern that extends far beyond the direct costs of ransom payments. The significant disruption of services, potential for regulatory fines, and reputational damage make ransomware a substantial threat to the region's economic security. It is, therefore, critical for both public and private entities to invest in robust cybersecurity measures, education, and **incident response (IR)** strategies.

Ransomware's economic impact in Asia – a detailed examination

As one of the most technologically advanced regions globally, Asia has also become a significant target for ransomware attacks, causing substantial economic impact. The extent of this issue varies widely, with economically prosperous countries such as Japan and South Korea being particularly affected due to their advanced digital infrastructure.

Economic impact

The precise economic costs of ransomware in Asia are difficult to calculate due to variations in reporting and data collection. However, a report from SonicWall Capture Labs indicates a notable spike in ransomware attacks in Asia, increasing by 31% from 2019 to 2020. This increase suggests a significant economic cost, given the disruptive potential of ransomware.

Japan and South Korea – a focus

Japan and South Korea, as highly digitalized societies, have been especially susceptible to ransomware attacks. In 2020, Symantec identified Japan as one of the top countries targeted by ransomware. In the same vein, South Korea has repeatedly been a target, with a notable incident in 2019 where the country's web hosting company, NAYANA, was attacked and had to pay a massive $1 million in ransom, one of the largest known ransom payments to date.

India – emerging threat landscape

India, with its rapidly growing digital economy, has also witnessed an increase in ransomware attacks. A report by Seqrite estimates that Indian businesses faced a potential economic loss of around $4 billion due to ransomware attacks in 2019 alone.

Potential future trends

The accelerating digitalization and development of smart cities, along with the increased adoption of IoT devices in Asia, potentially present new vulnerabilities that could be exploited by ransomware attackers. As such, the economic impact of ransomware attacks could potentially increase in the future if robust cybersecurity measures are not adopted.

In conclusion, ransomware poses a significant economic threat to Asia, with technologically advanced nations, in particular, finding themselves in the crosshairs of attackers. The potential for economic loss due to service disruption, ransom payments, and reputational damage is high, emphasizing the importance of a proactive approach to cybersecurity.

Ransomware's economic impact in Africa – an in-depth analysis

While Africa has not been as frequently targeted by ransomware attacks as other, more digitalized continents, the region is not immune to this growing cyber threat. Rapid digitalization and increased internet usage across the continent have begun to draw the attention of cybercriminals, making ransomware a rising concern for African nations.

Overall impact

The precise economic impact of ransomware attacks in Africa is difficult to quantify due to inconsistent reporting and data collection practices. However, it's clear that the threat is present and increasing. Symantec's *2020 Internet Security Threat Report* identified a notable rise in ransomware incidents in Africa, with South Africa emerging as the most targeted African country.

South Africa – a particular focus

South Africa's relatively advanced digital infrastructure compared to other African countries makes it an attractive target for cybercriminals. According to Kaspersky's *IT Threat Evolution Q1 2021* report, South Africa ranked among the top 10 countries worldwide with the highest percentage of users attacked by mobile malware. Moreover, in July 2020, South African port operator Transnet fell victim to a ransomware attack, disrupting port operations and causing significant economic damage.

Nigeria – an emerging digital economy

As Africa's largest economy, Nigeria has also seen an increase in cyber threats. A report from Serianu, a cyber threat intelligence body, showed that Nigerian businesses lost approximately $649 million to cybercrime in 2018. While this figure encompasses all forms of cybercrime, ransomware forms a significant portion of these attacks. Here are some additional recent findings from Serianu:

- In 2022, Serianu identified over 100 million malware infections in Africa, with Nigeria accounting for over 20% of these infections

- The most common types of malware in Africa are ransomware, Trojans, and adware

- SMEs are the most targeted sector in Africa, accounting for over 60% of all cyberattacks

The future of ransomware in Africa

While the current scale of ransomware attacks in Africa might not match those in other continents, rapidly increasing digitalization and internet penetration across the continent are likely to change this landscape. The COVID-19 pandemic has further accelerated this digital transition, as businesses and government services have moved online, potentially opening new avenues for cyberattacks.

In conclusion, despite lower levels of reported incidents compared to other regions, the economic impact of ransomware in Africa should not be underestimated. As digital transformation progresses across the continent, it is crucial for African nations to prioritize cybersecurity to protect their economies and citizens from potential cyber threats.

Ransomware's economic impact in South America – an extensive exploration

Ransomware has also posed a significant threat to countries in South America, leading to substantial economic impacts. As digitalization advances across the continent, the number of potential targets for cybercriminals is growing.

General impact

Quantifying the exact economic impact of ransomware in South America is challenging due to underreporting and variations in data collection. However, several reports indicate a growing problem. For example, a Kaspersky security bulletin from 2020 shows that South America faced a high number of ransomware attacks compared to other global regions.

Brazil – a major target

Brazil, with its vast economy and rapid digitalization, has been a prime target for ransomware attacks in South America. In 2020, the *Ransomware Year-in-Review* report by Cybereason noted that Brazil was among the countries most affected by ransomware attacks globally.

In one high-profile case, the Brazilian electrical energy company Light S.A. was targeted by a ransomware attack in June 2019. The attack led to the disruption of customer services and internal operations, representing not only direct costs from the attack but also indirect costs such as loss of business, recovery, and potential reputational damage.

Argentina – rising cyber threats

Argentina, another major economy in the region, has also experienced an uptick in ransomware incidents. A report from Argentina's national Ministry of Security indicated a sharp rise in cybercrime, including ransomware, from 2018 to 2019. This trend has continued with the growth in digital services.

Future risks

The future risk of ransomware attacks in South America is likely to increase due to the expanding digital landscape. The region has seen rapid growth in internet penetration, smartphone use, and digital services. This digital expansion, while beneficial for economic growth and development, also presents new opportunities for cybercriminals.

In conclusion, while South America may not have experienced the same scale of ransomware attacks as other continents, the threat is real and increasing. As digitalization continues to expand across the continent, so too does the potential for more extensive and damaging cyberattacks. Governments and organizations across South America must place an increasing focus on cybersecurity to mitigate the financial impact of these threats.

Economic impacts versus socio-economic impacts

There is a difference between economic impacts and socio-economic impacts, particularly when discussing the effects of events such as ransomware attacks.

Economic impacts refer directly to the measurable financial effects of an event. In the context of a ransomware attack, this might include the cost of the ransom, expenses related to system recovery and repair, the hiring of cybersecurity experts, or investment in better security infrastructure. It also includes the opportunity cost of downtime, the loss of business during the period of disruption, and any regulatory fines that might result from the breach.

Socio-economic impacts, on the other hand, encompass a wider range of effects that include both social and economic aspects. These impacts are often less tangible and more difficult to measure, but they can be just as significant.

In the context of a ransomware attack, socio-economic impacts could include the following:

- **Employment**: The attack could lead to job losses if the company is forced to downsize due to the financial strain. Conversely, it might also result in job creation in certain sectors, such as cybersecurity, as companies ramp up their security efforts.

- **Public services**: If the attack targets government systems, it could disrupt public services, affecting everything from healthcare and education to utilities and transportation. This can have a significant impact on the quality of life for citizens.

- **Trust and consumer behavior**: Repeated ransomware attacks can undermine trust in digital infrastructure and online services. This could potentially change consumer behavior, affecting the broader digital economy.

- **Inequality**: Ransomware attacks can exacerbate existing inequalities. For instance, those with lower digital literacy are more likely to fall victim to such attacks. Additionally, smaller businesses that cannot afford strong cybersecurity measures are often more vulnerable to attacks.

- **Policy and regulation**: Large-scale or repeated attacks often prompt changes in government policy and regulation. While this could lead to improved security in the long term, it may also impose additional costs on businesses.

So, while economic impacts focus strictly on financial effects, socio-economic impacts consider a broader range of consequences that a ransomware attack (or any event) might have on society and the economy.

Ransomware attacks and their impact on employment – an in-depth perspective

Ransomware attacks can have significant implications on employment, affecting both job security and the nature of job opportunities available. These implications can be seen from two major perspectives – job losses due to financial strain and job creation in the cybersecurity sector.

Job losses due to financial strain

Ransomware attacks have the potential to cause serious financial harm to businesses. The direct costs of a ransomware attack can include the ransom itself, downtime due to operational disruption, costs related to restoring the network, potential legal fees, and possible regulatory fines.

If a business suffers severe financial damage from a ransomware attack, it might be forced to lay off employees to cut costs. This is particularly likely for SMEs, which often operate with slim margins and may not have the financial reserves to weather the aftermath of a significant ransomware attack.

For instance, following the 2017 NotPetya ransomware attack, which is considered one of the most destructive cyberattacks to date, several businesses were severely affected. Among them was the international shipping firm Maersk, which reported an estimated loss of $300 million. Although Maersk did not announce layoffs as a direct result of the attack, it highlights the potential scale of financial damage that could lead other less resilient companies to reduce their workforce.

Job creation in the cybersecurity sector

Conversely, the rising threat of ransomware and other forms of cybercrime can lead to increased job creation in the cybersecurity sector. As businesses and governments recognize the importance of protecting their digital assets, there is increased demand for cybersecurity professionals to prevent and respond to attacks.

According to Cybersecurity Ventures, there will be 3.5 million unfilled cybersecurity jobs globally by 2021, up from 1 million positions in 2014. This indicates that the sector is growing rapidly in response to increasing cybersecurity threats. More recently, according to the **International Information Systems Security Certification Consortium**'s **(ISC2)** *2023 Cybersecurity Workforce Study*, the global cybersecurity workforce gap is still growing, with an estimated 3.4 million unfilled cybersecurity jobs in 2023. This is up from 3.1 million unfilled jobs in 2022.

Furthermore, the nature of ransomware attacks demands a wide range of expertise, leading to the creation of diverse job roles within the cybersecurity sector. These can range from ethical hackers who test system vulnerabilities to cybersecurity analysts who monitor and respond to threats, and cybersecurity consultants who advise organizations on best practices.

In conclusion, while ransomware attacks can lead to job losses in affected companies due to financial strain, they also contribute to job creation in the cybersecurity sector. The net impact on employment thus depends on various factors, including the resilience of affected companies and the pace at which the cybersecurity sector can grow and provide new job opportunities.

Ransomware attacks and their impact on public services – an elaborate examination

Ransomware attacks have increasingly targeted public sector organizations in recent years, disrupting essential public services ranging from healthcare and education to utilities and public transportation. These attacks not only cost governments substantial amounts of money to resolve but also have a significant societal impact.

Healthcare services

One of the most critical sectors affected by ransomware attacks is healthcare. Hospitals and healthcare systems are often targets because they hold sensitive patient data and because any disruption to their services can have life-threatening consequences, making them more likely to pay a ransom quickly.

For example, in 2020, a major German hospital was hit by a ransomware attack that caused a significant delay in emergency patient care, leading to the death of a patient who had to be diverted to a more distant hospital. Similarly, in the US, a widespread ransomware attack on the **Universal Health Services** (**UHS**) network in the same year led to the disruption of healthcare services across hundreds of its healthcare facilities.

Education services

Educational institutions, from primary schools to universities, have also been increasingly targeted by ransomware attacks. These attacks can disrupt learning, especially in the current digital age where many institutions rely on digital platforms for teaching and administrative functions.

For instance, in 2020, the Clark County School District in Nevada, US, suffered a ransomware attack that disrupted online learning for its over 300,000 students. The attack also led to the exposure of sensitive student and staff data.

Utilities and public transportation

Other public services that can be severely disrupted by ransomware attacks include utilities such as water and power supply and public transportation systems. For example, in 2020, the **San Francisco Municipal Transportation Agency** (**SFMTA**) fell victim to a ransomware attack that disrupted its ticketing services over a weekend.

In conclusion, the impact of ransomware attacks on public services extends beyond the direct financial costs associated with addressing the cyberattack. The disruption of these essential services can significantly affect citizens' quality of life, pose potential safety risks, and erode public trust in the government's ability to protect sensitive information. It highlights the urgency and importance of implementing robust cybersecurity measures within public sector organizations.

Ransomware and inequality – a closer look at the impact on small businesses

Ransomware attacks can exacerbate existing economic and social inequalities, and this is particularly evident when considering the impact of such attacks on small businesses.

Increased vulnerability of small businesses

SMEs are often more vulnerable to ransomware attacks than larger corporations for several reasons.

Firstly, SMEs often lack the financial resources to invest in robust cybersecurity infrastructure and may not have dedicated IT staff to manage and update their systems regularly. This can make them an easier target for cybercriminals.

Secondly, many SMEs may not fully understand the threat posed by ransomware and other forms of cybercrime, leading to a lack of awareness and training about how to prevent such attacks. A 2018 report by the Ponemon Institute found that 66% of small businesses would struggle to remain profitable after a cyberattack, underlining their vulnerability.

Finally, smaller businesses are less likely to be able to absorb the financial shock of a ransomware attack. The direct costs of dealing with the attack, coupled with the indirect costs of operational downtime, can be devastating for a small business.

Wider socio-economic implications

The vulnerability of SMEs to ransomware attacks has broader socio-economic implications. SMEs play a crucial role in most economies worldwide, providing a significant proportion of employment and contributing to economic growth. In the US, for example, the **Small Business Administration (SBA)** reports that small businesses account for 44% of US economic activity.

Therefore, the disruption caused by ransomware attacks on small businesses can have ripple effects throughout the economy, potentially leading to job losses, reduced economic output, and increased inequality.

Furthermore, if SMEs in certain sectors or regions are disproportionately targeted or affected by ransomware attacks, it can exacerbate regional and sectoral inequalities.

In conclusion, the inequality aspect of ransomware attacks is a critical component that often gets overshadowed by the focus on large-scale attacks on major corporations or public sector entities. Addressing this issue requires making cybersecurity tools and training accessible to SMEs and increasing awareness about the threat of ransomware and other forms of cybercrime.

Policy, regulations, and their downstream impact on smaller businesses and public services

The rise of ransomware attacks has led to increased attention from policymakers and regulators, leading to new laws and regulations aimed at boosting cybersecurity. While these regulations are crucial for enhancing cybersecurity, they can also impose additional burdens on smaller businesses and public services, creating downstream impacts.

Increased regulatory burdens

Policy changes often come in the form of stricter regulations, which, while essential for increasing the overall level of cybersecurity, can put a strain on smaller businesses. These businesses often operate on tight budgets and may struggle to find the resources to comply with new regulatory requirements.

For example, the EU's GDPR requires businesses to implement a high level of data protection and imposes hefty fines for non-compliance. While GDPR is necessary to protect individuals' data rights, its implementation can be challenging for smaller businesses due to its complexity and the costs associated with compliance.

In the US, various states have enacted laws requiring businesses to implement reasonable security measures to protect personal information. These laws, such as the **California Consumer Privacy Act (CCPA)**, can impose a significant compliance burden on small businesses.

Impacts on public services

Similar impacts can be seen in the public sector. Increased regulation can improve cybersecurity in public services, but it can also put a strain on already limited resources. Public services, especially in smaller municipalities, may struggle to meet the financial and administrative requirements of enhanced cybersecurity regulations.

This can lead to a difficult balancing act: diverting funds toward compliance with cybersecurity regulations may lead to short-term cuts in public services. However, failing to adequately invest in cybersecurity could lead to a costly ransomware attack, which would also impact service delivery.

Potential for positive change

Despite the challenges, regulatory changes can also drive positive change. They can incentivize businesses and public services to invest in cybersecurity, potentially preventing costly ransomware attacks. Regulations can also encourage innovation in the cybersecurity sector, leading to the development of more affordable and accessible cybersecurity solutions for smaller businesses and public services.

In conclusion, while policy and regulatory changes in response to the ransomware threat can impose additional burdens on smaller businesses and public services, they are a necessary part of the solution. To minimize downstream impacts, there is a need for support measures such as funding, training, and resources to help these entities comply with the regulations without compromising their operations or service delivery.

Regulatory changes due to malware impacts on small and mid-scale businesses

The increased focus on cybersecurity and subsequent regulatory changes have led to significant impacts on small and mid-scale businesses. While these changes are critical in an age where cyber threats such as malware and ransomware are prevalent, they also impose certain challenges and costs on these businesses.

Increased costs

Complying with cybersecurity regulations often means incurring additional costs for small and mid-scale businesses. These costs can be related to hiring or outsourcing cybersecurity professionals, investing in updated software and hardware, implementing new security protocols, and training staff on these protocols.

For instance, the GDPR in the EU, one of the most comprehensive data protection regulations globally, requires businesses to have adequate security measures in place to protect consumer data. Meeting these requirements could mean significant upfront costs for small and mid-scale businesses that previously did not have such security measures in place.

Operational challenges

In addition to financial costs, keeping up with regulatory changes also involves operational challenges. It often requires changing existing business processes, updating IT systems, and continuous monitoring to ensure compliance.

A business might also need to create new roles, such as a data protection officer as mandated by GDPR for organizations that process large amounts of sensitive data, adding to the operational complexity.

Penalties for non-compliance

Non-compliance with cybersecurity regulations can lead to severe penalties, including hefty fines. For small and mid-scale businesses, these penalties could potentially threaten their financial stability or even their very existence.

For instance, under GDPR, fines for non-compliance can reach up to 4% of the company's annual global turnover or €20 million, whichever is higher.

Opportunities

Despite these challenges, keeping up with regulatory changes also presents opportunities for small and mid-scale businesses. By improving their cybersecurity posture, businesses can increase trust with their customers and gain a competitive edge, particularly in sectors where data security is a priority for consumers.

Additionally, these businesses could potentially avoid the devastating costs of a cyberattack by investing in robust cybersecurity measures. Given that a report from Hiscox in 2020 indicated that the average cost of a cyberattack had risen to $200,000, such proactive investment can be financially prudent in the long run.

In essence, while regulatory changes due to the rise in cyber threats such as malware pose challenges for small and mid-scale businesses, they are a crucial part of modern business practice. Businesses that proactively adapt to these changes can protect themselves from cyber threats and possibly gain a competitive advantage in an increasingly digital marketplace.

A deeper dive into the operational challenges

Operational challenges associated with meeting cybersecurity regulations in the context of small and mid-scale businesses are multifold. Let's dive deeper into some key aspects.

Understanding regulatory requirements

The first operational challenge is simply understanding the regulations themselves. Laws such as the GDPR and the CCPA are complex and can be difficult to interpret, especially for small businesses without a legal team.

Understanding these laws involves more than just reading the text. It requires an understanding of the spirit of the law, precedent, and ongoing legal interpretations. For smaller businesses, this can mean hiring a lawyer or consultant with expertise in cyber law, which can be costly.

Implementing appropriate cybersecurity measures

Once a business understands the regulations it needs to comply with, the next challenge is implementing the appropriate cybersecurity measures. This could involve updating IT infrastructure, implementing new security software, or changing business processes to protect data.

However, implementing these measures can be complex and disruptive. It might require hiring or training staff with specific technical skills, and the process of updating systems can cause downtime or disrupt normal business operations.

Employee training

Another significant challenge is training employees on new processes and protocols. Human error is one of the most common causes of cybersecurity breaches, so it's essential that all employees understand and adhere to new security protocols.

This involves not only initial training but also ongoing education to keep employees updated as threats and regulations evolve. It can be a particular challenge for smaller businesses without a dedicated HR or training department.

Ongoing compliance monitoring and reporting

Ensuring ongoing compliance is another operational challenge. Cybersecurity is not a set-it-and-forget-it proposition. Continuous monitoring is necessary to ensure that security measures are working and that the business remains in compliance as regulations change.

Additionally, many regulations require businesses to report on their compliance, which can involve complex record-keeping and reporting processes. For example, under GDPR, businesses must be able to demonstrate compliance and could be required to provide this evidence in the event of an audit or a breach.

Managing third-party risk

In today's interconnected digital world, businesses often work with a range of third-party vendors, from **cloud service providers** (**CSPs**) to payment processors. Each of these third parties represents a potential security risk, and managing this risk is a significant operational challenge.

This involves not only ensuring that third-party vendors have appropriate security measures in place but also managing contracts to ensure that they include the necessary provisions around data security. This can be particularly challenging for smaller businesses that may have less bargaining power with large vendors.

IR planning

Finally, businesses must be prepared to respond quickly and effectively in the event of a breach. This involves developing an IR plan, regularly testing and updating the plan, and training staff on their roles in the event of a breach. Managing this process can be a significant operational challenge, particularly for smaller businesses with limited resources.

Translating operational challenges into increased cost

Translating operational challenges posed by cybersecurity regulations into financial terms requires understanding the various components that can potentially increase the expenses for small and mid-scale businesses. Let's look at how each of the operational challenges translates into increased costs.

Understanding regulatory requirements

Hiring legal consultants or cybersecurity experts to understand complex cybersecurity laws and regulations, such as GDPR and CCPA, can be a significant expense. According to the *Robert Half 2022 Salary Guide*, the median salary for a cybersecurity consultant in the US ranged from $91,000 to $161,000, depending on expertise and location.

Implementing appropriate cybersecurity measures

Investing in IT infrastructure updates, security software, and hardware necessary for compliance can lead to significant upfront and ongoing costs. According to Gartner, worldwide spending on **information security risk management (ISRM)** technology and services is forecast to grow 11.3% to reach more than $188.3 billion in 2023, indicating the considerable expenses businesses face in this area. Further, the ISRM market is expected to grow at a **compound annual growth rate (CAGR)** of 11.5% from 2023 to 2028, reaching $303.4 billion by 2028. Regarding 2024, according to Gartner, worldwide spending on ISRM technology and services is expected to grow 11.8% to reach more than $212 billion in 2024. This growth is being driven by multiple factors, including the increasing adoption of AI and ML in security solutions.

Employee training

Developing and delivering training programs for employees about new protocols and processes can be costly. According to *Training Magazine*'s *2021 Training Industry Report*, small companies spend an average of $1,290 per employee on training annually.

Ongoing compliance monitoring and reporting

Investing in monitoring tools and hiring personnel to oversee ongoing compliance can be another significant expense. The cost of non-compliance, however, can be much higher, with GDPR violations potentially resulting in fines up to 4% of annual global revenue or €20 million, whichever is greater.

Managing third-party risk

Ensuring the cybersecurity compliance of third-party vendors can also lead to increased costs, particularly if it necessitates the renegotiation of contracts or switching to more secure, and potentially more expensive, **service providers (SPs)**.

IR planning

Creating, testing, and updating an IR plan requires both time and resources. Businesses may need to hire consultants or dedicate internal resources to this task. Expenses, however, can be viewed as an investment, considering that IBM Security's *2020 Cost of a Data Breach Report* found that companies with an IR team and testing of IR plans could save an average of $2 million per breach. More recently, according to IBM Security's *2023 Cost of a Data Breach Report*, organizations with an IR team and regularly tested IR plans saved an average of $2.66 million per breach. This is a significant savings compared to organizations without an IR team or IR plan testing, which saved an average of $1.87 million per breach.

While the exact costs can vary depending on the size and nature of the business, the complexity of its data processing activities, and the specific regulations it needs to comply with, they can be substantial and should be factored into any cybersecurity budget.

Expansion of economic and socio-economic impacts on key industries globally

Economic and socio-economic impacts of cyber threats such as malware and ransomware have been widespread and have affected various key industries globally.

Healthcare

The healthcare sector is a prime target for cyber threats with both economic and socio-economic impacts. Economically, hospitals and healthcare systems incur significant costs due to breaches, including remediation costs, potential fines, and lost revenue due to disrupted operations. The *Protenus Breach Barometer* report estimated that healthcare data breaches cost the US healthcare industry approximately $6.2 billion each year.

Socio-economically, the disruption of healthcare services due to cyberattacks can have life-threatening implications. This was seen during the WannaCry attack, where hospitals across the UK had to cancel around 19,000 appointments, including operations.

Finance

The financial sector is also a prime target. The cost of cybercrime for financial services companies globally was estimated to be $18.5 million per firm in 2017, significantly higher than the average cost of $11.7 million per firm across industries, according to an Accenture and Ponemon Institute study. Even more, the cost of cybercrime for financial services companies is expected to continue to grow in the coming years. According to a report by Cybersecurity Ventures, the global cost of cybercrime is expected to reach $10.5 trillion annually by 2025, up from $6 trillion in 2021.

On the socio-economic front, attacks on financial institutions can undermine trust in the financial system, potentially affecting financial stability. Consumer trust, once damaged, can take years to restore, impacting the industry's long-term growth and prosperity.

Retail

In the retail sector, data breaches can lead to substantial financial losses due to remediation costs, regulatory fines, and lost business. Recent examples stemming the impact of data breaches in the retail sector are as follows:

- The average cost of a data breach in the retail industry has increased to $2.48 million in 2023, according to the IBM *2023 Cost of a Data Breach Report*. This is up from $2.0 million in 2020.
- The retail sector is the second most targeted industry for data breaches, after the healthcare sector.

- Data breaches in the retail sector can have a significant impact on consumer confidence. A recent study by Ponemon Institute found that 66% of consumers would stop doing business with a company after a data breach.

- Data breaches can also lead to job losses in the retail sector. A recent study by Cybersecurity Ventures found that data breaches cost the global economy $10.5 trillion in 2021, and this number is expected to grow to $15 trillion by 2025.

Here are some additional updates on the socioeconomic impact of data breaches:

- **Identity theft**: Identity theft is a serious crime that can have a devastating impact on victims. It can lead to financial losses, damage to credit scores, and even criminal prosecution.

- **Financial impact on customers**: Data breaches can also have a direct financial impact on customers. For example, if a customer's credit card information is stolen, they may be liable for fraudulent charges. Additionally, customers may need to spend time and money to protect themselves from identity theft after a data breach.

- **Loss of trust**: Data breaches can also lead to a loss of trust between businesses and their customers. Customers are more likely to do business with companies that they trust to protect their data.

Overall, the impact of data breaches in the retail sector is significant. Businesses in the retail sector need to take steps to protect their customers' data and mitigate the risk of data breaches.

Socio-economically, these breaches can lead to a loss of consumer trust, impacting consumer spending habits and potentially leading to job losses within the industry. Moreover, loss of sensitive customer data can result in identity theft and other personal financial impacts for the customers themselves.

Manufacturing

In manufacturing, cyber threats can lead to production shutdowns, with significant economic implications. A study by the cybersecurity firm Emsisoft estimated that ransomware downtime cost businesses globally at least $225 billion in 2020. The 5-year forecast for the cost of ransomware downtime in manufacturing is expected to reach $400 billion by 2025, according to a report by Cybersecurity Ventures. This is due to the increasing sophistication of ransomware attacks, the growing number of connected devices in manufacturing environments, and the lack of adequate cybersecurity measures in many manufacturing organizations.

Socio-economically, manufacturing shutdowns can lead to job losses and can also disrupt supply chains, impacting other industries and potentially leading to shortages of goods. This was seen in the NotPetya attack, where major global firms such as Maersk and FedEx had operations significantly disrupted.

Key downstream impacts on key industries globally

Downstream impacts refer to indirect or secondary consequences that occur as a result of an initial action or event. In the context of cyber threats such as malware and ransomware, these downstream impacts can be varied and widespread, affecting not only the targeted organizations but also various stakeholders and interconnected systems. Here are some of the key downstream impacts:

- **Supply chain disruptions**: Cyberattacks can disrupt supply chains, affecting not only the targeted business but also its suppliers and customers. For example, if a manufacturing company is hit by a ransomware attack that halts production, its suppliers could be left with unsold stock, and its customers may face shortages or delays. These disruptions can ripple through the economy, impacting various sectors and regions.

- **Job losses**: As discussed earlier, cyberattacks can lead to financial losses and business shutdowns, potentially resulting in job losses. This can have wide-ranging socio-economic impacts, affecting families and communities and contributing to economic inequality.

- **Increased cybersecurity costs**: The rise in cyber threats can lead to increased cybersecurity costs for all businesses, not just those directly targeted. These increased costs can affect profitability and potentially lead to higher prices for consumers. For smaller businesses, the additional cost burden may even threaten their viability.

- **Erosion of trust**: Cyberattacks, particularly those that involve data breaches, can erode trust in digital systems. This can affect consumer behavior, potentially slowing the adoption of digital technologies and hampering digital innovation. In certain sectors such as finance or healthcare, a loss of trust can have significant economic impacts.

- **Regulatory impacts**: Increased cyber threats can lead to tighter regulations, which can have downstream impacts on businesses, particularly small and mid-sized ones. These businesses may face increased costs and operational challenges in meeting these regulatory requirements, as discussed in previous sections.

- **Economic inequality**: Cyber threats can contribute to economic inequality, as larger, wealthier businesses and countries are better able to protect themselves. This can leave smaller businesses and developing countries more vulnerable to attacks, exacerbating existing economic disparities.

- **Impact on innovation**: Finally, the rise in cyber threats can impact innovation. Businesses may become more cautious in adopting new technologies due to potential cybersecurity risks, potentially slowing the pace of technological advancement and economic growth.

The use of AI systems with malware

AI systems can both help combat and potentially increase the likelihood of malware incidents, depending on their use.

On the one hand, AI is increasingly being used in cybersecurity solutions to detect and prevent malware attacks. ML, a subset of AI, can be used to recognize patterns and anomalies that suggest malicious activity, making it easier to identify and mitigate threats in real time. Sophisticated AI systems can analyze vast quantities of data much faster and more accurately than human analysts, leading to more efficient and effective threat detection and response.

However, on the other hand, AI can also be used maliciously to create more sophisticated malware. Cybercriminals can use AI to automate the creation of malware, making it easier to produce and disseminate threats. AI can also be used to create polymorphic malware, which changes its code as it spreads, making it harder to detect. Additionally, AI can be used to analyze the defenses of potential targets and identify vulnerabilities more efficiently.

There is also the potential for AI to be used in so-called deepfake attacks. Deepfakes use AI to create realistic-looking fake videos or audio recordings that can be used in sophisticated phishing attacks. This opens up a whole new avenue for cybercrime, beyond traditional malware.

Although there have been no widely reported and confirmed cases where AI was the primary tool used to create or disseminate malware, this does not mean that AI has not been used in this way – it is entirely possible that AI has been used in malware attacks that have not been publicly disclosed or identified. In fact, security researchers and professionals have been predicting the rise of AI-powered malware for several years.

What has been documented are instances where AI has been used in conjunction with malware, although not as the primary tool. For example, ML has been used to improve phishing attacks by training on successful examples to create more convincing fake emails.

Furthermore, AI has been used to analyze and classify malware. This can be seen as a kind of "arms race" where both defenders and attackers use AI to improve their capabilities. For example, researchers at BlackBerry Cylance demonstrated in 2015 that they could use ML to classify malware with a high degree of accuracy.

In conclusion, while there are theoretical concerns about the potential for AI to be used in the creation and dissemination of malware, there have been no widely reported and confirmed instances of this occurring.

Cybersecurity, malware, and the socio-economic fabric

The digital age, while revolutionary in many respects, has introduced a labyrinth of challenges. Among these challenges, cyber threats such as malware and ransomware loom large. As this thread illuminated, the consequences of such threats extend beyond mere technical vulnerabilities, having profound economic, socio-economic, and operational ramifications.

In a world that is highly interconnected, malware attacks have showcased vulnerabilities inherent in global systems. The healthcare, financial, retail, and manufacturing sectors are all part of this intricate web, with cyberattacks not only causing direct financial losses but also impacting the trust quotient essential to commerce and public life.

Healthcare cyber breaches, for instance, can have life-altering repercussions when critical patient care is interrupted. Financial institutions, the bulwarks of our economic systems, when compromised, can undermine the very trust that upholds global economic stability. Similarly, retail and manufacturing sectors face both the immediate economic impact and ripple effects that can disrupt global supply chains and job markets.

The increasing sophistication of malware attacks, with potential links to AI, hints at an arms race between cyber defenders and attackers. AI, with its vast potential, stands at a crossroads, being a tool for both fortifying defenses and complicating the threat landscape. While its full-fledged use in creating malware hasn't been extensively documented since 2021, the potential remains a significant concern.

The socio-economic implications of cyberattacks are multifaceted. Jobs, essential to the livelihoods of millions, can be compromised with a single successful attack on key industries. Public services, the bedrock of civic life, when disrupted, can impact essential utilities and erode public trust. And the strain on small businesses, often less equipped to deal with cyber threats, exacerbates economic inequalities in an already divided world.

However, the true complexity emerges in the intertwined relationship between policy, regulation, and their downstream impacts. While regulations aim to fortify defenses and establish cybersecurity standards, they inadvertently also burden small and mid-scale businesses with operational challenges. Navigating the regulatory maze often translates to increased costs, hampering growth and potentially leading to business closures. This dichotomy between security and operational ease underscores the need for more inclusive and adaptive policy frameworks.

In addressing these challenges, there's a global imperative. To build a resilient, secure digital future, nations, businesses, and individuals need to recognize the multi-dimensional impact of cyber threats. Beyond technological solutions, this requires a socio-economic and policy perspective, underlined by a commitment to equity, innovation, and collaboration.

The digital realm's challenges are not just a technical frontier but a profound societal concern. As malware evolves and cyber threats proliferate, understanding and addressing their wider implications becomes paramount. The task ahead is not just to secure bytes and networks, but also to protect the very fabric of modern society.

Summary

We covered a wide array of topics related to cybersecurity, specifically focusing on the broader impacts of malware and ransomware incidents. We discussed how these cyber threats have economic, socio-economic, and operational consequences, affecting not just individual businesses but the global economic landscape as well.

We delved into various downstream impacts, from supply chain disruptions and job losses to the erosion of public trust and the need for tighter regulations. Emphasis was given to how smaller businesses and public services are disproportionately affected by the cyber threat landscape and the challenges in keeping up with ever-changing regulations.

AI's role was also highlighted, noting its dual-edged potential as a powerful tool for enhancing cybersecurity measures and, conversely, for creating more sophisticated and potentially undetectable malware. However, there have been no widely reported incidents where AI was the primary tool for deploying malware.

The overarching sentiment is that the challenge of cyber threats is not solely a technical issue; it's deeply interwoven with social and economic fabrics. While technology evolves, the socio-economic and policy frameworks must adapt correspondingly to protect the multifaceted aspects of modern society.

The multifaceted and evolving nature of malware and ransomware threats demands innovative and robust detection and analysis techniques. Conventional methods often fall short in this regard, highlighting the need for sophisticated approaches that can discern anomalous patterns and uncover hidden structures in complex malware data. Looking forward to the next chapter, we will discover how **Topological Data Analysis** (TDA) emerges as a promising paradigm for addressing this challenge, offering a unique perspective to unravel the topological features of malware and develop more effective detection and analysis systems.

Part 2 –
The Current State of
Key Malware Science AI
Technologies

We will cover three key AI methodologies used for malware detection and analysis.

This part has the following chapters:

- *Chapter 3, Topological Data Analysis for Malware Detection and Analysis*
- *Chapter 4, Artificial Intelligence for Malware Data Analysis and Detection*
- *Chapter 5, Behavior-Based Malware Data Analysis and Detection*

Topological Data Analysis for Malware Detection and Analysis

The advent of internet technologies has ushered in unprecedented opportunities for global communication and the exchange of information. However, it has also introduced a plethora of security threats, notably malware. These malicious software are designed to infiltrate, damage, or disrupt computing systems, often with severe consequences. Traditional malware detection methods have had varying levels of success but have also highlighted the need for more sophisticated approaches. This chapter explores the application of **Topological Data Analysis (TDA)** in malware detection and analysis, underscoring its potential to enhance cybersecurity measures.

Applying TDA to malware analysis presents a novel, efficient, and robust technique to identify and categorize malware. Unlike conventional analysis methods, which often hinge on known malware signatures or heuristic rules, TDA does not require prior knowledge of the data. Instead, it creates a multi-dimensional representation of the data, making it possible to uncover intrinsic data structures, highlight unusual patterns, and extract significant features that could signify the presence of malware.

Topological analysis of malware begins with transforming the malware binary or behavioral data into a topological space, often a simplicial complex. Each vertex in the complex represents a data point, and connections (edges) are drawn based on some proximity measure. The overall structure of the resulting complex offers a high-level view of the data, facilitating the identification of clusters, loops, and outliers, which are then examined for potential malware.

TDA's strength lies in its persistence homology – a tool that identifies and quantifies topological features at various scales. These features, such as connected components and holes, translate to essential properties in malware, such as command sequences or control flow structures. By examining the persistence of these features across multiple scales, researchers can differentiate between benign software and various types of malware, even amidst noisy data.

For instance, benign software might demonstrate a predictable structure when subjected to TDA, with data points forming compact clusters and fewer loops. On the other hand, malware, with its purposeful obfuscation techniques, might exhibit more complex structures, including scattered data points and numerous loops. By comparing the persistence diagrams of different software, TDA can reveal differences and similarities, enabling robust malware classification.

Moreover, TDA's ability to work with high-dimensional data suits the complex nature of malware. Cybercriminals continually evolve their strategies, resulting in an increasing variety of malware exhibiting multifaceted behaviors. Traditional methods often struggle to handle such complexities, but TDA thrives in this environment. It can unravel the inherent structure of complex malware data, making it easier to detect new or unknown malware variants.

Finally, TDA is resilient to noise and minor modifications – a characteristic critical in malware detection. Malware often undergoes minor tweaks, known as polymorphism and metamorphism, to evade detection. While such changes can deceive traditional detection systems, they are unlikely to alter the fundamental topological structure, allowing TDA-based systems to detect even sophisticated, modified malware.

Despite these significant advantages, the application of TDA in malware analysis is not without challenges. The interpretation of topological features and their correlation to malware traits requires deep domain knowledge. Additionally, high computational costs can limit its application in real-time detection systems.

Nonetheless, with the burgeoning growth of machine learning techniques and computational power, the integration of TDA in malware detection and analysis systems appears promising. Not only can it enhance the detection rates, but it can also provide insights into the inherent structure and behavior of malware – knowledge that could help in the development of more robust cybersecurity measures.

As such, TDA offers a fresh perspective in the battle against malware. By taking advantage of TDA's unique capabilities, researchers can navigate the evolving landscape of cyber threats, enhancing our capacity to protect digital assets. Despite the challenges, its potential to revolutionize malware detection and analysis systems is significant and warrants further exploration and investment.

In this chapter, we will cover the following main topics:

- The mathematics of space and continuous transformations
- A deeper dive into the "shape of the data"
- How TDA creates a multi-dimensional data representation
- Transforming a malware binary into a topological space
- Homology
- Persistence homology distinguishes meaningful patterns from random data fluctuations
- Improving detection algorithms to predict the behavior of new malware

- TDA – comparing and contrasting the persistence diagrams of different software
- Using malware persistence diagrams to classify unknown software
- Persistence homology – filtering noise to find meaningful patterns
- Classifying unknown malware with characteristic persistent features
- Leveraging classification to manage threat response
- A deeper dive – employing TDA for threat management

The mathematics of space and continuous transformations

Topology is a fascinating and broad field of mathematics, and its concepts can seem abstract if you're not familiar with them. To illustrate topology, one often-used example is the *Rubber-Sheet Geometry* analogy.

Let's imagine three shapes: a coffee mug, a donut (torus), and a soccer ball. In the eyes of a topologist, the coffee mug and the donut are equivalent because they each have one hole. In contrast, the soccer ball is different as it has no hole. The essence of topology is not about exact measurements such as length, angle, or area, but about the properties that remain unchanged under stretching, bending, or twisting – what topologists refer to as "continuous transformations."

If you consider that the coffee mug is made of a flexible material such as rubber, you could imagine deforming it into a donut shape without tearing or gluing it. The handle of the mug represents the hole in the donut. However, no amount of stretching or squishing could make the soccer ball look like a donut or coffee mug without introducing a hole or closing one up, which is not allowed in continuous transformations. Thus, the coffee mug and the donut belong to one topological class, while the soccer ball belongs to another.

When translating this concept to a more complex realm such as data analysis, topological structures allow us to understand the **shape** of the data. For example, if you have a dataset where points are sampled from a circular pattern, applying a topological lens would allow you to detect the inherent **loop** in the data, even if it is obscured by noise or the data is high-dimensional. The key here is that topology is concerned with these fundamental properties, which don't change under certain transformations, a concept that proves valuable in various applications, including malware data analysis and detection.

A deeper dive into the "shape of the data"

The concept of shape in topological data analysis is quite different from how we traditionally understand shapes in geometry. Instead of focusing on rigid properties such as lengths, angles, and areas, the shape in topology refers to the broader, more flexible structure of data. It looks at how data points relate to each other and form a larger pattern or structure.

Imagine that you have a cluster of data points. At the simplest level, you could look at the points individually. However, this wouldn't provide much insight beyond each point's specific characteristics. In contrast, topological data analysis allows you to take a step back and view the dataset as a whole.

To visualize this concept, let's consider a simple example. Suppose you have a dataset comprising various species of animals recorded from different habitats. The data includes attributes such as size, diet, habitat type, and other traits. If we take these data points and plot them in a high-dimensional space (where each dimension represents an attribute), it might be challenging to discern any clear pattern using traditional methods.

However, using topological methods, we could visualize this high-dimensional data in a more digestible form. The topological approach would identify clusters of animals with similar traits and connect these clusters based on shared characteristics. This process would create a network or graph that captures the key relationships within the data, effectively giving our animal dataset a simplified shape.

The shape here does not refer to a physical form but a structure that encapsulates the essential relationships and patterns within the data. This structure can reveal hidden patterns or clusters and even identify outliers – animals that don't fit into any established group.

Additionally, the concept of shape in TDA is particularly resilient to noise, unlike other data analysis methods. A few extra data points or minor variations won't significantly alter the broad topological shape, making TDA a robust tool for analyzing complex, real-world data.

Now, extending this concept to malware detection, let's imagine that each data point is a piece of software. Each software could be represented by a host of features, such as its binary structure, control flow, system calls, and more.

When analyzing the shape of this software data, topological analysis would look for structures and patterns within the data. Just like in the animal example, it might find clusters of benign software that share similar characteristics. Similarly, it might find clusters of malware with shared features.

More importantly, it might identify bridges or connections between benign and malicious software – instances where malware has been designed to look like benign software. By looking at the shape of the data, topologists can identify these anomalies and use them to improve malware detection.

As such, when we say *"topological structures allow us to understand the shape of the data,"* we refer to the ability to see the broad, structural patterns in data – how points cluster together, the connections between them, and the overall network they form. This perspective allows us to understand our data at a much deeper level, revealing insights that might be missed by traditional data analysis techniques.

How TDA creates a multi-dimensional data representation

TDA creates a multi-dimensional representation of the data, making it possible to uncover intrinsic data structures, highlight unusual patterns, and extract significant features that could signify the presence of malware.

Recall that TDA is a powerful tool that leverages the concepts of topology to analyze complex and high-dimensional datasets. It gives us the capacity to simplify and understand the shape of the data, allowing us to discover intrinsic data structures, highlight unusual patterns, and extract significant features.

Data in the real world, particularly in cybersecurity, tends to be multi-dimensional. For instance, when we are analyzing software for potential malware, we might consider features such as the sequence of system calls made, the binary structure, network activity, and more. Each of these features constitutes a dimension, leading to a high-dimensional dataset.

However, making sense of this high-dimensional data is not straightforward. Traditional techniques, such as statistical analysis, often struggle with what is referred to as the "curse of dimensionality." As dimensions increase, the volume of the space increases so fast that the available data becomes sparse, making meaningful analysis challenging.

TDA, on the other hand, has unique methods to handle such high-dimensional data. It starts by creating a multi-dimensional representation of the data, often in the form of a simplicial complex – a generalization of a network that can capture higher-order relationships and structures in the data.

Each data point, characterized by its various features, is represented as a node in this network. Connections (edges) between nodes are formed based on some measure of similarity or proximity. This could be as simple as Euclidean distance for numerical data, or it could be a more complex measure tailored to the specific type of data.

The simplicial complex forms a shape that represents the structure of the data in its multi-dimensional form. This topological shape encapsulates the key patterns and relationships within the data. Clusters of nodes might represent groups of similar software, loops may indicate recurring patterns, and outliers might signify unusual behavior.

One key aspect of TDA is its use of persistent homology – a technique that captures the "shape" of data across different scales. By adjusting the threshold for connection between nodes, different structures emerge. For instance, with a low threshold, only the most similar data points connect, revealing fine-grained clusters. As the threshold increases, more nodes connect, larger structures form, and the overall connectivity can be assessed.

In the context of malware detection, these methods could be used to reveal the underlying structure of malware and benign software. Clusters could represent different types of software, and outliers could represent potential malware. Persistent homology could detect structures in the data that persist across different scales, which could be indicative of the obfuscation techniques used by malware.

By analyzing the data's shape, TDA can identify patterns and structures that other methods might miss. These could be used as features in a machine learning model for malware detection or directly analyzed to identify potential threats. This multi-dimensional approach provides a comprehensive analysis, improving the robustness and accuracy of malware detection.

To summarize, TDA's ability to create a multi-dimensional representation of data offers a novel approach to understanding complex datasets. Its application in malware detection exemplifies its potential to unearth deep insights from data, opening up new avenues for cyber security.

Transforming a malware binary into a topological space

Now, let's expand on how topological analysis of malware begins with transforming the malware binary or behavioral data into a topological space, often a simplicial complex. Topological analysis of malware is a modern approach to cybersecurity that involves converting complex data about malware into a form that can be better understood and studied. This process might sound abstract and complicated, but let's break it down into more relatable terms using an analogy.

Imagine that you're looking at a massive crowd of people from a bird's-eye view. Each person in this crowd can be thought of as a data point. Now, suppose you want to understand more about the people in the crowd – their relationships, groups, and any unusual behavior. Trying to examine each person individually would be an overwhelming task. A much more efficient approach would be to look for patterns within the crowd.

This is essentially what topological analysis of malware aims to do. Instead of people in a crowd, we have pieces of software or code that might be malware. We want to understand the "crowd" of software, look for patterns, and spot any potential threats.

The first step in this process is to transform this "crowd" of data points into something that can reveal these patterns. In the world of topology, this is referred to as a "topological space," often in the form of a simplicial complex.

If we return to our crowd analogy, creating a topological space would be like drawing lines between people who know each other. If two people are friends, you draw a line between them. Groups of friends would then form interconnected clusters, allowing you to easily see relationships in the crowd. Similarly, a simplicial complex connects data points that are similar or close to each other in some way, based on the features we're considering (such as system calls made, binary structure, and more for software).

In a simplicial complex, each data point (software) is a vertex, and the lines drawn between them based on their similarity are edges. When you step back and look at this network of vertices and edges, you start to see the shape of the data.

Clusters of vertices represent groups of similar software. Just like clusters of interconnected friends in the crowd, these clusters could be different types of benign software or different families of malware. If a new software shares a lot of characteristics with a known malware cluster, it might be a potential threat.

Loops in the simplicial complex represent recurring patterns in the data. In our crowd analogy, a loop might represent a group of friends who all know each other. In the context of software, it could represent a common sequence of system calls or a pattern in the binary structure. If a new software displays these patterns, it might be a potential malware.

Outliers, on the other hand, are vertices that don't connect to any major cluster. In the crowd, these might be people who don't know anyone else. In the software world, outliers could be pieces of software that are markedly different from the rest. They may represent new or unknown types of malware.

Once the topological space is created, topologists can study it to understand the patterns and structures within the malware data. This approach provides a high-level view of the "crowd" of software, revealing insights that might be missed when looking at individual data points.

By identifying clusters, loops, and outliers, topologists can highlight potential threats, refine malware detection algorithms, and even understand the behavior of different malware families. This makes the complex task of malware detection more manageable and efficient.

As such, topological analysis of malware is like examining a crowd from a bird's-eye view. By transforming the data into a topological space, topologists can understand the "crowd" of software at a high level, look for patterns, and identify potential threats. Despite its abstract nature, this approach is a powerful tool in the arsenal of cybersecurity experts.

Homology

Recall that I mentioned TDA's strength lies in its persistence homology – a tool that identifies and quantifies topological features at various scales. Persistence homology is one of the most powerful tools in the TDA toolbox. To explain it simply, let's use the analogy of taking photographs of a mountain range at different altitudes.

Imagine you're in a helicopter, ascending from the base to the peak of a mountain range. As you ascend, you take a series of photographs. At the base, you capture individual mountains. As you rise higher, you start to see groups of mountains and then entire sections of the mountain range. By the time you're at the peak, you have a complete, bird's-eye view of the range.

In this analogy, each photograph you take represents a scale. Just like how different scales reveal different details about the mountain range, persistence homology explores data at different scales to uncover various topological features.

Let's consider a simplified example. Suppose we have a 2D scatter plot of data points, which are scattered in a way that they vaguely form two concentric circles. If we were to draw a small circle around each data point, we may only see isolated data points or small clusters, similar to individual mountains at the base level.

However, as we start increasing the radius of the circles (analogous to ascending in the helicopter), the circles start to overlap and form bigger structures. At some point, the circles from the data points in each ring will overlap enough to form two separate loops, the equivalent of seeing groups of mountains. As we keep increasing the radius, eventually, all circles will overlap, and we will lose the two-loop structure, giving us a bird's-eye view where all details are lost.

The key idea of persistent homology is to track these features, such as clusters (connected components) and loops (holes), as we change the scale (in this case, increasing the circle's radius).

In the concentric circles example, persistence homology would help us identify the two loops. The fact that these loops persist over a range of scales suggests that they're significant and not just random noise. On the other hand, features that appear and disappear quickly at a certain scale might just be random fluctuations in the data.

Persistence homology produces something called a persistence diagram, which is a way of recording the birth and death of these topological features as the scale changes. In the diagram, the birth of a feature is when it first appears (for example, when a loop forms) and its death is when it disappears (for example, when a loop closes up).

The persistence of a feature is the difference between its birth and death, and it indicates the significance of a feature – the longer a feature persists, the more significant it is assumed to be. So, in our example, if the two loops appear for a considerable range of radii before they disappear, they would be deemed significant.

In the context of malware analysis, persistence homology could reveal significant structures in the data that persist across scales. These could correspond to underlying patterns or characteristics in the behavior or structure of malware. Because it identifies features that are consistent across multiple scales, persistence homology offers robustness against noise and the ability to distinguish meaningful patterns from random fluctuations in the data.

As such, persistence homology can be thought of as a multi-scale microscope for studying data. Identifying and quantifying features at various scales allows us to distill complex, high-dimensional data down to its most significant features. This makes it a powerful tool for analyzing complex datasets, such as those found in malware analysis.

Persistence homology distinguishes meaningful patterns from random data fluctuations

TDA and its tool, persistent homology, can provide innovative methods to fight cyber threats, particularly malware. To understand how it works, let's first consider what malware is and the challenges it presents.

Recall that malware comes in many forms, from viruses to ransomware, and is continually evolving. Cybersecurity professionals must analyze vast amounts of data to detect these threats and protect systems. However, the sheer volume of data, its complex structure, and the continuously changing nature of malware make this a challenging task.

This is where TDA and persistent homology come into the picture. Recall the mountain range analogy and how it was used to explain the concept of scale. Now, let's use a similar analogy to understand how these techniques can be applied to malware analysis.

Imagine you're a detective trying to find a crime syndicate in a bustling city. You start at the ground level, going street by street, inspecting every building and person. At this level, you can observe individual activities, but spotting organized crime patterns can be quite challenging amid the city's complexity and noise.

Now, imagine if you could rise above the city and view it from different altitudes. From higher up, you might start to see patterns that you couldn't spot at the ground level: groups of people meeting regularly, unusual movement patterns, or a particular building getting a lot of visitors.

Applying persistent homology to malware analysis is like being that detective with the ability to view the city from multiple altitudes. It involves studying the data at various scales to uncover structures and patterns that might indicate the presence of malware.

The data points, in this case, could be various characteristics of software or its behavior, such as system calls, binary structures, or network activity. These characteristics can be transformed into a topological space (such as our city viewed from different altitudes), and then persistent homology comes into play.

As we change the scale – similar to changing our altitude – we observe the birth and death of different topological features, such as clusters or loops. A cluster could represent a group of similar programs, while a loop might represent a recurring pattern of behavior in the software.

In malware analysis, a persistent feature – one that appears consistently across multiple scales – could indicate a significant pattern characteristic of malware. For example, a persistent cluster might represent a family of malware that shares a common structure or behavior. A persistent loop could represent a typical sequence of system calls that malware makes to infect a system.

This ability to identify persistent features makes persistent homology robust against noise in the data. In our city analogy, noise would be like random, everyday activities that don't have anything to do with the crime syndicate. Similarly, in malware analysis, there could be many random patterns in the data that are not related to malware. Persistent homology helps distinguish these random fluctuations from the significant, persistent patterns indicative of malware.

By identifying these persistent features, cybersecurity professionals can better understand the underlying structure and behavior of malware. This information can be used to improve malware detection algorithms and to predict the behavior of unknown or new malware, enhancing the overall security of the systems.

In summary, TDA and persistent homology offer a powerful, multi-scale perspective for analyzing complex data in malware detection. By identifying significant, persistent features in the data, they can help distinguish the signal from the noise, improving the efficiency and accuracy of malware detection.

Improving detection algorithms to predict the behavior of new malware

Persistent homology, a concept from TDA, offers a novel perspective in dealing with the constant threats posed by malicious software, known as malware. Its unique value lies in its ability to extract significant patterns and structures in complex data across multiple scales. By identifying these so-called persistent features, cybersecurity professionals gain insights into the core structure and behavior of malware, enabling them to enhance detection algorithms and predict the behavior of new or unknown malware strains. Let's explore this concept more deeply using a practical analogy.

Consider a game of chess. Each player maneuvers their pieces, trying to anticipate the opponent's moves and strategize accordingly. Skilled chess players often recognize patterns in their opponent's moves. They can distinguish a defensive player from an aggressive one, or identify specific strategies based on the arrangement of the pieces on the board. Recognizing these patterns helps the player anticipate future moves and plan their strategy accordingly.

In the world of cybersecurity, the situation is somewhat similar. Cybersecurity experts are engaged in a constant game against malicious actors who produce malware. Much like a chess player, these experts need to recognize patterns in the behavior and structure of malware to anticipate future threats and improve their defenses.

In this context, the chessboard is the vast, high-dimensional space of malware data. Each piece on the board is a piece of software, and its position on the board represents its features (such as binary structure, system calls, or network activity). The challenge for cybersecurity professionals is to recognize patterns in this complex, multi-dimensional space, identify potential threats, and predict the behavior of malware.

This is where TDA and persistent homology come in. These tools provide a way of viewing the chessboard from different altitudes and observing the data at various scales. By doing so, they can reveal persistent features – patterns that persist across different scales, much like a recurring strategy in a chess game.

Identifying these persistent features can significantly improve our understanding of malware. For example, a persistent cluster of data points could represent a family of malware that shares common behaviors or structures. Recognizing this cluster allows cybersecurity experts to identify other potential malware that share these common features, improving their detection capabilities.

Similarly, a persistent loop could represent a recurring sequence of system calls or a common pattern in the binary structure of malware. Detecting such loops helps in identifying malware that exhibits these persistent patterns, even if they are embedded in a sea of benign software.

These insights aren't just valuable for detecting known threats; they also have powerful implications for predicting the behavior of unknown or new malware. Once a persistent feature is identified as being indicative of malware, any new software exhibiting similar features can be flagged as a potential threat, even if it's a previously unseen variant. This predictive capability is crucial in a field where new malware strains are continually emerging.

Furthermore, the ability of persistent homology to distinguish significant patterns from random noise adds an additional layer of robustness to malware detection. In our chess analogy, this would be like distinguishing between a strategic move and a random one. By focusing on features that persist across different scales, TDA avoids being misled by random fluctuations in the data, which could lead to false detections.

By incorporating these insights from TDA and persistent homology into their strategies, cybersecurity professionals can enhance the overall security of the systems they protect. They can improve their malware detection algorithms, making them more efficient and accurate. They can also better anticipate future threats, allowing them to respond proactively rather than reactively.

As such, TDA, and in particular, persistent homology, offer powerful tools for understanding and combating malware. By identifying and focusing on persistent features in the data, these techniques can provide deeper insights into the underlying structures and behaviors of malware, significantly enhancing our ability to detect and predict threats.

TDA – comparing and contrasting the persistence diagrams of different software

The application of TDA and its technique of persistent homology offers a unique approach to differentiating benign software from malicious ones (malware), even amid the complexity and noise present in high-dimensional datasets.

Let's delve into this by further expanding on the examples provided. First, consider benign software – programs designed to perform legitimate, useful tasks without causing harm to the system. When subjected to TDA, the properties of benign software tend to form certain predictable patterns. These properties, which can include binary structures, system calls, or network activity, may cluster together in the topological space. This is like how people at a social gathering might group based on shared interests or common connections. In terms of our earlier analogy, these clusters can be viewed as "mountains" on our landscape.

In the context of persistent homology, benign software's topological features, such as clusters and loops, may form and dissolve over a smaller range of scales. For example, a cluster could form when certain system calls are frequently made together, and this cluster might persist only for a narrow range of scales. Similarly, benign software might have fewer loops, indicating less complex interconnections or dependencies between different functions or components within the software.

On the other hand, malware is designed with the express intention of evading detection and causing harm. Malware authors often use obfuscation techniques to make the malicious code harder to detect or analyze. This could involve making changes to the control flow, the use of non-standard library calls, or complex encryption techniques. When subjected to TDA, these techniques can lead to a more complex topological structure, including scattered data points and numerous loops. This would be analogous to a social gathering where people are purposefully disguising their true interests or connections to evade detection.

In the persistence homology framework, the birth and death of these topological features could occur over a broader range of scales compared to benign software. A persistent cluster could represent a family of malware with a common structure or behavior, while a persistent loop might signify a characteristic pattern of system calls or control flows employed by the malware.

Now, let's consider how comparing the persistence diagrams of different software can aid in malware classification. A persistence diagram is a graphical representation of the birth and death of topological features as the scale changes. By comparing these diagrams, we can discern similarities and differences between various software, whether benign or malicious.

For example, suppose we find that certain persistent clusters or loops are commonly seen in the persistence diagrams of known malware but not in benign software. In that case, we can use this information to classify new or unknown software. If a piece of software has similar persistent features as known malware, it can be flagged as potentially malicious. This comparison can also help identify different families or types of malware that share common persistent features.

Conversely, if the persistence diagram of a piece of software closely matches that of benign software and lacks the persistent features associated with malware, it can be classified as likely benign. This kind of comparison is especially useful for dealing with "zero-day" threats – new or previously unseen malware that do not match any known signatures. By focusing on the topological structure rather than specific signatures, TDA offers a robust way to detect these novel threats.

This comparative approach extends to analyzing changes in the landscape of malware over time. Cyber threats continually evolve, with new malware variants being developed and existing ones being modified to evade detection. By tracking changes in the persistence diagrams over time, cybersecurity professionals can gain insights into these evolving trends and adapt their detection and defense strategies accordingly.

As such, the comparison of persistence diagrams offers a powerful tool for malware classification. By identifying and focusing on persistent features across different scales, TDA can highlight the topological differences and similarities between benign software and malware. This approach improves the robustness and flexibility of malware detection, helping to safeguard our systems against both known and emerging threats.

Using malware persistence diagrams to classify unknown software

Cybersecurity experts leverage a variety of approaches to detect and counter malware threats. One of these approaches is the use of signatures or known patterns of behavior that are indicative of a specific malware. However, modern malware employs sophisticated techniques to evade such signature-based detection methods. This is where TDA and its associated method of persistent homology can provide a significant edge.

To further expand on the example given: persistent homology creates a topological summary of high-dimensional data in the form of a persistence diagram. This diagram shows the "birth" and "death" of topological features, such as clusters and loops, as we vary the scale. By observing these diagrams, we can identify certain recurring patterns or "persistent features" that are commonly seen in the persistence diagrams of known malware.

Take, for instance, a certain persistent cluster or loop that we frequently see in known malware samples. These persistent features could correspond to certain shared behaviors or structures in the malware code, such as a specific sequence of system calls, a particular control flow pattern, or a common method of obfuscation.

But how do we use this information for malware detection and classification?

When we analyze a new or unknown piece of software using persistent homology, we generate a persistence diagram for that software. If we find that this diagram has similar persistent features as the known malware (such as the persistent cluster or loop we identified earlier), it is a strong indicator that this software could be potentially malicious. By looking for these common persistent features, we can flag software as suspicious, even if it doesn't match any known malware signatures. This is particularly useful in identifying and countering zero-day threats.

However, the utility of this method doesn't stop at detection. It also offers valuable insights for malware classification. Different malware often belongs to different families or types, each with its own set of characteristics. For instance, ransomware is a type of malware that encrypts a user's files and demands a ransom to decrypt them, while a Trojan disguises itself as legitimate software to trick the user into installing it.

These different types of malware may exhibit different persistent features. For example, a specific persistent loop could be common among ransomware but rarely seen in Trojans. Conversely, a particular persistent cluster might be prevalent among Trojans but uncommon in ransomware. By identifying these characteristic persistent features, we can classify unknown malware into their respective families or types, improving our understanding of the threat and informing our response.

As such, persistent homology offers a powerful tool for both malware detection and classification. By identifying persistent features that are common among known malware and comparing them with new or unknown software, we can detect potentially malicious programs and classify them into different types or families. This methodology, while complex, provides an innovative approach to bolstering cybersecurity in the face of evolving threats.

Persistence homology – filtering noise to find meaningful patterns

TDA and its method of persistent homology provide a groundbreaking approach to cyber threat detection that complements traditional techniques. In a world where threats are constantly evolving and new malware is being developed, the ability to identify and classify potentially harmful software based on its inherent data structure is invaluable.

To better understand the usefulness of this approach, let's dig deeper into how persistence diagrams, the graphical representation of topological data, can be leveraged to identify benign software and detect novel threats.

As we explained earlier, benign software, when analyzed using persistent homology, typically presents a predictable structure. This might mean tight clusters of data points representing common or routine software activities, fewer loops indicating less intricate interactions, and simpler connections that align with the software's legitimate function. The persistence diagram of such benign software could be thought of as a relatively tame topographical map – few mountains, easy trails, and minimal surprises.

Comparing the persistence diagram of an unknown piece of software to that of known benign software serves as a baseline assessment. If they match closely and the unknown software lacks the persistent features typically associated with malware, the software can be tentatively classified as likely benign. This doesn't necessarily mean it's entirely safe, but the odds are in its favor.

On the contrary, if the unknown software exhibits complex or unusual topological features not found in the benign software, it could be flagged for further investigation. This nuanced approach to software analysis enables more accurate classification and reduces the number of false positives – a common problem with traditional signature-based malware detection methods.

The versatility of TDA truly shines when dealing with "zero-day" threats. These are new or previously unseen forms of malware that do not match any known signatures. They're called "zero-day" because they exploit vulnerabilities that are unknown to the software vendor, giving the vendor zero days to develop and distribute a patch. As you might imagine, these threats are particularly insidious and difficult to detect using conventional methods.

Signature-based detection, while effective against known threats, is inherently limited when faced with novel malware variants. These methods rely on identifying known patterns, so malware that doesn't follow any known pattern can easily slip through. But TDA, with its focus on the topological structure of data, offers a robust way to detect these novel threats.

Remember, TDA is about understanding the "shape" of the data. When faced with a zero-day threat, it can provide critical insights based on the intrinsic structure and properties of the malware, regardless of how different it might be from known threats. This is because, at its core, malware – regardless of its signature – tends to behave in certain ways that differ from benign software. These behaviors, though they might be obfuscated or modified, can cause distinctive topological features to emerge when analyzed via persistent homology.

For instance, consider a piece of zero-day malware that employs a novel method of obfuscation. Although its code might not match any known signatures, this obfuscation might cause certain loops to form in the topological space. These loops might be rare or non-existent in known benign software, but common in various forms of malware. By identifying this anomaly, the TDA method could flag this software as potentially malicious, even though it's a zero-day threat.

In this way, TDA offers a level of robustness and adaptability that is incredibly valuable in the ever-evolving landscape of cybersecurity. It's not about recognizing known threats but about understanding the inherent topological differences between benign and malicious software. This empowers cybersecurity professionals to identify potential threats based on their topological "fingerprint" rather than relying solely on known signatures.

As such, by focusing on topological structure, TDA and persistent homology offer a compelling solution to the challenges posed by zero-day threats and rapidly evolving malware. The methodology enriches the toolkit of cybersecurity professionals, complementing existing techniques, and enhancing our collective ability to safeguard digital systems.

Classifying unknown malware with characteristic persistent features

In the ongoing battle against cyber threats, malware detection and classification remain crucial components of a robust cybersecurity strategy. TDA, particularly its method of persistent homology, provides a powerful way to analyze and categorize malware based on their intrinsic topological features.

Let's delve deeper into how these tools can be employed to better understand and respond to different types of malware threats. At its core, TDA is about understanding the shape of data. With persistent homology, we convert the complex, high-dimensional data into a more interpretable form, called a persistence diagram. These diagrams show the **birth** and **death** of topological features such as clusters and loops as we vary the scale of analysis. Importantly, these features persist across different scales, allowing us to identify recurring patterns in the data that are robust against noise and small perturbations:

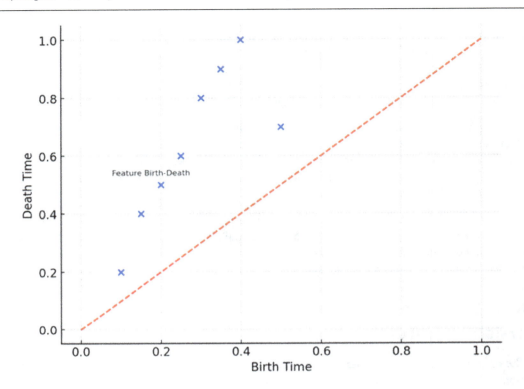

Figure 3.1 – Persistence diagram in the context of malware analysis using TDA

The preceding persistence diagram illustrates the concept of birth and death times of topological features, such as clusters and loops, in the context of malware analysis using **Topological Data Analysis (TDA)**. In this diagram, each point represents a topological feature, with the x-coordinate indicating its birth time and the y-coordinate its death time. The line \(y = x\) (shown in red) helps to visualize the minimum lifespan of these features. Points above this line represent features that persist over a range of scales, which can be crucial for identifying recurring patterns or "persistent features" in the data, especially in the analysis of malware.

Here's a copy of the python code I used to generate the diagram and description:

```
import matplotlib.pyplot as plt
import numpy as np

# Generate some sample data for the persistence diagram
# These are arbitrary points representing the birth and death times of
topological features
sample_data = np.array([
    [0.1, 0.2],
    [0.15, 0.4],
```

```
    [0.2, 0.5],
    [0.25, 0.6],
    [0.3, 0.8],
    [0.35, 0.9],
    [0.4, 1.0],
    [0.5, 0.7]
])

# Plotting the persistence diagram
plt.figure(figsize=(8, 6))
plt.scatter(sample_data[:, 0], sample_data[:, 1], color='blue')

# Adding labels and titles
plt.title("Sample Persistence Diagram")
plt.xlabel("Birth Time")
plt.ylabel("Death Time")
plt.grid(True)

# Drawing a line y=x to represent the minimum lifespan of features
plt.plot([0, 1], [0, 1], color='red', linestyle='--')

# Annotating a sample point
plt.annotate('Feature Birth-Death', (sample_data[2, 0], sample_data[2,
1]),
             textcoords="offset points", xytext=(-10,10), ha='center',
fontsize=8)

# Show plot
plt.show()
```

I then took the data set a step further:

```
import pandas as pd

# Number of samples
n_samples = 100

# Simulating different features that could be indicative of malware
behavior
np.random.seed(0)  # for reproducibility

# Memory usage pattern (e.g., sudden spikes could indicate malicious
activity)
memory_usage = np.abs(np.random.normal(loc=50, scale=10, size=n_
samples)) + np.random.exponential(scale=5, size=n_samples)
```

```
# Network activity (e.g., high network usage could be a sign of data
exfiltration)
network_activity = np.abs(np.random.normal(loc=20, scale=5, size=n_
samples)) + np.random.exponential(scale=10, size=n_samples)

# File access patterns (e.g., high rate of file access could indicate
scanning activity)
file_access = np.random.poisson(lam=5, size=n_samples)

# CPU usage (e.g., high CPU usage could indicate intensive processes
typical of some malware)
cpu_usage = np.abs(np.random.normal(loc=30, scale=10, size=n_samples))
+ np.random.exponential(scale=3, size=n_samples)

# Aggregating these features into a DataFrame
malware_data = pd.DataFrame({
    'MemoryUsage': memory_usage,
    'NetworkActivity': network_activity,
    'FileAccess': file_access,
    'CpuUsage': cpu_usage
})

malware_data.head()   # Displaying the first few rows of the dataset
```

I generated a synthetic dataset that would be better suited for the book. Please note that this data will be a simplified representation and won't capture the full complexity of real malware data.

The generated dataset above represents a simplified example of what malware data might look like, featuring various metrics such as memory usage, network activity, file access rates, and CPU usage. These features are designed to mimic potential indicators of malware behavior:

- **Memory usage**: Fluctuations in memory usage could indicate malicious processes.
- **Network activity**: High or irregular network usage might suggest data exfiltration or communication with a command-and-control server.
- **File access**: An unusually high rate of file access could signal scanning or corrupting files.
- **CPU usage**: Elevated CPU usage might be associated with intensive tasks performed by malware.

This synthetic dataset can serve as a starting point for TDA and the creation of a persistence diagram. However, it's important to remember that real-world malware data would be more complex and require sophisticated analysis methods to accurately identify and classify malware behavior.

Here is a conceptual representation of a persistence diagram created using the synthetic malware dataset:

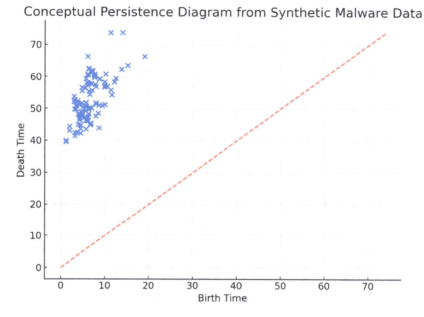

Figure 3.2 – Conceptual persistence diagram from synthetic malware data

In this simplified diagram, each point represents a feature in the dataset:

- The x-axis ("Birth Time") indicates the earliest point of significant change or emergence of a feature, as measured by its minimum distance to other points.

- The y-axis ("Death Time") represents the point at which the feature ceases to be relevant or distinct, as indicated by its maximum distance to other points.

- The red dashed line represents the threshold where the death time equals the birth time. Features (points) well above this line are considered more significant or persistent in the TDA context, potentially indicating notable characteristics in the malware data.

It's important to note that this diagram is a basic and conceptual illustration. In actual TDA applications, especially in complex fields like malware analysis, the analysis, and the resulting persistence diagram would involve more sophisticated computations and interpretations, typically performed using specialized TDA software.

Different types of malware often exhibit different persistent features. This could be due to differences in their coding structure, functionality, or behavior. For instance, ransomware, a type of malware that encrypts users' files and demands a ransom for decryption, may exhibit a certain persistent loop when analyzed via persistent homology. This loop could correspond to the sequence of operations the ransomware performs, such as searching for specific file types, encrypting them, and then initiating the ransom demand.

On the other hand, a Trojan, which disguises itself as a legitimate program to trick users into installing it, might exhibit a different topological structure. Instead of a loop, it might form a persistent cluster, reflecting its deceptive mode of operation. For example, this cluster could represent the steps the Trojan takes to mimic legitimate software, establish itself within the system, and then carry out its malicious activities.

These distinctive topological features serve as "fingerprints" that we can use to identify and classify different types of malware. By comparing the persistence diagrams of unknown malware to those of known malware types, we can determine which family or type the unknown malware most likely belongs to. For example, if an unknown malware's persistence diagram exhibits the loop commonly seen in ransomware, we might classify it as likely ransomware.

Classification is not only about assigning labels. It also improves our understanding of the threat and informs our response. Knowing that a piece of malware is likely ransomware can help cybersecurity professionals anticipate its behavior, such as which files it might target for encryption. This information can be used to develop appropriate countermeasures, such as isolating the affected systems to prevent further damage and using decryption tools that have been effective against similar ransomware in the past.

Additionally, this classification process can help uncover new variants or evolutions of known malware types. Suppose we encounter an unknown malware that exhibits the loop associated with ransomware but also has a new persistent feature not seen in known ransomware. This could indicate that it's a new variant of ransomware that has evolved to incorporate new **tactics, techniques, and procedures (TTPs)**. Recognizing this evolution can help us adapt our defenses accordingly.

This approach can also aid in the detection and understanding of advanced persistent threats APTs. APTs are sophisticated, long-term cyber-espionage campaigns that aim to gain unauthorized access to a network and remain undetected for an extended period. These threats often use a combination of different malware types and techniques, and their topological features could reflect this complexity. By identifying and analyzing these features, we can gain insights into the TTPs used by the APTs, which can help us devise more effective defensive strategies.

As such, the ability to identify and classify malware based on their persistent topological features adds a valuable dimension to our cybersecurity toolkit. Not only can it enhance our malware detection capabilities, but it can also improve our understanding of the threats we face and inform our response. As the landscape of cyber threats continues to evolve, these capabilities will become increasingly important in maintaining the security of our digital systems.

Leveraging classification to manage threat response

The domain of cybersecurity presents a unique challenge, characterized by a continual need to adapt to evolving threats. Each malware sample represents an ongoing effort by malicious actors to subvert digital systems. Understanding these threats at a deeper level can be the key to crafting effective defenses and neutralizing them. This is where TDA comes into play, offering an advanced methodology to classify and comprehend these threats.

In the context of malware analysis, classification is more than just about assigning labels to unknown samples. It's about understanding the fundamental nature of the threat. This is where TDA, and particularly persistent homology, can offer profound insights. When we classify malware using persistent homology, we're not simply assigning it into a category based on a shallow comparison of signatures. Instead, we're delving deeper, examining the topological shape of the data, which provides insight into its intrinsic structure and behavior.

Consider the hypothetical example of a piece of malware that, when analyzed through TDA, presents a persistent loop in its persistence diagram. This loop, a signature topological feature, could represent a particular sequence of activities or behaviors that the malware routinely executes. Ransomware might present such a loop, signifying the sequence of scanning, encrypting, and then demanding a ransom.

This loop isn't just a label or a signature – it's a representation of the malware's modus operandi. It provides valuable information about what malware does, how it operates, and, potentially, how it can be neutralized. For instance, knowing that a malware sample is likely ransomware based on its persistent loop, cybersecurity experts can anticipate the type of damage it might cause and implement appropriate countermeasures, such as isolating the compromised system or restoring files from a backup.

Beyond the immediate threat, persistent homology also offers insights into broader threat trends. By analyzing the topological features of different malware samples, we can identify patterns or similarities that indicate a shared origin or a common strategy among malicious actors. For instance, suppose we notice that multiple ransomware samples present a similar persistent loop. In that case, it could suggest that these samples were developed by the same group or that they're using a common ransomware-as-a-service platform.

Recognizing these patterns can provide strategic intelligence about the threat landscape. It can help us understand the TTPs employed by malicious actors, anticipate future threats, and devise effective defenses. For instance, if we find that many ransomware samples share a similar persistent loop, we might focus our efforts on developing defenses or countermeasures that disrupt this loop, effectively neutralizing a whole category of threats.

Persistent homology can also aid in the discovery and understanding of APTs. APTs are complex, multi-faceted threats that often employ a mix of different malware types and sophisticated techniques. Their persistence diagrams could present a variety of topological features, reflecting this complexity. By identifying and analyzing these features, we can gain valuable insights into the structure and operation of these APTs, which can guide our defensive strategies.

Moreover, the robustness of TDA against noise and its ability to identify significant features at multiple scales make it well-suited for detecting novel or evolving threats. Suppose we encounter an unknown malware sample that presents a new persistent feature not seen in known malware types. In that case, it could indicate a novel threat or an evolution in an existing threat. Recognizing these changes can help us stay ahead of the threat and adapt our defenses accordingly.

In essence, classification through persistent homology is a pathway to a deeper understanding of malware. It's not just about identifying what a piece of malware is; it's about understanding how it operates, how it fits into the broader threat landscape, and how we can best respond. As cybersecurity threats continue to evolve and become more sophisticated, such insights will become increasingly valuable.

A deeper dive – employing TDA for threat management

The use of TDA in malware detection represents a significant advancement in our ability to identify, understand, and counteract cyber threats. Its strength lies in the fact that it goes beyond superficial features of the data to understand its inherent structure, revealing persistent patterns that are consistent across multiple scales and resilient to noise. This allows the AI system to extract meaningful insights from the data, leading to improved threat detection and mitigation.

When an AI system employs TDA, particularly persistent homology, it essentially maps the high-dimensional malware data onto a simpler representation that preserves its fundamental topological features. This mapping process involves constructing a simplicial complex and then examining its structure at various scales to identify persistent features such as clusters and loops. These features serve as "signatures" of the malware, revealing underlying patterns in its structure or behavior.

The robustness of persistent homology against noise and its ability to identify significant features at multiple scales make it a valuable tool for detecting novel or evolving threats. Consider the example of an unknown malware sample that presents a new persistent feature not seen in known malware types. The AI system, using persistent homology, would be able to recognize this new feature and flag it for further investigation. This could lead to the discovery of a novel threat or an evolution in an existing threat.

The ability to recognize changes in the persistent features of malware samples is a key advantage of using TDA. It allows the AI system to stay ahead of the threat landscape by identifying new or evolving TTPs employed by malicious actors. This ability is especially valuable in the context of APTs, which are complex, multi-faceted threats that often involve a mix of different malware types and sophisticated techniques.

Adapting defenses accordingly involves using the insights gained from TDA to inform countermeasures. For instance, if a new persistent loop is identified that corresponds to a particular sequence of operations performed by ransomware, countermeasures could be developed to disrupt this sequence and neutralize the ransomware. Similarly, if a new cluster is identified that corresponds to the behavior of a Trojan, steps could be taken to enhance the detection of such behavior and prevent the Trojan from establishing itself within the system.

In the process of training the AI system, the trainer would feed the system a variety of malware samples and guide it in constructing their persistence diagrams. By comparing these diagrams and identifying common and unique persistent features, the system could learn to classify unknown malware samples and recognize new or evolving threats. The trainer would also validate the system's performance, adjust its parameters, and provide additional training data as necessary to improve its accuracy and reliability.

Moreover, the insights gained from TDA could be used to inform the development of new machine learning models or improve existing ones for malware detection. For instance, the persistent features identified by TDA could serve as novel features for training these models, enhancing their ability to distinguish between different types of malware and detect novel threats.

As such, employing TDA enables the AI system and trainer to recognize changes in the threat landscape and adapt defenses accordingly by providing a deeper understanding of the intrinsic structure and behavior of malware. This approach enhances our ability to detect and respond to cyber threats, thereby improving the overall security of our digital systems.

Summary

In this chapter, we explored various facets of TDA and its applicability in the domain of cybersecurity, particularly for malware detection. The discussion ranged from understanding the foundational principles of topology and its relevance in data analysis to diving into specialized topics such as persistence homology. We also touched on the benefits of employing TDA in AI systems for recognizing evolving cyber threats and how these advanced techniques can contribute to the ongoing battle against malware.

One of the key themes that we highlighted was the adaptability and robustness of TDA in filtering out noise and distinguishing meaningful patterns in complex datasets. This ability is especially crucial for detecting zero-day threats and classifying malware into different types or families based on their persistent features. The concept of classification as a nuanced approach, not just for labeling but also for understanding the threat landscape, was emphasized as well.

Several attempts were made to articulate these complex topics in layman's terms, and while the conversation faced some technical challenges, the overarching takeaway remains that TDA is a powerful tool for enhancing our cybersecurity frameworks. Its capabilities extend beyond traditional data analysis methods and offer a dynamic way to understand and combat cyber threats.

We also covered the topic of how long and detailed responses could be effectively managed in a chat-based interface, which brought into focus the limitations and optimization strategies that can be employed to achieve coherent and impactful communication.

Having explored the foundations of TDA for malware detection, in the next chapter, we'll delve into the realm of AI, which plays a crucial role in advancing malware data analysis and detection capabilities.

4

Artificial Intelligence for Malware Data Analysis and Detection

The increasing sophistication and frequency of malware attacks pose significant challenges to cybersecurity professionals. Traditional methods of detecting and analyzing malware are often unable to keep up with the evolving threat landscape. **Artificial intelligence (AI)** has emerged as a powerful tool for malware data analysis and detection, providing more accurate and efficient solutions to combat this growing problem.

This chapter provides an in-depth exploration of AI techniques that are used in malware data analysis, including machine learning and deep learning approaches. This chapter explores the role of AI in malware analysis, its benefits, challenges, and future prospects.

We will cover the following topics in this chapter:

- AI techniques used in malware data analysis
- Benefits of AI in malware detection
- Future prospects

AI techniques used in malware data analysis

AI techniques used in malware data analysis, such as machine learning and deep learning, have revolutionized malware data analysis. These techniques enable the development of models capable of automatically learning patterns and features from large datasets, facilitating the detection and classification of malware samples. By leveraging AI, security analysts can automate the analysis process, reduce human error, and enhance the overall efficiency and accuracy of malware detection.

Machine learning techniques are widely applied in malware detection and analysis. Machine learning models learn patterns and features from large datasets to identify and classify malware samples. Key machine learning techniques that are utilized in malware analysis include **supervised learning**, **unsupervised learning**, and **deep learning**.

Supervised learning

Supervised learning involves training machine learning models on labeled datasets, where each sample is associated with a known class label (for example, malware or benign). The models learn to classify new, unseen samples based on the patterns learned during training. Let's try to understand supervised learning in detail.

Understanding supervised learning

Supervised learning is a branch of machine learning where models are trained on labeled datasets, comprising input data and corresponding output labels. The goal is to learn a mapping function that can predict the correct output for unseen input data. In supervised learning, the learning process involves two main phases – the training phase and the inference phase.

Training phase

During the training phase, the model is exposed to a labeled dataset, and it learns from the input-output pairs to create a predictive model. The model adjusts its internal parameters based on the training data to minimize the discrepancy between predicted and actual outputs.

The training phase of supervised learning is a crucial step in developing accurate and reliable models. During this phase, the model learns from the labeled dataset to create a predictive model that can generalize well to unseen data. Here are some key aspects of the training phase:

- **Dataset splitting**: In supervised learning, it's common practice to partition the labeled dataset into two distinct subsets: a training set and a validation set. The training set plays a crucial role in allowing the model to learn the inherent relationships between input variables and their respective output labels. Conversely, the validation set serves to assess the model's effectiveness during its learning process. It aids in adjusting hyperparameters and ensures the model doesn't overfit the training data.

- **Feature engineering**: Feature engineering involves selecting or transforming the input features to make them more suitable for the learning algorithm. This process aims to extract the most relevant information from the raw data, enhancing the model's ability to capture important patterns. Feature engineering techniques may include scaling, normalization, dimensionality reduction, or creating new features through mathematical operations or domain knowledge.

- **Model selection**: Choosing an appropriate model architecture is an essential step in the training phase. Different supervised learning algorithms, such as decision trees, support vector machines, or neural networks, have different capabilities and characteristics. The choice of the model depends on the specific problem domain, the nature of the data, and the desired performance metrics. It is often necessary to experiment with different models and compare their performance on the validation set to determine the most suitable one.

- **Loss function and optimization**: During training, the model's parameters are adjusted iteratively to minimize a chosen loss function, which quantifies the discrepancy between the predicted outputs and the true labels. The optimization process aims to find the optimal set of parameters that yields the lowest loss. Gradient-based optimization algorithms, such as **stochastic gradient descent (SGD)** and its variants, are commonly used to update the model's parameters based on the computed gradients of the loss function.

- **Hyperparameter tuning**: Supervised learning models often have hyperparameters that control the behavior of the learning algorithm but are not learned from the data. These hyperparameters can significantly impact the model's performance and generalization ability. Examples of hyperparameters include learning rate, regularization strength, network architecture, or tree depth. Hyperparameter tuning involves selecting the best combination of hyperparameters to optimize the model's performance. Techniques such as grid search, random search, or Bayesian optimization can be employed for hyperparameter tuning.

- **Model evaluation**: Throughout the training phase, the model's performance is evaluated on the validation set. Common evaluation metrics depend on the specific task and can include accuracy, precision, recall, F1 score, mean squared error, or **area under the receiver operating characteristic curve (AUC-ROC)**. These metrics provide insights into how well the model is learning and allow for comparisons between different models or hyperparameter configurations.

- **Early stopping and regularization**: To prevent overfitting, which occurs when the model performs well on the training set but poorly on unseen data, techniques such as early stopping and regularization are employed. Early stopping stops the training process if the performance on the validation set starts to deteriorate, indicating that further training may lead to overfitting. Regularization methods, such as L1 or L2 regularization, impose additional constraints on the model's parameters to discourage complex or overfitting models.

By carefully managing the training phase of supervised learning, it is possible to develop robust models that accurately predict or classify unseen data. Proper dataset splitting, feature engineering, model selection, loss function optimization, hyperparameter tuning, and regularization techniques contribute to successfully training supervised learning models.

Inference phase

Once the model has been trained, it can be used to make predictions or classifications on new, unseen data. The model generalizes its knowledge from the training data to make intelligent decisions on previously unseen examples. During this phase, the trained model is utilized to make predictions or classifications on new, unseen data. Here are some important aspects of the inference phase:

- **Data preprocessing**: Before making predictions, it is essential to preprocess the new, unseen data similarly to the training data. This involves applying the same preprocessing steps used during the training phase, such as scaling, normalization, or feature transformation. Consistency in preprocessing ensures that the input data is in a suitable format for the model to process.

- **Forward propagation**: In the inference phase, the preprocessed data is fed into the trained model for prediction. For example, in neural networks, the input data is passed through the network's layers in a process called forward propagation. Each layer applies a set of learned weights to the input data, processes it, and passes it to the next layer until the final output layer is reached.

- **Prediction or classification**: Based on the learned patterns and relationships acquired during the training phase, the model generates predictions or classifications for the input data. The output can vary depending on the specific problem domain. For instance, in classification tasks, the model assigns class labels to the input data, while in regression tasks, it predicts continuous or numerical values.

- **Confidence estimation**: In addition to making predictions or classifications, the model can often provide an estimate of its confidence or uncertainty in its predictions. This is particularly useful in decision-making scenarios where the model's reliability is important. Confidence estimation helps identify cases where the model may be less certain, allowing for additional scrutiny or potential human intervention if necessary.

- **Post-processing**: After obtaining the predictions or classifications from the model, post-processing steps may be applied, depending on the specific application. This can include thresholding, filtering, or additional domain-specific rules to refine the output. Post-processing aims to improve the final prediction quality or tailor it to specific requirements.

- **Performance evaluation**: Once the model has made predictions on the new data, it is essential to assess its performance. This involves comparing the model's predictions against the true labels or ground truth. Performance metrics, such as accuracy, precision, recall, F1 score, or mean squared error, are calculated to evaluate the model's effectiveness on the unseen data. The performance evaluation helps determine the model's reliability and provides insights into its generalization capabilities.

- **Iterative refinement**: Supervised learning is an iterative process, and the inference phase provides valuable feedback for model improvement. If the model's performance on the new data is not satisfactory, the feedback can be used to retrain the model with additional labeled data, refine the model architecture, or adjust hyperparameters. This iterative refinement ensures that the model continues to learn and adapt to the evolving patterns in the data.

By going through the inference phase, the trained supervised learning model can provide accurate predictions or classifications on new, unseen data. Preprocessing the data, propagating it through the model, generating predictions, and evaluating the model's performance form the core steps of the inference phase. Iterative refinement based on the inference results allows for continuous improvement and adaptation of the model.

Supervised learning algorithms

Various algorithms are used in supervised learning, each with its strengths and applicability to different problem domains. Some common supervised learning algorithms include the following:

- **Decision trees**: Decision trees represent a hierarchical structure that uses a series of `if-else` conditions to make predictions. Each internal node of the tree represents a decision based on a specific feature, leading to different branches and outcomes.

- **Support vector machine (SVM)**: SVM is a popular algorithm that's used for both classification and regression tasks. It separates data points using a hyperplane in high-dimensional space to maximize the margin between classes.

- **Naive Bayes**: Naive Bayes is based on the Bayesian theorem and assumes independence between features. It calculates the probability of a particular class given the input features and selects the most probable class as the prediction.

- **Neural networks**: Neural networks consist of interconnected layers of artificial neurons called nodes or units. They learn complex patterns by adjusting the weights between nodes. Neural networks, particularly deep learning models, have shown remarkable success in various domains, including image recognition and natural language processing.

Benefits and applications of supervised learning

Let us look at the benefits and applications of supervised learning:

- **Accurate predictions**: Supervised learning allows models to make accurate predictions by leveraging labeled data. The models can generalize from known examples to make informed decisions on unseen instances.

- **Classification and recognition**: Supervised learning is widely used for classification tasks, such as spam detection, sentiment analysis, and object recognition. By training on labeled data, models can classify new instances into predefined categories accurately.

- **Regression analysis**: Supervised learning is also employed for regression analysis, where models predict continuous or numerical values. It finds applications in stock market prediction, housing price estimation, and demand forecasting.

- **Personalization and recommendation systems**: Supervised learning techniques enable personalized recommendations in various domains, such as e-commerce, streaming platforms, and content filtering. Models learn from users' preferences and behaviors to provide tailored recommendations.

Challenges and considerations

While supervised learning offers significant advantages, there are challenges and considerations to keep in mind.

Labeled data requirements

One of the significant challenges in supervised learning is the requirement for labeled data. Labeled data consists of input samples paired with their corresponding output labels, which serve as the ground truth for training the model. However, acquiring and preparing labeled data can present several challenges and considerations:

- **Data collection and annotation**: Collecting a large and representative dataset that encompasses the variations and complexities of the problem domain can be a time-consuming and resource-intensive process. Additionally, labeling the data often requires human expertise or domain knowledge to correctly assign the appropriate labels. Manual annotation can be subjective, leading to potential labeling biases or inconsistencies. Ensuring high-quality labeled data necessitates careful planning, expertise, and thorough quality control measures during the data collection and annotation process.

- **Imbalanced datasets**: In many real-world scenarios, datasets can be imbalanced, meaning that the number of instances in different classes or categories is significantly skewed. Imbalanced datasets can lead to biased models that favor the majority class, resulting in poor performance for the minority class. Addressing this challenge requires techniques such as over-sampling, under-sampling, or generating synthetic samples to balance the class distribution and provide the model with sufficient information from all classes.

- **Label noise and quality**: Labeled data may contain noise or errors, which can be introduced during the annotation process or due to inherent ambiguities in the data. Noisy labels can negatively impact the model's performance and generalization ability. Cleaning and verifying the quality of labeled data through extensive quality control measures, inter-annotator agreement analysis, or semi-supervised learning approaches can help mitigate these issues.

- **Limited labeled data**: Obtaining a large amount of high-quality labeled data may not always be feasible, especially in domains with complex or specialized tasks. Limited labeled data can lead to overfitting, where the model fails to generalize well to unseen instances. Techniques such as transfer learning, data augmentation, or active learning can be employed to address the limited labeled data challenge. Transfer learning leverages knowledge from pre-trained models on related tasks or domains, data augmentation artificially expands the labeled data by creating new samples with modifications or variations, and active learning focuses on iteratively selecting the most informative samples for annotation.

- **Data distribution shift**: Supervised learning models assume that the distribution of the training data is representative of the distribution of the test or inference data. However, in real-world scenarios, the distribution of the test data may differ from the training data due to various factors, such as evolving trends, domain shifts, or deployment environments. This distribution shift can lead to a degradation in model performance. Techniques such as domain adaptation, continual learning, or retraining the model with updated data can help address the challenge of data distribution shift.

- **Ethical and privacy considerations**: Labeled data may contain sensitive or **personally identifiable information** (**PII**). Ensuring data privacy, compliance with regulations, and ethical considerations are of paramount importance. Organizations must implement robust data anonymization techniques, secure data storage and access controls, and adhere to legal and ethical guidelines when collecting, storing, and using labeled data.

By recognizing and addressing the challenges related to labeled data requirements, practitioners can mitigate biases, improve model performance, and build trustworthy and reliable supervised learning systems. Leveraging techniques for data collection, annotation, balancing imbalanced datasets, managing label noise, handling limited labeled data, adapting to distribution shifts, and ensuring ethical considerations are key to successfully overcoming these challenges.

Overfitting and generalization

Overfitting and generalization are critical challenges in supervised learning that impact the performance and reliability of the trained models. Understanding these challenges and adopting appropriate strategies is crucial to developing models that generalize well to unseen data. Models trained on labeled data may sometimes overfit the training set, failing to generalize well to unseen data. Techniques such as cross-validation, regularization, and feature selection can help address overfitting and improve generalization. Here are some key considerations related to overfitting and generalization:

- **Overfitting**: Overfitting occurs when a model learns the training data too closely, capturing noise or random fluctuations in the data rather than the underlying patterns. As a result, the model performs well on the training data but fails to generalize well to unseen data. Overfitting can lead to poor performance, low accuracy, and an inability to make accurate predictions or classifications.

- **Model complexity**: One common cause of overfitting is an overly complex model that has too many parameters or features compared to the available training data. A complex model can memorize the training data instead of learning the underlying patterns, leading to poor generalization. It is crucial to strike a balance between model complexity and the amount of available training data to avoid overfitting.

- **Insufficient training data**: When the training data is limited, the risk of overfitting increases. With a small dataset, the model may try to fit the noise or random variations in the data, leading to poor generalization. Collecting more labeled data or employing techniques such as data augmentation, transfer learning, or active learning can help mitigate the effects of insufficient training data and reduce overfitting.

- **Regularization**: Regularization techniques are employed to prevent overfitting by adding additional constraints on the model's parameters during training. Regularization methods, such as L1 or L2 regularization, penalize large parameter values, encouraging the model to learn simpler representations. Regularization helps to control model complexity and reduce overfitting.

- **Cross-validation**: Cross-validation is a technique that's used to evaluate the model's performance and assess its generalization ability. Instead of relying solely on a single train-test split, cross-validation involves partitioning the available labeled data into multiple subsets or folds. The model is trained and evaluated iteratively on different combinations of training and validation folds, allowing for a more robust estimation of its performance and potential overfitting.

- **Early stopping**: Early stopping is a regularization technique that helps prevent overfitting by monitoring the model's performance on a validation set during training. If the model's performance on the validation set starts to deteriorate or plateau, training is stopped to avoid further overfitting. Early stopping helps find the optimal trade-off between model complexity and generalization.

- **Ensembling**: Ensembling techniques combine the predictions of multiple models to improve generalization and robustness. By training several models with different initializations, architectures, or hyperparameters and aggregating their predictions, ensembling helps reduce overfitting by capturing a more diverse range of patterns from the training data.

- **Feature selection and dimensionality reduction**: Feature selection or dimensionality reduction techniques aim to identify the most informative and relevant features for training the model. Removing irrelevant or redundant features can help simplify the model, reduce overfitting, and improve generalization. Techniques such as **principal component analysis (PCA)** or feature importance analysis can aid in feature selection and dimensionality reduction.

Addressing the challenges of overfitting and generalization requires careful model selection, regularization, sufficient training data, cross-validation, early stopping, ensembling, and feature selection techniques. By employing these strategies, practitioners can develop models that strike the right balance between complexity and generalization, leading to improved performance and reliable predictions or classifications of unseen data.

Unsupervised learning

Unsupervised learning techniques aim to discover patterns, structures, or relationships in unlabeled data without the need for predefined output labels. Feature selection and feature extraction are crucial steps in unsupervised learning that help us identify relevant and informative features from the input data. Here, we will delve into the concepts of feature selection and extraction in unsupervised learning.

Feature selection and extraction

Machine learning models rely on relevant features to accurately classify malware. Feature selection and extraction techniques help identify the most informative attributes from raw data, reducing dimensionality and improving detection performance.

Feature selection

Feature selection is the process of selecting a subset of the original features from the input data that are most relevant to the underlying patterns or structures. The objective is to reduce the dimensionality of the data by discarding irrelevant or redundant features, thereby improving the efficiency and performance of unsupervised learning algorithms. The key aspects of feature selection include the following:

- **Filter methods**: Filter methods rank features based on statistical measures such as correlation, mutual information, or variance, without considering the learning algorithm. By selecting the top-ranked features, filter methods aim to capture the most discriminative and informative aspects of the data. Common techniques include chi-square, information gain, and correlation-based feature selection.

- **Wrapper methods**: Wrapper methods assess the performance of the learning algorithm using different subsets of features. They search through the space of possible feature subsets and select the subset that optimizes the performance of a specific learning algorithm. This iterative process evaluates the learning algorithm's performance on a validation set with different feature subsets, allowing for more fine-grained feature selection. However, wrapper methods can be computationally expensive, especially for high-dimensional data.

- **Embedded methods**: Embedded methods incorporate feature selection directly into the learning algorithm's training process. These methods use a specific criterion, such as regularization, to jointly optimize the model's performance and feature selection. Algorithms such as **Least Absolute Shrinkage and Selection Operator** (**LASSO**) and Elastic Net employ regularization techniques that encourage sparsity in the feature space, effectively performing feature selection as part of the learning process.

Feature extraction

Feature extraction aims to transform the input data into a lower-dimensional representation while preserving or enhancing the relevant information. Unlike feature selection, feature extraction creates new feature representations rather than selecting from the original set. Feature extraction methods project the data into a new feature space, typically of lower dimensionality, while capturing the most important and discriminative aspects of the data. Some common techniques are as follows:

- **PCA**: PCA is a widely used technique for feature extraction that transforms the input data into a set of linearly uncorrelated variables called principal components. Each principal component captures the maximum variance in the data, allowing for dimensionality reduction while retaining the essential information. PCA is particularly effective for data with high dimensionality or multicollinearity.

- **Independent component analysis (ICA)**: ICA is a technique that separates the input data into statistically independent components by estimating the underlying sources. Unlike PCA, which focuses on capturing variance, ICA aims to identify components that are statistically independent and non-Gaussian. ICA is useful for scenarios where the data sources are assumed to be independent, such as separating mixed audio signals or identifying distinct patterns in images.

- **Manifold learning**: Manifold learning methods aim to uncover the underlying nonlinear structure or manifold in the data. Techniques such as **t-Distributed Stochastic Neighbor Embedding (t-SNE)** and Isomap map the high-dimensional data onto a lower-dimensional space while preserving the local or global relationships between data points. Manifold learning allows for the visualization and exploration of complex data structures.

- **Autoencoders**: Autoencoders are neural network models that learn to encode the input data into a lower-dimensional representation and reconstruct it back to the original input. By imposing a bottleneck layer with fewer neurons, autoencoders force the model to capture the most salient features in the data. Autoencoders are effective for unsupervised feature extraction and can learn hierarchical representations of the input data.

Feature selection and extraction techniques in unsupervised learning play a vital role in reducing dimensionality, eliminating irrelevant information, and capturing the essential patterns or structures in the data. By selecting the most relevant features or creating meaningful representations, unsupervised learning models can discover valuable insights and uncover hidden patterns in unlabeled data.

Deep learning for malware analysis deep learning

Deep learning, a subset of machine learning, utilizes artificial neural networks with multiple layers to automatically learn complex representations from raw data. Deep learning techniques have demonstrated remarkable success in various domains, including malware analysis. Let's take a look at the key deep learning techniques that are employed in malware analysis.

Convolutional neural networks (CNNs)

Deep learning, a subfield of machine learning, has gained significant attention in malware analysis due to its ability to automatically learn complex patterns and features from raw data. **Convolutional neural networks (CNNs)** are deep learning models that are specifically designed for processing grid-like data, such as images or sequences. They consist of multiple interconnected layers, including convolutional layers, pooling layers, and fully connected layers. CNNs are particularly effective for extracting spatial and hierarchical features from data. Let's explore the key concepts and advantages of CNNs in malware analysis:

- **Convolutional layers**: Convolutional layers are the core building blocks of CNNs. They apply a set of learnable filters or kernels to the input data, which convolve (slide) over the data in a systematic manner. Each filter captures specific local patterns or features, detecting edges, textures, or higher-level structures. Convolutional layers enable CNNs to automatically learn relevant features directly from the raw data.

- **Pooling layers**: Pooling layers are often used after convolutional layers to reduce the spatial dimensions of the feature maps, capturing the most salient information. Pooling operations, such as max pooling or average pooling, downsample the feature maps by aggregating neighboring values. Pooling helps in reducing computational complexity, extracting important features, and providing invariance to small spatial transformations.

- **Hierarchical feature learning**: CNNs excel in hierarchical feature learning, where lower layers capture simple and local features (for example, edges), and deeper layers learn more abstract and complex features (for example, shapes or objects). This hierarchical representation allows CNNs to automatically discover meaningful patterns and hierarchies in the data, making them well-suited for analyzing the complex structures and relationships present in malware code or binary files.

- **Transfer learning**: Transfer learning is a technique that leverages pre-trained CNN models on large-scale datasets, such as ImageNet, to tackle related tasks with limited labeled data. By fine-tuning or reusing the lower layers of a pre-trained CNN, malware analysts can benefit from the learned feature representations, reducing the need for extensive training on small malware datasets. Transfer learning helps in overcoming the limitations of limited labeled malware samples and improves the model's generalization capabilities.

- **Adversarial detection**: CNNs have shown promise in detecting adversarial malware samples that are specifically designed to evade traditional detection methods. The ability of CNNs to learn complex and robust features makes them effective in capturing subtle variations and patterns in malware code, even when subjected to obfuscation or evasion techniques. However, ongoing research is necessary to improve the robustness of CNN models against advanced adversarial attacks.

- **Scalability and efficiency**: CNNs can efficiently process large volumes of data, making them suitable for analyzing massive malware datasets. They can leverage the parallel processing capabilities of modern GPUs or distributed computing frameworks, enabling fast and scalable analysis. This scalability is particularly important in real-time threat detection and response scenarios.

- **Interpretability and explainability**: Interpretability and explainability are important considerations in malware analysis. While CNNs are known for their black-box nature, efforts are being made to develop techniques that provide insights into the decision-making processes of CNN models. Researchers are exploring methods to visualize the learned features, highlight important regions in the input data, or generate explanations to increase the transparency and trustworthiness of CNN-based malware analysis systems.

CNNs have demonstrated significant potential in malware analysis, enabling the automatic extraction of meaningful features and patterns from malware code and binary files. Their hierarchical feature learning capabilities, transfer learning advantages, scalability, and efficiency make them valuable tools in the fight against malware. However, ongoing research is necessary to improve interpretability and robustness against adversarial attacks, as well as the development of specialized CNN architectures tailored to the unique characteristics of malware analysis.

Recurrent neural networks (RNNs)

In addition to CNNs, **recurrent neural networks (RNNs)** have gained prominence in the field of malware analysis. RNNs are a class of deep learning models specifically designed to capture sequential dependencies and temporal dynamics in data by maintaining an internal memory state. Let's explore the key concepts and advantages of RNNs in the context of malware analysis:

- **Long Short-Term Memory (LSTM)**: A variant of RNNs that's commonly used in malware analysis is the LSTM network. LSTMs have specialized memory cells that can selectively retain or forget information over time, enabling the model to capture long-term dependencies in sequential data. LSTMs are particularly effective when analyzing sequences of variable length as they can handle varying time lags and patterns.

- **Sequential modeling**: RNNs and LSTMs excel in modeling sequential data, making them well-suited for analyzing malware-related sequences, such as network traffic, API calls, or system logs. By processing the sequential data in a step-by-step manner, RNNs can capture the temporal dynamics and behavior patterns of malware, allowing for the detection of malicious activities or anomalies.

- **Capturing temporal dependencies**: RNNs are designed to capture dependencies between past and future time steps in a sequence. This property is beneficial for identifying patterns in malware behavior that unfold over time. For example, RNNs can capture the sequence of system calls made by malware, enabling the detection of suspicious sequences or deviations from normal behavior.

- **Variable-length sequences**: Malware-related sequences, such as network traffic or API call sequences, often have variable lengths. RNNs, particularly LSTMs, can handle sequences of different lengths without requiring fixed-length inputs. This flexibility is crucial in malware analysis, where the length of sequences may vary significantly between different samples or instances.

- **Bidirectional RNNs (Bi-RNNs)**: To capture dependencies in both forward and backward directions, Bi-RNNs are employed in malware analysis. Bi-RNNs process the input sequence in both directions simultaneously, allowing the model to access future as well as past information at each time step. This helps in capturing a more comprehensive understanding of the sequence dynamics and improves the model's ability to identify relevant patterns.

- **Anomaly detection**: RNNs are effective in anomaly detection, a critical task in malware analysis. By learning the normal patterns and behavior of a system or network, RNNs can detect deviations or anomalies in the sequences. Anomalies can indicate the presence of malware or malicious activities, allowing for timely detection and response.

- **Transfer learning and ensemble techniques**: Similar to CNNs, RNNs can benefit from transfer learning and ensemble techniques. Pre-trained RNN models, trained on large-scale datasets or related tasks, can be fine-tuned or combined with domain-specific data for malware analysis. This allows for leveraging learned representations and knowledge from existing models, even with limited labeled malware samples.

- **Limitations**: RNNs can face challenges when dealing with very long sequences or capturing long-range dependencies. The vanishing gradient problem, where gradients become exponentially small over time, can affect the learning of long-term dependencies. Techniques such as **gated recurrent units** (**GRUs**) and LSTMs mitigate this problem to some extent. Additionally, RNNs may require substantial computational resources for training and inference due to their sequential nature.

RNNs and LSTMs have demonstrated their effectiveness in capturing sequential patterns and temporal dependencies in malware analysis. Their ability to model variable-length sequences and detect anomalies makes them valuable tools for identifying malicious activities in network traffic, system logs, or API call sequences. Combining RNNs with transfer learning and ensemble techniques can further enhance their performance in detecting and analyzing malware. Ongoing research in optimizing RNN architectures and addressing their limitations is necessary to advance the field of deep learning in malware analysis.

Generative adversarial networks (GANs)

Generative adversarial networks (**GANs**) are a powerful deep learning framework that has shown promise in various domains, including malware analysis. GANs consist of two neural networks – a generator and a discriminator – that compete against each other in a game-theoretic setting. The generator network synthesizes data samples that resemble the target distribution, while the discriminator network aims to distinguish between real and fake samples. Both networks are trained iteratively, with the generator learning to generate increasingly realistic samples and the discriminator learning to become better at differentiating real from fake samples. GANs have unique characteristics that make them valuable for malware analysis tasks. Let's explore the key concepts and advantages of GANs in the context of malware analysis:

- **Synthetic data generation**: One of the primary applications of GANs in malware analysis is the generation of synthetic malware samples. By training a GAN on a dataset of real malware samples, the generator can learn the underlying patterns and generate new, realistic malware samples. Synthetic data generation using GANs can significantly augment the available training data, allowing for improved model training and better generalization.

- **Data augmentation**: GANs can be used to augment the existing malware dataset by generating additional samples with variations or perturbations. This augmentation technique helps in improving the model's robustness and ability to handle different variations of malware. By generating diverse samples, GANs can help in training models that are more resilient to evasion techniques or previously unseen malware variants.

- **Unsupervised representation learning**: GANs can learn meaningful feature representations of malware samples without requiring explicit labels. The generator network learns to capture the underlying structure and variations in the data, leading to latent representations that encode relevant information about the malware. These learned representations can be further utilized for downstream tasks, such as clustering, similarity analysis, or anomaly detection.

- **Adversarial detection and evasion**: GANs can be employed in the context of adversarial detection, where the generator is trained to generate adversarial malware samples that are specifically designed to evade detection by security systems. By training the discriminator on a combination of real and adversarial samples, the discriminator network learns to distinguish between benign and adversarial samples, enhancing the robustness of the detection system.

- **Privacy-preserving analysis**: GANs can assist in privacy-preserving malware analysis by generating synthetic representations of sensitive or proprietary malware samples. Instead of directly sharing or analyzing the original samples, synthetic samples generated by the GAN can be used for analysis, preserving the privacy and confidentiality of the actual malware instances.

- **Limitations**: Despite their potential, GANs also come with challenges. Training GANs can be computationally demanding and require significant resources. GANs can suffer from mode collapse, where the generator produces limited variations, or from unstable training dynamics. Proper architectural design, training strategies, and regularization techniques are necessary to mitigate these challenges.

GANs have demonstrated their utility in generating synthetic malware samples, augmenting datasets, learning meaningful representations, and improving adversarial detection in malware analysis. The ability to generate diverse and realistic malware samples can greatly enhance the effectiveness of models and contribute to better threat detection and understanding of malware behavior. Continued research and development are essential to addressing the challenges associated with GANs and advancing their application in the field of malware analysis.

Benefits of AI techniques in malware data analysis

In this section, we will delve into the multifaceted advantages of utilizing AI in malware analysis, illustrating how it acts as a catalyst in bolstering the overall efficacy and responsiveness of security systems. Here, we will explore the significant enhancement in detection accuracy enabled by AI, demonstrating how the strategic use of AI algorithms and models fine-tunes the precision and effectiveness of malware detection processes. This exploration will extend to real-time threat detection, revealing how AI techniques empower systems to instantaneously analyze diverse data streams, enabling the immediate identification of and response to imminent malware threats. Moreover, the last subsection will shed light on the scalability and efficiency attained through AI, showcasing how these techniques facilitate organizations in efficiently processing extensive data volumes, thereby effectively addressing the growing complexities in the cybersecurity landscape. Each section will unravel the key factors that underline the transformative benefits of implementing AI techniques in the domain of malware data analysis.

Enhanced detection accuracy

AI techniques offer numerous advantages in the field of malware data analysis, with enhanced detection accuracy being a significant benefit. Leveraging AI algorithms and models can greatly improve the accuracy and effectiveness of malware detection. Here are the key factors that contribute to enhanced detection accuracy through AI techniques:

- **Learning from large-scale datasets**: AI techniques can analyze vast amounts of labeled and unlabeled data, allowing for the identification of complex patterns and relationships that may not be apparent to traditional rule-based or signature-based approaches. Machine learning algorithms, such as supervised learning, unsupervised learning, and deep learning, can process extensive datasets to learn from the diverse characteristics of malware samples. This ability to learn from large-scale datasets enhances the accuracy of malware detection models.

- **Automated feature extraction**: AI techniques, particularly deep learning algorithms such as CNNs and RNNs, excel at automated feature extraction. Instead of relying on manually crafted rules or signatures, these models automatically learn relevant features and representations directly from the raw malware data. This automated feature extraction eliminates the need for human experts to specify or update explicit features, leading to more accurate and adaptive detection systems.

- **Capturing complex and evolving malware characteristics**: Malware threats are continuously evolving, with new variants and attack techniques emerging regularly. AI techniques are well-suited to capture the complex and evolving characteristics of malware. Machine learning models can detect subtle changes and variations in malware behavior, enabling accurate identification of both known and previously unseen malware. Additionally, AI techniques can adapt and update their models based on new malware samples, improving detection accuracy in real time.

- **Handling unknown and zero-day malware**: Traditional signature-based antivirus systems often struggle to detect unknown or zero-day malware, which lack known signatures or behavioral patterns. AI techniques offer the potential to address this challenge by utilizing anomaly detection, unsupervised learning, and generative models. These techniques can identify deviations from normal system behavior, detect previously unseen malware variants, and generate synthetic samples for training models to recognize new threats accurately.

- **Ensembling and combining multiple models**: AI techniques allow for the ensemble or combination of multiple models, leading to improved accuracy in malware detection. Ensembling involves training and combining multiple models with different architectures or training strategies to leverage their strengths and collectively achieve higher accuracy. By combining diverse models, such as CNNs, RNNs, SVMs, or decision trees, the detection system can benefit from their complementary capabilities and enhance overall accuracy.

- **Real-time and continuous monitoring**: AI-based malware detection systems can operate in real time, continuously monitoring incoming data streams, network traffic, or system logs. This real-time monitoring allows for immediate detection and response to malware threats, minimizing the potential damage caused by malicious activities. The ability to analyze and process data in real time ensures that the detection system remains effective and up to date in rapidly evolving malware landscapes.

- **Reduced false positives**: AI techniques can significantly reduce false positive rates, minimizing the occurrence of false alarms or misidentifications. By leveraging the learning capabilities of AI models, detection systems can accurately differentiate between benign and malicious activities, reducing the number of false alerts and improving the efficiency of security operations. This reduction in false positives helps security analysts focus their efforts on legitimate threats, leading to more effective and timely responses.

The benefits of AI techniques in malware data analysis, particularly the enhanced detection accuracy, contribute to building robust and reliable security systems. By leveraging large-scale datasets, automated feature extraction, adaptive learning, and the ability to handle unknown malware, AI techniques offer significant improvements over traditional approaches. The integration of AI models, ensembling, and real-time monitoring enables accurate and proactive detection, leading to more effective threat mitigation and enhanced cybersecurity.

Real-time threat detection

AI techniques offer several advantages in the field of malware data analysis, and one of the significant benefits is real-time threat detection. AI-powered systems can rapidly analyze data streams, network traffic, or system logs in real time, allowing for immediate identification and response to malware threats. Here are the key factors that contribute to real-time threat detection through AI techniques:

- **Rapid processing and analysis**: AI techniques, such as machine learning and deep learning algorithms, are designed to process and analyze data efficiently. These algorithms can quickly evaluate and classify incoming data, enabling near real-time analysis of potential malware threats. By leveraging the computational power of modern hardware and parallel processing capabilities, AI-based systems can analyze large volumes of data in a fraction of the time required by traditional approaches.

- **Adaptive learning and continuous improvement**: AI techniques allow for adaptive learning and the continuous improvement of malware detection models. These models can dynamically update their knowledge and adapt to emerging threats by incorporating new data and patterns. By continuously learning from real-time data, AI-based systems can enhance their accuracy and stay up to date with the evolving nature of malware attacks. This adaptability enables real-time threat detection and response, even in the face of rapidly changing threat landscapes.

- **Anomaly detection**: AI techniques, such as unsupervised learning and anomaly detection, are effective in identifying deviations from normal system behavior. By establishing baselines of normal activities, these models can detect and raise alerts when anomalous patterns indicative of malware activities are observed. The ability to detect anomalies in real time allows for the timely identification of potential threats and enables immediate action to mitigate the impact of malware.

- **Behavioral analysis**: AI-based systems can perform behavioral analysis to identify suspicious or malicious activities in real time. By analyzing patterns of system behavior, network traffic, or user interactions, these systems can recognize deviations from expected norms and raise alarms accordingly. Behavioral analysis enables the detection of malware that exhibits evasive or stealthy behaviors, helping to detect advanced threats that may bypass traditional signature-based approaches.

- **Deep packet inspection (DPI)**: AI techniques, combined with deep learning models, can facilitate DPI for real-time threat detection. DPI involves analyzing the content and structure of network packets to identify potential malware or malicious activities. By employing AI models, such as CNNs, deep packet inspection can rapidly examine packet payloads, metadata, and traffic patterns, allowing for the immediate detection of malware-related indicators and anomalies.

- **Threat intelligence integration**: AI-based malware detection systems can integrate with threat intelligence feeds and databases in real time. By continuously monitoring and incorporating up-to-date threat intelligence, these systems can identify known malware signatures, IP addresses, or behavioral patterns associated with malicious activities. The integration of threat intelligence enables real-time threat detection by leveraging the collective knowledge of the cybersecurity community.

- **Automated response and mitigation**: AI techniques can facilitate automated response and mitigation actions in real time. When a potential malware threat is detected, AI-powered systems can trigger automated responses, such as isolating affected systems, blocking network connections, or initiating remediation processes. This real-time automated response capability allows for immediate containment and mitigation of malware incidents, reducing the time for threat actors to exploit vulnerabilities and minimizing the impact of attacks.

The benefits of AI techniques in malware data analysis, particularly real-time threat detection, provide organizations with the ability to proactively respond to malware threats. By rapidly processing and analyzing data, leveraging adaptive learning and behavioral analysis, and integrating threat intelligence, AI-based systems can identify and respond to malware in real time. This capability enables swift detection, containment, and mitigation of threats, enhancing the overall security posture and minimizing potential damages caused by malware attacks.

Scalability and efficiency

AI techniques offer significant advantages in the field of malware data analysis, particularly in terms of scalability and efficiency. By leveraging AI algorithms and models, organizations can tackle the challenges of processing large volumes of data efficiently and effectively. Here are the key factors that contribute to the scalability and efficiency benefits of AI techniques in malware data analysis:

- **Processing large-scale datasets**: Malware data analysis often involves processing massive volumes of data, including malware samples, network traffic logs, system logs, and other relevant information. AI techniques, such as machine learning and deep learning, excel at handling big data. These techniques can efficiently process and analyze vast amounts of data, enabling organizations to gain insights from the extensive malware datasets without being limited by traditional manual or rule-based approaches.

- **Parallel processing and distributed computing**: AI techniques can take advantage of parallel processing and distributed computing architectures to enhance scalability and efficiency. With the help of modern hardware, such as **graphics processing units (GPUs)** or specialized accelerators, AI algorithms can perform computations in parallel, significantly reducing the time required for analysis. Additionally, distributed computing frameworks, such as Apache Spark or TensorFlow's distributed training, can distribute the workload across multiple machines, enabling faster processing and analysis of large-scale malware datasets.

- **Real-time and near real-time analysis**: AI techniques enable real-time and near real-time analysis of malware data, providing timely insights and responses. With the ability to process and analyze data streams, network traffic, or system logs in real time, AI-powered systems can detect and respond to malware threats as they occur. This real-time analysis capability is crucial for organizations that require immediate detection and mitigation of malware incidents to minimize potential damages.

- **Efficient feature extraction and selection**: AI techniques, such as deep learning models, can automatically extract relevant features from raw malware data, eliminating the need for manual feature engineering. Deep learning architectures, such as CNNs or RNNs, can learn hierarchical representations of data, capturing both low-level and high-level features automatically. This automated feature extraction not only improves detection accuracy but also reduces the time and effort required for manual feature selection and engineering.

- **Transfer learning and pre-trained models**: AI techniques, particularly transfer learning, can enhance scalability and efficiency in malware data analysis. Transfer learning allows organizations to leverage pre-trained models on large-scale datasets or related tasks, reducing the need for extensive training from scratch. By transferring the knowledge and learned representations from pre-trained models, organizations can achieve faster model training and better generalization on smaller malware datasets, thus increasing scalability and efficiency.

- **Automated analysis and decision-making**: AI-powered systems can automate the analysis and decision-making processes in malware data analysis. Once trained, AI models can automatically process and classify malware samples, network traffic, or system logs without the need for manual intervention. This automation not only saves time and resources but also allows security analysts to focus on more complex or critical tasks, improving the overall efficiency in malware detection and response.

- **Continuous learning and adaptation**: AI techniques enable continuous learning and adaptation to evolving malware landscapes. AI models can be trained with new malware samples or updated datasets to stay up to date with the latest threats. The ability to continuously learn and adapt ensures that the detection models remain effective and relevant in the face of emerging malware variants or attack techniques, enhancing both scalability and efficiency.

The benefits of AI techniques in malware data analysis, particularly scalability and efficiency, enable organizations to handle large-scale datasets, process data in real time, automate analysis tasks, and continuously adapt to evolving threats. By leveraging parallel processing, distributed computing, automated feature extraction, and transfer learning, organizations can achieve faster and more efficient malware detection and response, ultimately strengthening their cybersecurity defenses.

Challenges in AI-based malware analysis

Now, let's shift our focus to the challenges in AI-based malware analysis. Despite AI's notable benefits in malware analysis, it grapples with several hurdles. First, we'll explore adversarial attacks and how they manipulate AI model vulnerabilities. Subsequently, we'll address the ethical concerns and data privacy issues inherent in utilizing AI for analyzing sensitive information. Lastly, we'll examine the challenges in interpreting and explaining AI models, underscoring the importance of transparency and understanding in AI's decision-making processes. The upcoming sections will delve deeper into these intricate challenges, offering a well-rounded view of AI's role in malware analysis.

Adversarial attacks

While AI techniques offer significant advantages in malware analysis, they also face challenges, particularly in dealing with adversarial attacks. Adversarial attacks aim to manipulate or deceive AI models, exploiting their vulnerabilities and causing misclassifications or false negatives. Here are the key challenges that are related to adversarial attacks in AI-based malware analysis:

- **Evasion and camouflage techniques**: Adversarial attacks in malware analysis often involve the creation of malware samples specifically designed to evade detection. Attackers employ evasion and camouflage techniques to modify or obfuscate the characteristics of malware, making it difficult for AI models to recognize or classify them correctly. These techniques can include code obfuscation, polymorphism, encryption, or the use of anti-analysis mechanisms.

- **Adversarial examples and perturbations**: Attackers generate adversarial examples by introducing subtle perturbations or modifications to legitimate or benign inputs. These modifications are often imperceptible to human observers but can significantly impact the performance of AI models. Adversarial perturbations can alter the features or characteristics of malware samples, leading to misclassifications or evading detection by AI-based malware analysis systems.

- **Transferability of adversarial attacks**: Adversarial attacks can have transferability across different models or systems. Adversarial samples generated to deceive one AI model can often fool other models trained on different architectures or datasets. This transferability poses a challenge as it means that an attacker's crafted adversarial samples can have a broad impact across multiple AI-based malware detection systems, making them less reliable and susceptible to attacks.

- **Limited robustness and generalization**: AI models in malware analysis can lack robustness and generalization capabilities in the face of adversarial attacks. Models that perform well on clean or benign samples may exhibit reduced accuracy or vulnerability when confronted with adversarial examples. Adversarial attacks can exploit the model's weaknesses, resulting in incorrect classifications or evasion, even though the model performs well on normal data.

- **Lack of adversarial training data**: Training AI models to defend against adversarial attacks requires access to labeled adversarial training data. However, collecting such data is challenging as it involves crafting and labeling samples with adversarial characteristics. The scarcity of labeled adversarial samples limits the ability to train models to detect and defend against adversarial attacks, making AI-based malware analysis systems more vulnerable to such attacks.

- **Constantly evolving adversarial techniques**: Adversarial attacks are continually evolving as attackers develop new techniques and exploit vulnerabilities in AI models. Attackers adapt their strategies to bypass detection mechanisms and exploit weaknesses in the model's decision boundaries. This dynamic nature of adversarial attacks requires continuous research and development efforts to improve the robustness and resilience of AI-based malware analysis systems.

- **A trade-off between robustness and accuracy**: Enhancing the robustness of AI models against adversarial attacks often involves a trade-off with accuracy. Techniques such as adversarial training or defensive distillation can improve the model's resilience but may lead to reduced accuracy on clean data. Striking a balance between robustness and accuracy is a challenge as organizations must ensure that the model remains effective in detecting malware while being capable of withstanding adversarial attacks.

Addressing the challenges of adversarial attacks in AI-based malware analysis requires ongoing research and development efforts. Robust countermeasures are needed to detect and mitigate adversarial attacks, such as adversarial training, model regularization, or ensemble methods. The development of large-scale labeled adversarial datasets, improved detection techniques, and collaborative efforts among researchers and organizations can enhance the resilience and reliability of AI-based malware analysis systems in the face of adversarial threats.

Data privacy and ethical considerations

While AI techniques offer significant benefits in malware analysis, they also present challenges related to data privacy and ethical considerations. The use of AI models for analyzing malware data raises concerns regarding the privacy of sensitive information and potential ethical implications. Here are the key challenges related to data privacy and ethical considerations in AI-based malware analysis:

- **Data privacy and confidentiality**: Malware analysis often involves the use of sensitive data, such as network traffic logs, system logs, or malware samples, which may contain PII or sensitive business data. Protecting the privacy and confidentiality of this data is crucial. Organizations must ensure that appropriate data protection measures, such as data anonymization, encryption, or access controls, are in place to prevent unauthorized access or disclosure of sensitive information during the analysis process.

- **Informed consent and data usage**: When collecting malware samples or conducting analysis, it is important to consider the issue of informed consent. Organizations need to ensure that the data that's used for training or validating AI models has been obtained legally and ethically, with proper consent from relevant stakeholders. Additionally, organizations must communicate how the collected data will be used and ensure compliance with applicable privacy regulations and guidelines.

- **Bias and fairness**: AI models can be susceptible to bias, both explicit and implicit, which can impact the fairness and accuracy of malware analysis. Bias in training data or algorithmic design can lead to unfair or discriminatory outcomes. It is crucial to address and mitigate bias during the training and evaluation of AI models to ensure fairness in the analysis process and prevent unintended consequences or discriminatory practices.

- **Transparency and explainability**: The black-box nature of some AI models poses challenges in understanding the decision-making process. Transparency and explainability are important considerations, especially in malware analysis, where the ability to interpret and understand the reasoning behind a model's classification or detection is critical. Techniques for model interpretability, such as generating explanations or providing visualizations of decision processes, can help increase transparency and facilitate trust in AI-based malware analysis systems.

- **The adversarial use of AI**: AI techniques, if misused, can also contribute to the development of sophisticated malware or hacking tools. Adversaries can leverage AI algorithms to craft more evasive or intelligent malware, capable of bypassing traditional security measures. The potential for the malicious use of AI in malware creation or attack strategies highlights the need for ethical considerations and the responsible use of AI techniques in malware analysis.

- **Data retention and disposal**: AI-based malware analysis systems generate and accumulate vast amounts of data during their operation. It is essential to have proper data retention and disposal policies in place to prevent data breaches or unauthorized access to collected data. Organizations must establish guidelines for data retention periods and implement secure processes for the disposal of data once it is no longer required.

- **Adherence to regulatory and legal frameworks**: AI-based malware analysis systems must comply with applicable legal and regulatory frameworks related to data privacy, security, and ethical considerations. Organizations should adhere to regulations such as the GDPR or specific industry guidelines when handling personal or sensitive data. Compliance with these frameworks ensures the protection of individual privacy rights and mitigates the potential risks associated with AI-based malware analysis.

Addressing the challenges of data privacy and ethical considerations in AI-based malware analysis requires a multidisciplinary approach. Organizations must adopt privacy-by-design principles, implement appropriate data protection measures, and ensure transparency and fairness in the analysis process. Collaboration between data scientists, malware analysts, legal experts, and policymakers is necessary to navigate the complex landscape of data privacy, ethics, and AI-based malware analysis effectively.

Interpretability and explainability

One of the significant challenges in AI-based malware analysis is the interpretability and explainability of AI models. While AI techniques excel at processing large volumes of data and making accurate predictions, the lack of transparency and understanding in their decision-making process can hinder their acceptance and trustworthiness. Here are the key challenges related to interpretability and explainability in AI-based malware analysis:

- **The black-box nature of AI models**: Many AI models, such as deep learning architectures such as CNNs or RNNs, are often considered black boxes. They are highly complex and lack explicit rules or explanations for their predictions. This lack of interpretability makes it challenging to understand the factors or features that contribute to the model's decision in malware analysis tasks.

- **Trust and confidence**: Interpretability and explainability are crucial for establishing trust and confidence in AI-based malware analysis systems. Security analysts, auditors, or regulatory bodies may require insights into the rationale behind a model's decisions to assess its reliability and determine if the model is operating as intended. The ability to provide clear explanations for predictions helps build trust and confidence in the system and facilitates better decision-making.

- **Compliance with regulations and standards**: Interpretability and explainability are important considerations for compliance with regulations and standards. Legal frameworks such as the GDPR or industry-specific regulations may require organizations to provide explanations for automated decisions made by AI systems. Compliance with these regulations necessitates having AI models that can provide interpretable and explainable outputs in malware analysis processes.

- **Detecting and addressing bias**: Interpretability and explainability can aid in detecting and addressing biases in AI models that are used for malware analysis. Bias can arise from various sources, including biased training data or algorithmic design choices. Understanding how AI models make decisions allows analysts to identify potential biases, correct them, and ensure fairness in malware detection processes.

- **Debugging and error analysis**: Interpretability and explainability play a crucial role in debugging and analyzing errors in AI models. When a model misclassifies or fails to detect malware, interpretable outputs can help analysts understand the reasons behind the error. Insights into the decision-making process can guide improvements in model architecture, training data, or feature engineering to address such errors effectively.

- **Human-machine collaboration**: Interpretability and explainability facilitate effective collaboration between humans and AI models in malware analysis. Providing interpretable outputs allows security analysts to understand and trust the decisions that are made by AI models. This collaboration leverages the strengths of both humans and machines, with AI models supporting analysts by automating tasks and providing insights while allowing analysts to exercise their expertise and domain knowledge.

- **A trade-off with performance**: Enhancing interpretability and explainability may come at the cost of performance in terms of accuracy or efficiency. Techniques that increase interpretability, such as simplified model architectures or rule-based models, may sacrifice some predictive power or require additional computational resources. Striking a balance between interpretability and performance is crucial to ensure that the interpretability efforts do not compromise the effectiveness of AI-based malware analysis systems.

Addressing the challenges of interpretability and explainability in AI-based malware analysis requires ongoing research and development efforts. Techniques such as model visualization, feature importance analysis, rule extraction, or attention mechanisms can contribute to improved interpretability. The development of **Explainable AI (XAI)** models tailored to malware analysis and the establishment of standards and guidelines for explainability contribute to more transparent and trustworthy AI-based malware analysis systems.

AI techniques, including machine learning and deep learning, have revolutionized malware data analysis, significantly improving the ability to detect and classify malware samples accurately. The benefits of AI in malware analysis, such as enhanced detection accuracy, real-time threat monitoring, and scalability, are invaluable in combating the ever-evolving threat landscape. However, challenges related to adversarial attacks, data privacy, and interpretability must be addressed to maximize the potential of AI in malware analysis. With ongoing research and development, AI will continue to play a vital role in bolstering cybersecurity defenses against malware attacks.

Benefits of AI in malware detection

Navigating the realm of malware detection, AI technologies bring forth pronounced advantages. In this section, we'll delve into how AI enhances detection accuracy, amplifying the precision of malware detection systems. Then, we'll discuss real-time threat monitoring, highlighting how AI facilitates continuous scrutiny and rapid response to threats. Lastly, we'll spotlight AI's role in achieving scalability and efficiency, enabling organizations to process vast data volumes effectively. Each section will underscore the transformative benefits of AI in malware detection methodologies.

Enhanced detection accuracy

AI techniques offer significant advantages in the field of malware detection, with enhanced detection accuracy being a primary benefit. Leveraging AI algorithms and models can greatly improve the accuracy and effectiveness of malware detection systems. Here are the key factors that contribute to enhanced detection accuracy through AI in malware detection:

- **Pattern recognition and anomaly detection**: AI techniques, such as machine learning and deep learning, excel at pattern recognition and anomaly detection. These techniques can analyze large volumes of data, such as network traffic, system logs, or file behavior, to identify patterns indicative of malware or detect anomalies that deviate from normal behavior. By leveraging sophisticated algorithms, AI-based malware detection systems can accurately differentiate between malicious and benign activities, leading to improved detection accuracy.

- **Learning from large-scale datasets**: AI models can learn from large-scale datasets, including labeled malware samples and diverse characteristics of benign software. By training on extensive and diverse data, AI algorithms can capture intricate patterns and relationships that may not be apparent to traditional signature-based or rule-based approaches. This ability to learn from large-scale datasets enhances the accuracy of malware detection models and enables the detection of both known and previously unseen malware variants.

- **Adaptability and generalization**: AI models can adapt and generalize to new and evolving malware threats. Through continuous learning and exposure to new samples, AI-based malware detection systems can update their knowledge and improve their ability to recognize and classify emerging malware variants. The adaptability and generalization capabilities of AI models allow for more accurate detection in real time, even when faced with previously unknown or zero-day malware.

- **Automated feature extraction**: AI models, particularly deep learning architectures such as CNNs or RNNs, can automatically extract relevant features from raw malware data. This automated feature extraction eliminates the need for manual feature engineering, which can be time-consuming and limited in its ability to capture complex characteristics. By automatically learning discriminative features, AI models enhance the accuracy of malware detection by effectively capturing the distinguishing traits of malware samples.

- **Ensemble learning**: AI-based malware detection systems can benefit from ensemble learning, where multiple models are combined to improve accuracy. Ensembling techniques, such as model averaging, boosting, or bagging, leverage the diversity of multiple AI models to enhance detection performance. By combining the strengths of different models, such as decision trees, SVMs, or deep learning architectures, ensemble learning improves accuracy by reducing false positives and false negatives.

- **Rapid analysis and real-time detection**: AI techniques enable rapid analysis and real-time detection of malware threats. These techniques leverage the computational power of modern hardware, such as GPUs or specialized accelerators, to process and analyze data streams, network traffic, or system logs in real time. The ability to perform fast and accurate analysis enables the timely detection and mitigation of malware incidents, reducing the potential damage caused by malicious activities.

- **Continuous improvement and adaptation**: AI-based malware detection systems can continuously improve and adapt to evolving threats. By leveraging techniques such as transfer learning, reinforcement learning, or active learning, these systems can incorporate new data, update models, and refine their detection capabilities over time. This continuous improvement and adaptation ensure that the detection accuracy remains high, even as new malware variants and attack techniques emerge.

The benefits of AI in malware detection, particularly enhanced detection accuracy, provide organizations with more reliable and effective defense mechanisms against malware threats. By leveraging pattern recognition, learning from large-scale datasets, automated feature extraction, ensemble learning, real-time detection, and continuous improvement, AI-based malware detection systems can accurately identify and mitigate malware, enabling organizations to proactively protect their systems and networks.

Upon recognizing the profound benefits of AI in refining detection accuracy, it becomes imperative to explore the specific aspects of these advancements. Consequently, our focus shifts to real-time threat monitoring, a pivotal aspect of AI in malware detection that offers immediate identification and response capabilities to organizations.

Real-time threat monitoring

AI techniques offer significant advantages in the field of malware detection, with real-time threat monitoring being a crucial benefit. By leveraging AI algorithms and models, organizations can actively monitor their systems and networks in real time, enabling immediate identification and response to malware threats. Here are the key factors that contribute to the benefits of real-time threat monitoring through AI in malware detection:

- **Rapid detection and response**: AI-based malware detection systems can monitor network traffic, system logs, or other data sources in real time. These systems analyze incoming data streams as they occur, allowing for the rapid detection of malware threats. Real-time monitoring enables organizations to identify and respond to malware incidents immediately, minimizing the potential damage caused by malicious activities.

- **Continuous monitoring**: AI techniques enable continuous monitoring of systems and networks for malware threats. Instead of relying on periodic scans or manual inspections, AI-based systems can continuously analyze data streams, detecting any anomalies or suspicious behaviors. Continuous monitoring ensures that potential malware threats are identified promptly, allowing for quick response and mitigation.

- **Proactive threat mitigation**: Real-time threat monitoring through AI-based malware detection systems enables proactive threat mitigation. By actively monitoring for malware indicators or anomalies, organizations can detect and address threats at their early stages, preventing their escalation or spread. Proactive mitigation measures, such as isolating affected systems, blocking network connections, or initiating remediation processes, can be implemented swiftly to minimize the impact of malware incidents.

- **Immediate alerting and notifications**: AI-based systems can generate immediate alerts or notifications when malware threats are detected in real time. These alerts can be sent to security personnel or administrators, providing them with timely information about the detected threats. Immediate alerts enable prompt investigation and response, facilitating swift actions to mitigate the risks associated with malware incidents.

- **Dynamic adaptation to emerging threats**: Real-time threat monitoring through AI techniques allows for dynamic adaptation to emerging malware threats. AI models can be continuously trained and updated with new data, enabling them to learn and adapt to the evolving nature of malware attacks. This adaptability ensures that the detection system remains effective and up to date, even in the face of rapidly changing threat landscapes.

- **Enhanced visibility and situational awareness**: Real-time threat monitoring provides organizations with enhanced visibility and situational awareness of their systems and networks. AI-based systems can provide real-time visualizations, dashboards, or reports that highlight the current state of malware threats and their impact. This enhanced visibility allows security analysts to quickly assess the severity of threats, prioritize response efforts, and make informed decisions to protect critical assets.

- **Reduction in dwell time**: Dwell time, the period between a malware intrusion and its detection, is a critical factor in mitigating the impact of attacks. Real-time threat monitoring helps minimize dwell time by rapidly detecting and responding to malware incidents. By reducing dwell time, organizations can limit the extent of damage caused by malware, prevent data exfiltration, and minimize the disruption to operations.

The benefits of real-time threat monitoring through AI in malware detection empower organizations to proactively protect their systems and networks. Rapid detection, continuous monitoring, proactive mitigation, immediate alerts, dynamic adaptation, enhanced visibility, and reduced dwell time contribute to a more robust and resilient security posture. By leveraging AI techniques for real-time threat monitoring, organizations can strengthen their defense against malware threats and respond effectively to potential incidents.

Scalability and efficiency

AI techniques offer significant advantages in the field of malware detection, with scalability and efficiency being key benefits. By leveraging AI algorithms and models, organizations can tackle the challenges of processing large volumes of data efficiently and effectively. Here are the key factors that contribute to the benefits of scalability and efficiency through AI in malware detection:

- **Processing large-scale datasets**: Malware detection often involves analyzing vast amounts of data, including malware samples, network traffic logs, system logs, and other relevant information. AI techniques, such as machine learning and deep learning, excel at handling big data. These techniques can efficiently process and analyze massive volumes of data, enabling organizations to gain insights from extensive malware datasets without being limited by traditional manual or rule-based approaches.

- **Parallel processing and distributed computing**: AI techniques can take advantage of parallel processing and distributed computing architectures to enhance scalability and efficiency. With the help of modern hardware, such as GPUs or specialized accelerators, AI algorithms can perform computations in parallel, significantly reducing the time required for analysis. Additionally, distributed computing frameworks, such as Apache Spark or TensorFlow's distributed training, can distribute the workload across multiple machines, enabling faster processing and analysis of large-scale malware datasets.

- **Real-time and near real-time analysis**: AI techniques enable real-time and near real-time analysis of malware data, providing timely insights and responses. With the ability to process and analyze data streams, network traffic, or system logs in real time, AI-powered systems can detect and respond to malware threats as they occur. This real-time analysis capability is crucial for organizations that require immediate detection and mitigation of malware incidents to minimize potential damages.

- **Automated analysis and decision-making**: AI-powered systems can automate the analysis and decision-making processes in malware detection. Once trained, AI models can automatically process and classify malware samples, network traffic, or system logs without the need for manual intervention. This automation not only saves time and resources but also allows security analysts to focus on more complex or critical tasks, improving overall efficiency in malware detection and response.

- **Efficient feature extraction and selection**: AI techniques, such as deep learning models, can automatically extract relevant features from raw malware data, eliminating the need for manual feature engineering. Deep learning architectures, such as CNNs or RNNs, can learn hierarchical representations of data, capturing both low-level and high-level features automatically. This automated feature extraction not only improves detection accuracy but also reduces the time and effort required for manual feature selection and engineering.

- **Scalable model training and deployment**: AI techniques enable scalable model training and deployment in malware detection. With the availability of powerful computing resources, organizations can train AI models on large-scale datasets, leveraging techniques such as distributed training or transfer learning to improve efficiency. Once trained, AI models can be deployed and applied to real-time malware detection on a large scale, efficiently processing incoming data streams or analyzing large volumes of network traffic.

- **Continuous learning and adaptation**: AI techniques enable continuous learning and adaptation in malware detection systems. AI models can be trained with new malware samples or updated datasets to stay up to date with the latest threats. The ability to continuously learn and adapt ensures that the detection systems remain effective and relevant in the face of emerging malware variants or attack techniques, enhancing both scalability and efficiency.

The benefits of AI in malware detection, particularly scalability and efficiency, enable organizations to handle large-scale datasets, process data in real time, automate analysis tasks, and continuously adapt to evolving threats. By leveraging parallel processing, distributed computing, automated feature extraction, scalable model training, and continuous learning, AI-based malware detection systems can efficiently and effectively identify and mitigate malware threats, ultimately strengthening the organization's cybersecurity defenses.

To summarize this section, we highlighted the broad advantages of using AI in malware analysis, illustrating its essential role in enhancing the efficacy and responsiveness of security systems. We explored how AI improves detection accuracy and refines malware identification processes. We discussed how AI enables the rapid analysis of various data streams, allowing for quick detection and response to threats. We also examined AI's contributions to scalability and efficiency in handling extensive data and addressing increasing cybersecurity challenges. In essence, this section has underscored the key benefits and substantial impacts of employing AI techniques in the realm of malware data analysis.

Future prospects

The future of AI in malware analysis is promising, with several potential advancements on the horizon. Let's take a look at them.

Improved adversarial defense

The future state of AI in adversarial defense is likely to be characterized by the following trends:

- **Increased use of adversarial training**: Adversarial training is becoming increasingly popular in improving the robustness of machine learning models. As this technique becomes more sophisticated, it is likely to become even more effective at defending against adversarial attacks.

- **Development of new adversarial defenses**: Researchers are constantly developing new techniques to defend against adversarial attacks. These techniques are likely to become more effective as AI technology continues to advance.

- **Increased use of XAI**: XAI is becoming increasingly important for understanding and defending against adversarial attacks. As XAI techniques become more sophisticated, they are likely to play an even more important role in adversarial defense.

The future state of AI in adversarial defense is promising. As AI technology continues to advance, new and more effective techniques for defending against adversarial attacks are likely to be developed. This will help keep computer systems safe from these increasingly sophisticated cyberattacks.

Hybrid approaches

Signature-based detection is effective at detecting known malware, but it is not as effective at detecting new malware or malware that has been modified to evade detection. This is because signature-based detection only looks for specific patterns that are known to be associated with malware. If a malware author changes the pattern, the signature-based detection system will not be able to detect it.

AI-based detection methods can offer a more comprehensive and accurate solution to malware detection. AI-based methods can learn to identify malware by looking for patterns that are not necessarily known to be associated with malware. This means that AI-based methods can be more effective at detecting new malware and malware that has been modified to evade detection.

In addition, AI-based methods can be used to analyze the behavior of files. This can help with identifying malware that is not detected by signature-based detection methods. For example, an AI-based method could be used to identify a file that is trying to connect to a known malicious server.

By integrating AI with traditional signature-based detection methods, it is possible to create a more comprehensive and accurate solution to malware detection. This can help protect organizations from a wider range of malware threats.

Here are some of the benefits of integrating AI with traditional signature-based detection methods:

- **Improved accuracy**: AI-based methods can be more effective at detecting new malware and malware that has been modified to evade detection

- **Enhanced visibility**: AI-based methods can analyze the behavior of files, which can help identify malware that is not detected by signature-based detection methods

- **Reduced false positives**: AI-based methods can be more precise than signature-based detection methods, which can help reduce the number of false positives

However, there are also some challenges associated with integrating AI with traditional signature-based detection methods that will need to be considered:

- **Cost**: AI-based methods can be more expensive to implement than traditional signature-based detection methods

- **Complexity**: AI-based methods can be more complex to implement and manage than traditional signature-based detection methods

- **Data requirements**: AI-based methods require large amounts of data to train, which can be a challenge for some organizations

Overall, integrating AI with traditional signature-based detection methods can offer a more comprehensive and accurate solution to malware detection. However, it is important to be aware of the challenges associated with this approach and to take steps to mitigate these challenges.

Explainable AI (XAI)

Malware is a type of software that is designed to harm a computer system. It can steal data, install other malware, or disrupt the normal operation of a computer. Malware analysis is the process of identifying and understanding malware. This can be done by examining the malware's code, behavior, and other characteristics.

Traditionally, malware analysis has been a manual process. However, machine learning has enabled the development of automated malware detection systems. These systems can be very effective at detecting known malware. However, they can also be fooled by new malware that has not been seen before.

XAI is a branch of AI that focuses on making machine learning models more interpretable. This means that XAI techniques can be used to explain why a machine learning model made a particular decision. This can be helpful for malware analysis because it can help security analysts understand how a malware detection system works and why it made a particular decision.

Several different XAI techniques can be used for malware analysis. Some of the most common techniques are as follows:

- **Feature importance**: This technique identifies the features that are most important for a machine learning model's decision. This can help security analysts understand what characteristics of a malware sample are most likely to trigger a detection.

- **Model explanation**: This technique generates a text or graphical explanation of a machine learning model's decision. This can help security analysts understand how the model arrived at its decision and why it might have made a mistake.

- **Counterfactual explanation**: This technique generates a sample that is similar to a malware sample but that is not detected by the machine learning model. This can help security analysts understand what changes would need to be made to a malware sample for it to evade detection.

Benefits of XAI in malware analysis

There are several benefits to using XAI in malware analysis:

- **Improved detection accuracy**: XAI can help security analysts identify and understand new malware that has not been seen before. This can improve the accuracy of malware detection systems.

- **Increased trust in machine learning models**: XAI can help security analysts understand how machine learning models work and why they make particular decisions. This can increase the trust that security analysts have in these models.

- **Enhanced security operations**: XAI can be used to improve the efficiency and effectiveness of security operations. For example, XAI can be used to prioritize malware samples for analysis or to identify patterns in malware attacks.

Challenges of XAI in malware analysis

There are several challenges to using XAI in malware analysis:

- **Limited data:** There is often limited data available for training XAI models. This can make it difficult to develop accurate and reliable XAI models.

- **Model complexity:** Machine learning models for malware analysis can be very complex. This can make it difficult to understand how these models work and why they make particular decisions.

- **Interpretability**: There is no single definition of interpretability. This can make it difficult to develop XAI techniques that are both accurate and interpretable.

XAI is a promising new technology that has the potential to improve malware analysis. However, several challenges need to be addressed before XAI can be widely adopted. Despite these challenges, XAI is a valuable tool for security analysts and is likely to play an increasingly important role in malware analysis in the future.

Summary

AI has revolutionized malware data analysis and detection, empowering organizations to combat the ever-evolving threat landscape more effectively. By leveraging AI techniques, such as machine learning and deep learning, organizations can enhance detection accuracy, monitor threats in real time, and improve overall efficiency. However, challenges related to adversarial attacks, data privacy, and interpretability must be addressed to maximize the potential of AI in malware analysis. With ongoing research and development, AI will continue to play a vital role in bolstering cybersecurity defenses against malware attacks in the future.

Having understood the transformative impact and the potential challenges of AI in malware analysis, it's essential to delve deeper into specific methods that embody this revolution. In the next chapter, we will explore one such method – behavior-based malware data analysis and detection – that moves away from the traditional reliance on known malware signatures. This dynamic approach aims to bridge the gap between static defenses and rapidly evolving threats, highlighting the direction in which modern cybersecurity is headed.

5

Behavior-Based Malware Data Analysis and Detection

Behavior-based malware data analysis and detection is a subset of computer security that revolves around detecting and preventing malicious software (malware) based on its behavior or activity, rather than relying on pre-existing, known malware signatures. It represents a more dynamic approach to cybersecurity that goes beyond static defenses as it's capable of identifying unknown threats that might be missed by traditional antivirus solutions.

In the increasingly complex world of digital technologies, growing cyber threats necessitate the adoption of advanced and comprehensive cybersecurity strategies. A pivotal part of these strategies is behavior-based malware analysis and detection, a proactive method that focuses on software behavior rather than its code structure. This approach has revolutionized malware detection and mitigation, but it's not a mere plug-and-play solution. Its implementation demands a significant transformation in the organization's maturity and operational processes.

A guiding beacon in this transformation journey is the **Capability Maturity Model Integration (CMMI)**. It's a recognized framework that measures and improves an organization's processes, marking a path from Level 1, characterized by ad hoc and chaotic processes, to Level 3, featuring well-understood and defined processes. Achieving this leap requires extensive planning, process improvements, training, and a cultural shift.

In this chapter, we'll delve into the intricacies of behavior-based malware analysis and detection, explore the significance of CMMI in operational maturity, and understand the transition from Level 1 to Level 3. We'll also uncover the challenges in this transition and discuss strategies to navigate them effectively, providing a roadmap for organizations to bolster their cybersecurity capabilities while enhancing their process maturity.

We will cover the following main topics in the chapter:

- Behavior-based malware data analysis
- Behavior-based malware detection

- Normalcy and anomaly detection
- Overcoming the increased complexity of evolving cyber threats
- Operational challenges and mitigation strategies to enhance organizational cybersecurity capabilities

First, we'll delve deeper into the aspects of this concept and its operational parameters.

Behavior-based malware data analysis

Behavior-based malware data analysis is a proactive approach to cybersecurity that focuses on the actions that are performed by a piece of software rather than its static attributes, such as its code signature. This shift in focus enables us to detect previously unknown or evolved threats that might not have a known signature but exhibit malicious behavior. The approach can be divided into two main stages:

- Data collection
- Behavior analysis

Let's take a closer look.

Data collection

In this stage, software behavior is monitored and recorded. This can be done through various methods, such as system call tracing, API function call tracking, memory and CPU usage monitoring, network traffic analysis, and more. The objective is to capture as much relevant behavior data as possible without overly impacting system performance.

Behavior analysis

This is where the collected data is analyzed to identify potential malicious activity. This analysis can be done using various techniques:

- **Heuristic analysis:** This method involves creating and using rules that define known malicious behavior. If a piece of software behaves according to these rules, it's flagged as potentially malicious.
- **Machine learning/artificial intelligence** (**AI**): Machine learning models can be trained on labeled datasets to learn what constitutes normal and abnormal behavior. Simply put, normal behavior is the expected behavior of a system or application, while abnormal behavior is any deviation from this norm. Once trained, these models can detect anomalies in new, unseen data, potentially identifying malicious activity.
- **Stateful analysis:** This method tracks the state changes in a system over time due to software behavior. Unusual or unexpected state changes can signal potential malicious activity.

Behavior-based malware data analysis is particularly effective at detecting zero-day threats, polymorphic and metamorphic malware, and **advanced persistent threats** (**APTs**) that traditional signature-based detection methods might miss. The approach does, however, require comprehensive data collection and advanced analysis techniques, which can be resource-intensive. Moreover, the effectiveness of this approach is highly dependent on the quality of the behavior data collected and the robustness of the analysis methods employed.

Heuristic analysis

Heuristic analysis is a cybersecurity strategy that uses rules to scrutinize a program's behavior rather than its file signature, making it especially good at spotting new and unknown threats. This method is proactive, meaning it aims to catch potential dangers before they can do any harm. It excels in detecting elusive threats such as unknown zero-day vulnerabilities and sophisticated malware that use tricks to evade traditional detection methods. Essentially, heuristic analysis offers a robust, preemptive defense against a wide range of evolving cyber threats.

Concept

In cybersecurity, heuristic analysis is a method that is used to identify malicious behaviors or potential threats based on a set of rules or algorithms. Unlike signature-based detection, which matches files against a database of known malware signatures, heuristic analysis focuses on the behavior or characteristics of the program to identify if it's potentially harmful.

Heuristic techniques can identify malicious activities or traits such as code obfuscation, attempts to access sensitive information, modification of system files, suspicious network activities, or exploiting system vulnerabilities.

Background

The term **heuristic** is derived from the Greek word *heuriskein*, which means *to discover*. In the field of computer science and particularly in cybersecurity, heuristic techniques represent a method of problem-solving that employs a practical, non-optimal solution under complex and uncertain scenarios.

These methods have been employed in various domains, such as AI, search optimization, and, importantly, malware analysis and detection. Heuristic methods were introduced in malware detection as an answer to the limitations of the traditional signature-based techniques that were ineffective against rapidly evolving and unknown malware.

Let's look at the operational aspects:

- **Static analysis heuristics**: In static analysis, heuristics are used to analyze the program's code, structure, and properties without actually executing it. Techniques such as control flow analysis, data flow analysis, and pattern matching can be employed. For example, the heuristic method might look for embedded, obfuscated code that's often used in malware to evade detection.

- **Dynamic analysis heuristics**: Dynamic analysis involves executing the program in a controlled environment (such as a sandbox) and observing its behavior. Heuristics can be applied to detect suspicious actions such as modifying system files and registry entries, creating or launching other executable files, or establishing network connections.

- **Fileless malware detection**: Fileless malware resides in the system's memory rather than a file, making it hard to detect with traditional methods. Heuristic analysis can identify fileless malware by monitoring behaviors such as the invocation of PowerShell scripts or commands that are commonly used by such threats.

- **Zero-day threat detection**: Heuristics can also help in detecting unknown or zero-day threats. By focusing on the behavior and traits of the program rather than known signatures, heuristic analysis can flag previously unseen malware.

- **Anomaly detection**: By establishing a baseline of normal system or network behavior, heuristic techniques can help identify anomalies or deviations from the norm that could indicate a potential threat.

- **False positives management**: While heuristic techniques are powerful, they can sometimes result in false positives. This is because legitimate programs may occasionally exhibit behavior that appears suspicious. Effective heuristic systems often incorporate methods to manage and minimize false positives, such as whitelisting, user feedback, or cross-verification using other detection methods.

In conclusion, heuristic analysis forms an integral part of a robust cybersecurity defense, allowing for proactive threat detection by focusing on the behavior and characteristics of a program rather than relying solely on known malware signatures. They can be particularly effective against unknown, zero-day threats, and sophisticated malware that uses evasion techniques to avoid detection.

Stateful analysis

Stateful analysis, also known as **stateful inspection** or **dynamic behavior analysis**, is a powerful and comprehensive method that's used in behavior-based malware analysis and detection. Unlike static or signature-based analysis, stateful analysis doesn't merely look at the code or signatures of a program. Instead, it observes and analyzes the **state** changes in a system or network that are induced by the software's behavior over a specific period. This dynamic approach helps in identifying unusual or malicious activities that might otherwise go unnoticed.

The concept of **state** refers to the conditions of various systems or network elements at a particular point in time. For instance, in a computing environment, a state could reflect open network connections, the values stored in memory, files being accessed, CPU usage, and more. In a network context, a state could represent active network sessions, source and destination IP addresses, port numbers, packet sequence information, and more. Any change in these conditions represents a state change, and tracking these changes forms the basis of stateful analysis.

Implementation and operation

Implementing stateful analysis begins with comprehensively monitoring a system or network to capture a wealth of data related to state changes. This might involve monitoring system calls, API function calls, memory, CPU usage, network traffic, filesystem changes, and registry changes, among other elements. This step requires careful planning to balance the need for extensive data collection with potential performance impacts.

Once the monitoring setup is in place, the collected data is analyzed to identify potential anomalies or malicious activities. This analysis is typically carried out using a combination of statistical methods, machine learning algorithms, and heuristic rules. The goal is to identify patterns of behavior that deviate significantly from the norm or match known patterns of malicious behavior.

Use cases

Stateful analysis has numerous use cases in cybersecurity. It is particularly effective at detecting zero-day threats, APTs, and polymorphic or metamorphic malware, which can evade traditional signature-based detection methods.

Zero-day threats, which exploit previously unknown vulnerabilities, may not have known signatures, making them invisible to signature-based detection methods. However, their actions within a system or network, such as exploiting a vulnerability or creating a backdoor, often lead to noticeable state changes that can be picked up by stateful analysis.

APTs involve attackers gaining unauthorized access to a network and remaining undetected for extended periods. These threats are typically characterized by subtle and stealthy behaviors designed to avoid detection. By continually monitoring state changes, stateful analysis can potentially identify the small but unusual changes associated with APTs.

Polymorphic and metamorphic malware change their code structure to avoid signature-based detection, but their behavior often remains consistent. Stateful analysis can detect the state changes induced by these types of malware, effectively identifying them despite their code changes.

Challenges and mitigation strategies

Stateful analysis is not without its challenges. The comprehensive data collection that's required can be resource-intensive and may impact system or network performance. Additionally, the method can generate false positives if normal behavior deviates from the established baseline or if the baseline is not representative of normal behavior.

Balancing the need for comprehensive data collection with potential performance impacts requires careful planning and the use of efficient monitoring tools. To manage false positives, continuously tuning the analysis algorithms and updating the baseline as the normal behavior evolves can be beneficial. Despite these challenges, stateful analysis is a powerful tool for behavior-based malware detection that's capable of detecting sophisticated threats that evade traditional detection methods. Its effectiveness is likely to increase with advances in machine learning and AI, making it a promising technique for future cybersecurity solutions.

Behavior-based malware detection

It is widely understood that signature-based detection and behavior-based malware detection serve as complementary pillars in a robust cybersecurity framework. While signature-based methods are quick and efficient for identifying known threats via a database of malware signatures, they lack the flexibility to adapt to new, "zero-day" threats and sophisticated malware that can change its code to evade detection. In contrast, behavior-based malware detection fills these gaps by being a proactive approach that focuses not on the malware's code structure, but on its actions when executed. It monitors for suspicious activities, anomalous behaviors, or policy violations such as keystroke logging, unauthorized system access, data theft, and network traffic manipulation.

By watching out for these activities, behavior-based detection can potentially identify and block even zero-day attacks, which are new and unknown to signature-based systems. This multi-layered approach, which incorporates both signature and behavior-based detection, provides a comprehensive, agile defense against a wide spectrum of evolving cybersecurity threats.

Operationally, behavior-based malware detection involves several key processes, including data collection, behavior modeling, behavior monitoring, and response:

- **Data collection**: The first step in the process is collecting data about the software's behavior. This might involve monitoring system calls, API calls, user actions, network activity, and other software interactions that might indicate malicious behavior.

- **Behavior modeling**: The next step is creating a model of normal software behavior. This model might be derived from historical data or pre-configured parameters and serves as a baseline for comparison. Behavior modeling is often done using machine learning or AI algorithms that can learn to distinguish between normal and abnormal behavior.

- **Behavior monitoring**: Once a model has been established, the system monitors ongoing behavior and compares it to the model. This can be done in real time, or the data can be logged for later analysis. The system might monitor all software running on a system or focus on certain high-risk areas.

- **Response**: When the system detects behavior that deviates from the model, it responds according to predefined rules. This might involve blocking the suspicious activity, alerting an administrator, or taking some other action. The key here is that the response is based on the behavior, not the identity of the malware.

Behavior-based systems use a variety of techniques to identify malicious behavior, including heuristics, anomaly detection, and specification-based techniques:

- **Heuristic techniques** involve using rules or algorithms to estimate outcomes. They are often used when an exhaustive search is impractical. In the context of *malware detection*, heuristic analysis might involve rules that trigger a warning when a program tries to write data to an unusual location, or when it uses certain system calls associated with malicious activity.

- **Anomaly detection** is a technique that's used to identify items, events, or observations that do not conform to an expected pattern in a dataset. Anomaly detection is frequently applied in many domains such as fraud detection, network intrusion, system health monitoring, and so on. In the context of malware detection, this could involve identifying when a program's behavior deviates from a baseline of normal activity.

- **Specification-based techniques** involve monitoring system activity to ensure that it complies with a set of defined specifications. These specifications could be a set of rules describing the correct usage of system resources, or they could be a more formal mathematical model of system behavior.

One important point to note is that behavior-based detection is not perfect; it can result in false positives (flagging benign behavior as malicious) or false negatives (missing actual malicious behavior). To mitigate this, these systems often employ a degree of "fuzziness" in their detection algorithms, tolerating minor deviations but escalating responses for more significant anomalies.

In conclusion, behavior-based malware data analysis and detection are vital approaches to cyber defense. They offer dynamic and adaptable solutions to the ever-evolving threat of malware, especially in an age where new threats emerge rapidly and traditional defenses struggle to keep up. However, it's also important to remember that they're part of a broader security posture and that they should be used in conjunction with other security measures for a more comprehensive and effective defense.

The concept of proactive behavior-based malware detection

The essence of behavior-based malware detection as a proactive technique lies in its underlying philosophy: instead of waiting to react to a known threat, this method actively monitors and assesses system activities to identify potential threats based on anomalous behavior.

Theoretical foundation

The theory behind behavior-based malware detection begins with the observation that all malware, regardless of its underlying code structure, ultimately manifests through a series of actions or behaviors when executed. These behaviors might include sending unauthorized network packets, accessing or modifying files, attempting to escalate privileges, disabling security software, and more.

The key insight here is that while malware signatures – the unique patterns of code that define a particular piece of malware – can change easily, the fundamental behaviors that define malicious activities are more consistent. This is the theoretical premise that behavior-based malware detection is built on.

Proactivity

The proactive nature of behavior-based detection lies in its operational model. It continuously monitors system activities, looking for patterns that deviate from the norm. This allows it to potentially detect new threats or variants of known malware that signature-based methods might miss.

In other words, it doesn't wait for a known malicious signature to trigger an alarm; instead, it constantly analyzes the behavior of the system and applications in real time. If something starts behaving unusually – for example, a text editor suddenly starts sending data to an external IP – the behavior-based detection system would flag this as suspicious.

Concept of normalcy

One of the fundamental aspects of behavior-based detection is the concept of normal behavior. The system establishes a baseline of normalcy, which could be pre-defined or based on historical behavior patterns. This baseline provides a point of comparison for ongoing activities.

To establish this baseline, the system might monitor the system and user behavior over time, learning what constitutes normal behavior. This could involve analyzing system and network logs, monitoring user actions, studying system call sequences, and so on. Machine learning techniques are often used in this process, enabling the system to adapt to changing behavior patterns and minimize false positives.

Concept of anomaly detection

Central to the proactive nature of behavior-based detection is the idea of anomaly detection. Once a baseline of normal behavior has been established, the system looks for deviations or anomalies from this baseline.

This is a continuous, real-time process that allows the system to respond quickly to potential threats. The system isn't simply looking for known threats; it's actively seeking out unusual behavior that could indicate a new, unknown threat.

In essence, behavior-based malware detection is proactive because it's constantly looking for trouble, not waiting for it to appear. By continuously monitoring system behavior and comparing it to a baseline of normalcy, it can potentially identify and mitigate threats before they cause significant damage.

While behavior-based detection is a powerful tool in your cybersecurity arsenal, it should be noted that it is not a panacea. False positives can occur, where benign activities are flagged as malicious, and false negatives are also possible, where actual threats go undetected. As a result, it's typically used as part of a layered security strategy, complementing other detection and prevention techniques.

The concept of malware's behavioral characteristic

Traditional methods of malware detection, such as signature-based detection, focus heavily on analyzing a piece of software's static properties, such as its code structure. Signature-based methods maintain a database of known malware signatures, which are unique sets of characteristics or patterns in a malicious software's code. When a new piece of software or a file enters a system, it's compared against this database, and if there's a match, it's flagged as malicious.

While this approach has been successful in the past, it has significant limitations in today's rapidly evolving threat landscape. It is inherently reactive – it can only detect malware that it has already seen and cataloged. This makes it less effective against new and unknown threats, such as zero-day exploits, polymorphic malware, or metamorphic malware, which change their code structure to evade detection.

This limitation led to a shift in focus from what a piece of malware is to what it does – a shift from static properties to dynamic behaviors. This is the foundation of behavior-based malware detection.

Behavior-based detection theory

The behavior-based approach is built on the understanding that while the code structure of malware can vary greatly and can be easily changed by attackers, the fundamental behaviors necessary to achieve the malware's goal are more consistent and harder to conceal.

For example, a piece of ransomware, regardless of its specific code, will exhibit certain behaviors to achieve its goal: it will typically scan the hard drive for specific file types, encrypt them, and then display a ransom message to the user. Similarly, a keylogger would need to monitor user input, and a piece of spyware might attempt to access the system's camera or microphone.

The behavior-based approach, therefore, is to monitor these types of activities and flag them as potentially malicious when detected. The behaviors it looks for could be anything that deviates from what is considered normal for a system or application: unusual system calls, abnormal API usage, strange network traffic, and so forth.

Operationalizing behavior-based detection

Operationally, behavior-based detection is more complex than signature-based detection. It typically involves the following steps:

1. **Establish a baseline of normal behavior**: This can be a complex process in itself, involving machine learning algorithms that analyze historical data on the system and user behavior to understand what is "normal." This baseline can then be used as a point of comparison for ongoing activities.

2. **Monitor system activities**: This is a continuous, real-time process. The system watches for activities such as file access, network connections, system calls, and so on.

3. **Analyze activities for anomalies**: The system compares ongoing activities to the baseline. Any deviation from the baseline is considered an anomaly.

4. **Flag or block anomalous activities**: When an anomaly is detected, the system can alert an administrator, block the activity, quarantine the software, or take some other pre-defined action.

The behavior-based approach provides a more dynamic and proactive form of malware detection. By focusing on what software does rather than what it is, it can potentially detect new, unknown threats that signature-based methods would miss. However, it also presents new challenges, such as establishing a reliable baseline of normal behavior and dealing with the potential for false positives or false negatives. Despite these challenges, it represents an essential tool in the ongoing fight against cyber threats.

Operational aspects of software behavior data collection

The process of collecting data about software behavior is a fundamental aspect of behavior-based malware detection systems. It's an essential step that serves to both establish a baseline of normal behavior and provide ongoing surveillance to identify anomalous activities. This can include actions taken by software applications, system calls, network communications, filesystem operations, memory usage patterns, user inputs, and other forms of interactions that software may have with the system and its resources.

Purpose and objective

The purpose of data collection in this context is two-fold:

- **Establish a baseline**: One of the core principles of behavior-based malware detection is the concept of "normal" behavior. By collecting data on software behavior, a system can establish a baseline that represents what is considered normal for that particular environment. This could be based on the historical behavior of applications, user activities, network traffic patterns, and so on.

- **Identify anomalies**: Once a baseline has been established, ongoing data collection allows the system to continuously monitor for any deviations from the norm. The objective here is to identify any anomalous behavior that might indicate malicious activity.

Operational aspects

Operationally, collecting data about software behavior typically involves the following steps:

1. **Monitoring system activities**: The first step is to monitor the relevant system activities. This can be a complex process due to the multitude of potential data sources and the high volume of data. The system might monitor activities such as application processes, system calls, network traffic, file access, and user activities. The specifics of what is monitored can vary, depending on the system and the particular approach used.

2. **Data recording and storage**: Once the data has been collected, it needs to be stored for further analysis. This can involve logging system activities and storing the logs in a database or some other form of data storage system. The system needs to be designed to handle potentially large volumes of data and to store it in a way that facilitates easy retrieval and analysis.

3. **Data preprocessing**: Before the data can be analyzed, it might need to be preprocessed to transform it into a suitable format. This could involve data cleaning (removing or correcting erroneous data), data transformation (converting the data into a standard format), and data reduction (reducing the volume of data to make it more manageable).

4. **Data analysis**: The collected data is then analyzed to identify any anomalous behavior. This could involve comparing current activities to the established baseline, using machine learning algorithms to identify patterns, and so on.

The data collection process is a continuous, ongoing activity. It's a fundamental part of the operation of behavior-based malware detection systems, providing the raw data that these systems need to identify potential threats.

In conclusion, the process of collecting data about software behavior is an integral part of behavior-based malware detection. It allows for the creation of a baseline of normal behavior and enables the ongoing identification of anomalies that might indicate malicious activities. The operational aspects of this process involve monitoring system activities, storing the collected data, preprocessing it, and then analyzing it to identify threats.

Operational aspects of behavior modeling using machine learning or AI

In an era where cyber threats are increasingly sophisticated and ever-changing, traditional methods of malware detection, such as signature-based approaches, are no longer sufficient on their own. Combining the established power of signature-based detection with the dynamic capabilities of machine learning and AI offers a more comprehensive and adaptive strategy. Behavior-based malware detection, empowered by machine learning or AI, provides an essential layer of proactive security that complements traditional methods. This hybrid approach aims to identify not just known threats but also new, evolving, and even unseen types of malicious activity by monitoring behavioral patterns within a system. Through this lens, we'll explore the concept, purpose, objectives, and operational workflow of behavior modeling using machine learning or AI in the cybersecurity landscape.

Concept

Behavior modeling in the context of behavior-based malware detection involves the use of machine learning or AI algorithms to learn and understand what constitutes normal behavior in a system, and thereby recognize deviations from this norm (that is, abnormal or potentially malicious activities).

These models, once trained, can generalize from the observed behavior to identify suspicious activities in new, unseen data. This capacity to extrapolate from known to unknown instances is a significant advantage over traditional signature-based methods.

Purpose and objective

The main purposes of behavior modeling in this context are as follows:

- **Understanding normal behavior**: By analyzing a large amount of system behavior data, machine learning or AI algorithms can "learn" what is considered normal for that particular system or environment. This understanding forms a baseline against which future behavior can be compared.

- **Identifying abnormal behavior**: Once a model of normal behavior is established, it can be used to identify behavior that deviates from this norm. This deviation, or anomaly, might indicate malicious activity.

Operational aspects

The operational aspects of behavior modeling using machine learning or AI in behavior-based malware detection typically involve the following steps:

1. **Data preprocessing**: Before the data can be fed into the machine learning or AI algorithms, it needs to be preprocessed. This could involve cleaning the data (removing outliers or noise), normalizing or standardizing the data (scaling the values to a certain range), and selecting relevant features (choosing the most informative attributes for the learning task).

2. **Training the model**: The next step is to feed the preprocessed data into the machine learning or AI algorithm. The algorithm uses this data to learn the patterns and relationships that define normal behavior. Depending on the complexity of the system and the amount of data, this could take anywhere from a few minutes to several hours or even days.

3. **Validating the model**: Once the model has been trained, it needs to be validated to ensure it has accurately learned the concept of normal behavior. This is usually done by testing the model on a separate set of data (the validation set) that wasn't used in the training process. The model's performance on the validation set indicates how well it has learned and its ability to generalize to unseen data.

4. **Applying the model**: Once the model has been validated, it can be used to monitor system behavior in real time. It analyzes ongoing system activities and flags any behavior that it considers abnormal based on what it learned during training.

5. **Updating the model**: Systems and behaviors can change over time, so it's important to periodically update the model. This involves collecting new data, retraining the model, and validating it again.

In behavior-based malware detection, the use of machine learning or AI algorithms for behavior modeling is key to distinguishing between normal and abnormal behavior. By learning from historical data, these algorithms can recognize potential threats that are not yet known or have never been seen before, making them a crucial tool in proactive cybersecurity efforts. The operational process involves data preprocessing, model training, validation, and application, along with continuous updates to adapt to changing behaviors and threat landscapes.

Operational aspects of behavior monitoring

In the field of cybersecurity, traditional signature-based detection methods are becoming less effective. Behavior monitoring serves as a more dynamic and proactive alternative for identifying potential threats. This approach involves continuously tracking and analyzing system or network activities to identify any unusual or suspicious behavior. Unlike methods that rely solely on code signatures, behavior monitoring can identify new or modified threats based on deviations from established norms. This section outlines the concept, purpose, and operational aspects of behavior monitoring, focusing on its role in identifying abnormal behaviors, detecting unknown threats, and serving as a proactive defense mechanism. It covers key operational steps, including establishing a baseline for normal activities, ongoing monitoring, analysis, and response protocols, and making adjustments to the baseline as needed.

Concept

Behavior monitoring, in the context of cybersecurity and malware detection, is a proactive approach that involves continuously observing and analyzing the activities that are happening within a system or network to detect any abnormal or suspicious activities that may indicate a potential security threat.

Purpose and objective

The main purposes of behavior monitoring are as follows:

- **Identify abnormal or malicious behavior**: By continuously monitoring system activities, behavior monitoring tools can spot behavior that deviates from established norms or patterns. This behavior could be indicative of a malware infection or another form of cyber threat.

- **Detect unknown threats**: Behavior monitoring is an effective way to detect new and unknown threats that haven't been cataloged in malware signature databases. By focusing on behavior rather than code signatures, behavior monitoring can identify malicious activity, even if the malware itself is brand new or has been modified to evade signature-based detection.

- **Proactive defense**: Instead of waiting for a threat to be recognized, behavior monitoring provides a proactive defense mechanism that's constantly on the lookout for signs of intrusion or malicious activity.

Operational aspects

The operational aspects of behavior monitoring typically involve the following steps:

1. **Establishing a baseline**: Before abnormal behavior can be identified, the system must first understand what constitutes "normal" behavior. This typically involves a learning phase, during which system activities are monitored and analyzed over time to establish typical patterns of behavior. These patterns form a baseline against which future behavior can be compared.

2. **Continuous monitoring**: Once a baseline has been established, the system continuously monitors activities. This could involve monitoring system processes, network traffic, user activities, file operations, and more. The specifics of what is monitored can vary depending on the system and the particular behavior-monitoring solution used.

3. **Behavior analysis**: The system analyzes the monitored activities in real time, comparing them to the baseline to identify any deviations. This analysis can involve a variety of techniques, ranging from simple rule-based methods to complex artificial intelligence algorithms.

4. **Alerts and response**: If the system identifies behavior that deviates from the norm, it can trigger an alert or take some pre-defined action. This could involve notifying an administrator, blocking suspicious activity, isolating the affected system, or any other response that has been configured.

5. **Adjusting the baseline**: Over time, "normal" behavior may change. Users may start using new applications, network traffic patterns may evolve, and so on. Behavior monitoring systems must be able to adjust the baseline to reflect these changes, either through manual reconfiguration or automated learning processes.

In behavior-based malware detection, behavior monitoring plays a crucial role in identifying potential threats. By continuously observing and analyzing system activities, behavior monitoring systems can identify suspicious behavior that deviates from the norm, providing a proactive defense mechanism against both known and unknown threats. The operational process involves establishing a baseline of normal behavior, continuous monitoring, behavior analysis, and a response when anomalies are detected, along with adjustments to the baseline as necessary.

Operational aspects of malware behavior-based response

In behavior-based malware detection, the response to a potential threat is determined by the behavior being observed, not the identity of the malware. This approach stands in contrast to signature-based methods, which respond to threats based on their identity – that is, whether the code of a file or program matches a known malware signature in the database.

Behavior-based systems are more concerned with *what* the software does rather than *who* the software is. This focus on behavior allows these systems to react to a wider range of threats, including new and unknown malware variants that may not be recognized by their code but can be detected by their activities.

Purpose and objective

The main purposes of behavior-based response are as follows:

- **Proactive defense**: By focusing on behavior, the system can proactively defend against threats that have not yet been recognized or cataloged. This includes zero-day threats and polymorphic or metamorphic malware that changes its code to evade signature-based detection.

- **Mitigate damage**: If malicious behavior is detected, immediate action can be taken to mitigate the potential damage. This can be especially important in cases of ransomware or other types of malware that can cause significant harm if not quickly stopped.

- **Prevent propagation**: Responding to the behavior can help prevent the spread of malware within the network by interrupting the activities that allow it to propagate, such as network connections or file modifications.

Operational aspects

The operational aspects of a behavior-based response typically involve the following steps:

1. **Detection**: The first step is to detect abnormal behavior. This involves monitoring system activities and comparing them to a baseline of normal behavior, as discussed in previous sections.

2. **Alert generation**: If abnormal behavior is detected, the system generates an alert. The specifics of this alert can vary but it typically includes information about the behavior detected, the system or process involved, the time of detection, and so on.

3. **Response action**: The system then takes some pre-defined action in response to the alert. The specifics of this action can vary, depending on the system and the severity of the threat. It might involve blocking the suspicious activity, isolating the affected system, terminating the offending process, or simply notifying an administrator for further investigation.

4. **Incident analysis and learning**: After the immediate threat has been dealt with, the event is often analyzed to learn more about the threat and improve future detection and response. This could involve a more in-depth analysis of the behavior, updating the behavior baseline or adjusting the behavior model, updating the response protocol, and so on.

In behavior-based malware detection, the response to potential threats is determined by the behavior observed, not the identity of the malware. This allows the system to proactively defend against a wide range of threats, including those that have not yet been recognized or cataloged. The operational aspects of a behavior-based response involve detecting abnormal behavior, generating an alert, taking some response action, and analyzing the event for future learning and improvement.

Operational aspects of anomaly detection

Anomaly detection, also known as outlier detection, has its roots in the field of statistics and has been utilized in various domains, including finance, health care, manufacturing, and, notably, cybersecurity. The fundamental principle behind anomaly detection is that abnormal or anomalous behaviors often represent significant, and potentially harmful, events.

In the context of cybersecurity, anomaly detection emerged as a way to detect new, unknown threats that cannot be caught by traditional signature-based methods. By monitoring normal behavior and identifying deviations from this norm, anomaly detection systems can flag potential security threats that haven't been previously identified or cataloged.

Concept

In cybersecurity, anomaly detection is a technique that's used to identify abnormal behavior or patterns that deviate significantly from expected behavior (the "norm"). This could involve unusual network traffic, abnormal user behavior, unexpected system processes, or any activity that deviates from what's considered normal for a particular system or environment.

These anomalies, while not always representing a security threat, are often indicative of potential malicious activities, such as malware infections, intrusions, system vulnerabilities, or insider threats.

Anomaly detection systems typically employ statistical, machine learning, or AI algorithms to establish a model of normal behavior and then use this model to identify anomalies.

Operational aspects

Anomaly detection is a key component in cybersecurity that focuses on identifying irregularities that deviate from an established baseline of normal system behavior. It encompasses a multi-step operational process that includes establishing a behavioral baseline, continuous monitoring, anomaly identification, alerting, investigation, response, and model refinement, aiming to proactively identify and mitigate potential security threats:

1. **Establishing a baseline**: The first step in anomaly detection is to establish a baseline of *normal* behavior. This involves collecting and analyzing data over a certain period to understand the normal state and variance in a system's behavior.

2. **Continuous monitoring**: Once a baseline has been established, the system continuously monitors the environment, which could be network traffic, user behavior, system processes, and so on.

3. **Anomaly identification**: Using statistical, machine learning, or AI algorithms, the system identifies instances that significantly deviate from the established baseline. These instances are flagged as anomalies.

4. **Alerting and investigation**: The anomaly detection system then generates alerts for these anomalies so that they can be investigated. The level of detail in these alerts can vary, but they typically provide enough information for security analysts to begin an investigation.

5. **Response and mitigation**: If an anomaly is confirmed to be a security threat, appropriate response and mitigation strategies are executed. This could involve stopping a malicious process, blocking network traffic, or patching a system vulnerability.

6. **Model update and refinement**: As systems and networks evolve, the definition of what is "normal" can change. Therefore, anomaly detection models need to be periodically updated and refined to account for these changes.

Anomaly detection plays a crucial role in cybersecurity, offering the ability to detect unknown, zero-day threats, and subtle, low-and-slow attacks that might not trigger signature-based systems. However, one challenge of anomaly detection is managing false positives as not all anomalies represent security threats. Therefore, effective anomaly detection often involves a combination of automated detection and human analysis for accurate threat identification and response.

Operational aspects of specification-based techniques

Traditional malware detection systems have limitations, such as the inability to detect zero-day attacks and a high rate of false positives and negatives. To address these issues, researchers and practitioners have proposed using specification-based techniques to capture the essential behavior of a system or a protocol, allowing for a deeper and more nuanced understanding of whether the system's behavior is malicious or benign.

Concept

Specification-based detection, also known as policy-based or rule-based detection, is a method of identifying malicious activity based on a set of predefined rules or specifications that describe the correct operation of a system, program, or protocol. When a behavior is observed that deviates from this specification, it's flagged as potentially malicious.

In this method, the "specification" represents the expected or allowed behavior of a system. It can be developed using expert knowledge, industry standards, or through an analysis of the system's design and intended functionality.

Operational aspects

The operational aspects of specification-based techniques typically involve the following steps:

1. **Specification development**: This is the initial phase and is where the rules or specifications are defined. This can be done manually by security experts, though it can be automated using machine learning techniques. The specifications describe the correct behavior of a system or network.

2. **Monitoring**: The system or network is then continuously monitored and the behavior of various elements is compared to the defined specifications. This monitoring can cover a wide range of activities, from network traffic patterns to user behavior and system processes.

3. **Detection**: If a behavior is observed that deviates from the defined specification, it is flagged as an anomaly. For instance, if a specification states that a particular system process should not make network connections, but such a connection is observed, this would be flagged as an anomaly.

4. **Alerting**: Upon detecting an anomaly, the system generates an alert. This alert will usually contain information about the detected anomaly and the associated specification.

5. **Investigation and response**: The alert will be investigated by security analysts to determine whether it represents a genuine security threat. If it does, appropriate response actions will be taken, such as blocking the anomalous activity, isolating the affected system, or launching a more detailed forensic investigation.

6. **Specification update**: Over time, the specifications may need to be updated to reflect changes in the system's normal operation or to improve detection accuracy.

One of the main advantages of specification-based detection is its ability to detect zero-day exploits and unknown threats. Since it doesn't rely on the signatures of known malware, but rather on deviations from correct behavior, it can potentially detect new types of attacks.

However, the effectiveness of this technique heavily relies on the accuracy and completeness of the specifications. If the specifications are not accurately defined or if they do not cover all aspects of the system's behavior, the detection capability can be compromised. Furthermore, like other anomaly detection techniques, specification-based techniques can lead to a high number of false positives. This can be mitigated to some extent through careful specification development and regular updates.

Normalcy and anomaly detection

In cybersecurity, the concepts of normalcy and anomaly detection are fundamental for establishing robust protective mechanisms. Normalcy refers to the expected, routine behaviors and operations within a system or network. This understanding of normalcy acts as a reference point for identifying irregularities or suspicious activities. However, the notion of what is considered "normal" is dynamic; it evolves with changes in system configurations, network traffic, and user behaviors. On the other hand, anomaly detection aims to identify deviations from this baseline of normalcy, often indicative of potential security threats such as malware or unauthorized intrusions. Operationalizing anomaly detection involves several key steps: establishing a baseline of normal behavior, continuous monitoring of systems or networks, identifying anomalies, investigating these irregularities for potential threats, initiating appropriate responses if threats are validated, and iteratively refining the baseline to keep pace with changes in the environment.

Concept of normalcy

In the context of cybersecurity, the concept of normalcy is concerned with the usual, expected, and non-harmful operations and behaviors of a system, network, or user. This includes routine patterns of network traffic, standard system processes, typical user behaviors, and other activities that are part of the day-to-day functioning of the system or network.

Establishing a sense of normalcy is crucial for many security systems as it serves as a baseline or reference point against which unusual or suspicious activities can be identified. The concept of normalcy, however, is not static. It can change over time as systems are updated, network configurations change, and user behaviors evolve. Therefore, maintaining an up-to-date understanding of what constitutes normal behavior in a specific context is a continual process.

Concept of anomaly detection

Anomaly detection, also known as **outlier detection**, is the process of identifying patterns in data that do not conform to the expected or *normal* behavior. These deviations or anomalies can be indicative of a wide range of issues, from system faults and errors to malicious activities and security threats.

In cybersecurity, anomaly detection is used to identify potential threats such as malware, intrusions, and other security compromises. These threats often manifest as anomalous behaviors, such as unusual network traffic, unexpected system processes, or abnormal user activities.

Operational aspects of anomaly detection

In cybersecurity, the framework for anomaly detection relies on a series of steps designed to recognize and counter threats based on deviations from established norms. From setting a baseline of typical behavior to continuously monitoring data and responding to detected anomalies, this structured approach enables security experts and automated systems to act preemptively against both known and emerging threats:

- **Establishing a baseline of normalcy**: This is the foundational step in anomaly detection. Security analysts, often with the aid of machine learning algorithms, analyze historical data to establish a baseline of what is considered normal behavior within a specific system or network.

- **Continuous monitoring**: Once the baseline has been established, continuous monitoring takes place. This can involve real-time data collection and analysis or periodic checks, depending on the specific requirements and capabilities of the organization.

- **Anomaly identification**: Using the baseline, the system or analyst identifies behavior or patterns that significantly deviate from the norm. The detection process can involve statistical methods, clustering algorithms, classification techniques, or other machine learning approaches.

- **Investigation and validation**: Once potential anomalies have been identified, they need to be investigated to determine whether they represent a genuine threat. This often involves a combination of automated analysis and human expertise.

- **Response and mitigation**: If a detected anomaly is determined to be a security threat, appropriate response and mitigation strategies are initiated. This could involve shutting down a malicious process, blocking a suspicious network connection, or patching a software vulnerability.

- **Update and refine the normalcy baseline**: As the system or network changes over time, so too does the definition of what constitutes normal behavior. Regular updates and refinement of the normalcy baseline are crucial for maintaining the effectiveness of the anomaly detection process.

The concepts of normalcy and anomaly detection are at the core of many cybersecurity strategies. By understanding what constitutes normal behavior and identifying significant deviations from this norm, security systems and analysts can proactively detect and respond to potential threats.

Future concepts of normalcy and anomaly detection

In the future, the concepts of normalcy and anomaly detection could see significant evolution and innovation driven by advancements in technology, AI, and machine learning. The proliferation of connected devices and the increasing complexity of cyber threats will also contribute to the evolution of these concepts:

- **Adaptive normalcy**: Future systems will likely have the capability to continually learn and adapt their understanding of "normal" based on the ever-evolving behaviors of users and systems. This adaptive normalcy would account for the dynamic nature of user behavior and system states, reducing false positives and increasing the accuracy of threat detection.

- **Predictive anomaly detection**: Predictive analytics could be used to forecast future anomalies based on current and historical data. This will allow organizations to act proactively against potential threats, securing their systems even before the anomalous behavior occurs.

- **Enhanced AI and machine learning techniques**: AI and machine learning will continue to play a significant role in defining normalcy and detecting anomalies. With advancements in deep learning, we can expect these systems to become more accurate, scalable, and capable of understanding complex patterns and behaviors. These techniques may also become better at understanding the context in which anomalies occur, further improving the precision of threat detection and response.

- **Distributed normalcy and anomaly detection**: With the rise of edge computing and the **Internet of Things** (IoT), the concept of normalcy and anomaly detection will likely become more distributed. Each edge device or IoT device may have a unique definition of normalcy and a capability for detecting anomalies, allowing for threat detection and response at the edge of the network.

- **Automated response and mitigation**: As systems become better at detecting anomalies and identifying threats, they'll likely also become more capable of responding to these threats automatically. Automated response systems could potentially isolate affected network segments, patch vulnerabilities, or even deploy decoy resources to distract attackers.

- **Privacy-preserving normalcy and anomaly detection**: As privacy regulations become stricter, new techniques will be needed to ensure the privacy of user data while still effectively modeling normal behavior and detecting anomalies. Techniques such as federated learning and differential privacy could allow systems to learn from data without directly accessing it, helping to balance security and privacy needs.

- **Cross-domain anomaly detection**: As businesses and operations become increasingly interconnected, anomaly detection will likely expand to consider multi-domain, cross-organizational data. For example, abnormal behavior might not just be detected in your network; anomalies might be detected across a supply chain network, a cloud ecosystem, or a system of interlinked IoT devices.

While the future of normalcy and anomaly detection will face challenges such as dealing with increased complexity, data volume, privacy regulations, and evolving cyber threats, advancements in technology, AI, and machine learning will likely provide new and innovative ways to meet these challenges.

Overcoming the increased complexity of evolving cyber threats

Addressing the future challenges of increased complexity, data volume, privacy regulations, and evolving cyber threats in the realm of normalcy and anomaly detection will require multi-pronged strategies encompassing technology innovation, regulatory compliance, and cybersecurity best practices. In this section, we will look at some possible ways to overcome these challenges:

- Handling increased complexity and data volume

- Navigating privacy regulations

- Mitigating evolving cyber threats

Let's get started.

Handling increased complexity and data volume

Let us look at ways to overcome this challenge.

- **Advanced machine learning and AI**: To handle the increased complexity and data volume, the use of more sophisticated machine learning and AI models will be essential. These models can effectively analyze large datasets and complex relationships. Techniques such as deep learning and reinforcement learning can be useful in identifying nuanced patterns and anomalies that simpler models might miss.

- **Distributed computing and edge analytics**: To handle large volumes of data, especially in IoT networks, distributed computing and edge analytics can be employed. By processing data closer to the source, we can reduce the need for data transfer, improve response times, and manage the data volume effectively.

- **Data management strategies**: Implementing robust data management strategies, including data cleansing, transformation, and dimensionality reduction techniques, can help in managing large data volumes and enhancing the efficiency of the detection algorithms.

Navigating privacy regulations

Let us look at ways to overcome this challenge.

- **Privacy-preserving machine learning**: Techniques such as federated learning, differential privacy, and homomorphic encryption can allow systems to learn from data while preserving privacy. These methods can be particularly useful in complying with privacy regulations while still benefiting from machine learning.

- **Anonymization and pseudonymization**: Anonymization techniques can help to protect individual privacy by removing **personally identifiable information (PII)** from datasets. Pseudonymization replaces PII with artificial identifiers, adding an extra layer of security.

- **Consent management**: Implementing robust consent management systems can also help in meeting privacy regulations. These systems ensure that data is only collected and processed when necessary and with the appropriate consent.

Mitigating evolving cyber threats

Let us look at ways to overcome this challenge.

- **Continuous learning and adaptation**: Systems will need to continuously learn about and adapt to new threats. This might involve regularly retraining machine learning models on updated data and incorporating feedback loops that allow the system to learn from its predictions and mistakes.

- **Threat intelligence sharing**: Collaborative threat intelligence sharing among organizations can help in identifying new types of cyber threats early. By sharing information about threats and attacks, organizations can collectively improve their defenses.

- **Proactive cybersecurity measures**: Adopting a proactive approach to cybersecurity that involves regular security audits, vulnerability assessments, and penetration testing can help organizations stay ahead of potential threats.

The combination of technology innovation, regulatory adherence, and evolving cybersecurity strategies can help overcome future challenges in normalcy and anomaly detection. By remaining adaptable and continuously improving systems and strategies, organizations can navigate the complex cybersecurity landscape of the future.

Implementing the solutions

Implementing the solutions to handle increased complexity, data volume, privacy regulations, and evolving cyber threats involves a strategic process that covers multiple stages. The steps can be adjusted based on the organization's specific needs, but a general approach might look like this:

1. **Assessment and planning**: Firstly, conduct an assessment of the current system capabilities, data management strategies, privacy measures, and threat detection mechanisms. Identify potential areas of weakness and areas for improvement. Use this assessment to formulate a strategic plan for implementing the solutions.

2. **Technology upgrade and integration**: Based on the strategic plan, introduce necessary technological upgrades. This could involve investing in advanced machine learning or AI capabilities or integrating distributed computing or edge analytics into the existing infrastructure. Work with data scientists, IT personnel, and cybersecurity experts to ensure a smooth transition.

3. **Data management improvements**: Improve the organization's data management practices. This could involve introducing new data cleansing, transformation, or dimensionality reduction techniques. It could also mean optimizing data storage and transfer practices to better handle large data volumes.

4. **Implementation of privacy-preserving techniques**: Incorporate privacy-preserving techniques such as federated learning, differential privacy, or homomorphic encryption where necessary. Work with legal and compliance teams to ensure that these techniques align with applicable privacy regulations.

5. **Anonymization and consent management**: Implement or improve anonymization and pseudonymization techniques to further enhance data privacy. Improve consent management systems to ensure that data is only collected and processed with appropriate consent.

6. **Security improvement and threat intelligence sharing**: Enhance the organization's security measures by integrating continuous learning and adaptation capabilities into the system. Consider participating in threat intelligence sharing networks to stay informed about new types of cyber threats.

7. **Regular audits and updates**: Finally, perform regular security audits and vulnerability assessments to evaluate the effectiveness of the implemented solutions. Use the results of these audits to update and refine the systems as necessary. This could involve retraining machine learning models, updating data management practices, or enhancing security measures.

Throughout this process, it's important to maintain open communication and collaboration between different teams within the organization, including IT, data science, cybersecurity, and legal/compliance. It's also critical to provide necessary training to all relevant staff to ensure that they are equipped to work with the new systems and practices. By following a systematic and collaborative approach, organizations can successfully implement solutions to overcome the challenges of the future in normalcy and anomaly detection.

Starting with the basics – organizational capability maturity

In an era where cyber threats are growing exponentially in scale and sophistication, organizations must go beyond conventional reactive security measures to implement proactive, robust cybersecurity systems. A key pillar in this defense strategy is behavior-based malware analysis and detection, a forward-thinking approach that focuses on identifying malicious activities based on the behavior of software, rather than relying solely on traditional signature-based detection methods.

In parallel, there is a rising necessity for organizations to enhance their operational and technological capabilities to maintain competitive advantage and resilience. The CMMI, a model that gauges and augments the maturity of an organization's processes, plays a pivotal role in this endeavor. Transitioning from a CMMI Level 1, characterized by unpredictable and poorly controlled processes, to Level 3, where processes are well-characterized and understood, is an integral stride.

This leap facilitates an improved quality of work, increased customer satisfaction, and an enhanced ability to manage growing complexities and cyber risks. A significant aspect of this transition is not merely implementing new processes, such as behavior-based malware detection, but also institutionalizing these procedures within the organization's operations. As such, understanding and effectively managing this transition is vital for any organization aspiring to secure and thrive in today's digital and risk-laden environment.

Moving an organization from a CMMI Level 1 to Level 3 involves significant planning, process improvements, training, and cultural change. The transition requires not just the implementation of new processes, but also the institutionalization of these processes throughout the organization. The following is a general roadmap for this transition, with specific reference to implementing the solutions for handling increased complexity, data volume, privacy regulations, and evolving cyber threats:

1. **Commitment to process improvement**: The first step is gaining commitment from the top management and key stakeholders for the process improvement plan. Make them understand the benefits of advancing to a higher maturity level and how it can help address the challenges of increased complexity, data volume, privacy regulations, and cyber threats.

2. **Gap analysis**: Carry out a gap analysis to understand the current state of the organization and the desired state (Level 3). The gap analysis should identify the processes that need to be defined, improved, and standardized. This will provide a clear roadmap for what needs to be achieved.

3. **Process definition and standardization**: Start defining and documenting the processes based on the findings from the gap analysis. For a Level 3 organization, the processes need to be well-defined, standardized, and tailored from the organization's set of standard processes according to the project's established tailoring guidelines.

4. **Process implementation**: Implement the defined processes. This involves deploying the necessary tools and technology, training the team members on the new processes, and ensuring they are used consistently throughout the organization.

5. **Institutionalization and cultural change**: It's crucial to institutionalize the processes and bring a cultural change where the team members understand the benefits of these processes and follow them consistently. This could be achieved through regular training and communication, and by demonstrating the benefits of these processes.

6. **Process measurement and control**: For a Level 3 organization, it's important to have processes that are measured and controlled. This involves setting up metrics to measure the effectiveness of the processes, collecting the metrics data, and using it to control and improve the processes.

7. **Continuous improvement**: Once the processes are in place and being measured, work on continuous improvement. Use the insights from the collected metrics data to identify the areas of improvement and optimize the processes.

8. **Independent audits and validation**: Regularly carry out internal audits to ensure that the processes are being followed. Once you feel that the organization is ready for Level 3, go for an independent CMMI appraisal to validate the maturity level.

Keep in mind that moving from Level 1 to Level 3 is a significant transition and it requires a considerable amount of time, effort, and cultural change throughout the organization. It's a journey of continuous improvement and learning, and it's important to celebrate the small wins along the way to keep the team motivated.

The relationship between the CMMI maturity process and the increased complexity of threat management

Combining the CMMI maturity process with strategies to handle increased complexity, data volume, privacy regulations, and evolving cyber threats would require an integrated approach that aligns the process improvement plan with the specific objectives of handling these challenges. Here's a potential approach:

- **Commitment to process improvement and security upgrades**

  The commitment to process improvement must extend to an understanding and acknowledgment of the importance of cybersecurity, data management, and privacy controls. This includes recognizing the importance of technology upgrades, implementing AI and machine learning, and integrating more sophisticated data management strategies.

- **Gap analysis and risk assessment**

  Conduct a gap analysis that includes assessing the current state of your cybersecurity measures, data management practices, and privacy compliance. Carry out a risk assessment to identify potential vulnerabilities and areas for improvement. This process will help you understand where you stand and what measures need to be taken to reach Level 3.

- **Define and standardize processes with cybersecurity and privacy in mind**

    When defining and documenting the processes, ensure that they are designed with cybersecurity best practices and privacy regulations in mind. Processes must be able to handle large volumes of data, manage complexity, and address privacy requirements. Standardization should also consider evolving cyber threats and create protocols that help in their early detection and mitigation.

- **Implement processes and technological solutions**

    Implement the processes across the organization. This involves not just the application of new methods, but also the deployment of necessary technology solutions. Introduce the necessary tools and systems that can effectively handle data, manage complexity, detect anomalies, and ensure data privacy.

- **Training and institutionalization**

    Ensure that all staff are properly trained in the new processes and technologies. This includes understanding data management, anomaly detection, privacy regulations, and how to respond to potential cyber threats. Cultivate a culture of security awareness, ensuring that cybersecurity becomes a fundamental part of everyone's role.

- **Measure, monitor, and control**

    Establish metrics and **key performance indicators (KPIs)** to measure the effectiveness of the new processes and technologies. Monitor these metrics regularly to ensure that they're effective in managing complexity, data volumes, and privacy compliance, and in mitigating cyber threats. Use the insights gained from monitoring to control and further improve the processes.

- **Continuous improvement and adaptation**

    Cyber threats, privacy regulations, and technological landscapes are continuously evolving. So, the organization needs to constantly learn and adapt to these changes. Encourage a culture of continuous improvement and learning, regularly updating processes and technologies to keep pace with the changing environment.

- **Regular audits and independent validation**

    Conduct regular internal audits to ensure compliance with defined processes and effectiveness in handling challenges. Once you're ready, go for an independent CMMI appraisal to validate the maturity level and ensure that the organization is effectively managing complexity, data volume, privacy regulations, and evolving cyber threats.

By taking an integrated approach that aligns the CMMI process improvement plan with strategies to handle these specific challenges, the organization can effectively progress in maturity while also enhancing its capabilities in managing complexity, handling large data volumes, ensuring privacy compliance, and mitigating cyber threats.

Operational challenges and mitigation strategies to enhance organizational cybersecurity capabilities

Implementing such a comprehensive program to enhance an organization's cybersecurity capabilities and move up the maturity levels of the CMMI will involve several operational challenges. These can be anticipated and mitigated with effective strategies. Here are some of the potential challenges and mitigation strategies:

- **Resistance to change**:

  - **Challenge**: In any organization, there can be resistance to changes in processes, particularly when they impact daily routines or require new skills.

  - **Mitigation strategy**: Create a clear communication plan outlining the reasons for the changes, the benefits they'll bring, and how they will be implemented. Regular training and support will also help team members adapt to the new processes and technologies.

- **Lack of necessary skills**:

  - **Challenge**: The introduction of advanced technologies such as AI and machine learning may reveal a lack of necessary skills within the organization.

  - **Mitigation strategy**: Invest in training programs to upskill existing staff and consider hiring new team members with the required expertise. It's also beneficial to establish relationships with external consultants or service providers who can provide necessary support.

- **Integration of new technologies**:

  - **Challenge**: The integration of new technologies with existing systems can present logistical and compatibility challenges.

  - **Mitigation strategy**: Carefully plan the technology integration process to minimize disruptions. This could involve running pilot projects, gradually phasing in new technologies, or using middleware to bridge compatibility gaps.

- **Resource constraints**:

  - **Challenge**: Implementing new processes and technologies can be resource-intensive, and there may be constraints in terms of budget, time, or personnel.

  - **Mitigation strategy**: Prioritize tasks and phase the implementation process to spread the resource demands over time. Seek external funding or partnerships if necessary.

- **Data security and privacy concerns:**

  - **Challenge**: With the increased use of data, particularly for AI and machine learning, there can be increased concerns around data security and privacy.

  - **Mitigation strategy**: Implement robust data security measures and ensure all activities comply with relevant privacy regulations. Regular audits and assessments can help identify any potential vulnerabilities and address them proactively.

- **Performance metrics and control:**

  - **Challenge**: Establishing effective performance metrics and control measures for new processes and technologies can be complex.

  - **Mitigation strategy**: Work with experts to develop meaningful metrics and control measures. Ensure these metrics are regularly reviewed and updated as necessary.

Remember, the successful execution and delivery of such a program requires strong leadership, clear communication, and the involvement of all team members. By taking a proactive approach to anticipating potential challenges and implementing effective strategies to mitigate them, an organization can navigate this transition smoothly and effectively.

In the current digital landscape, where cyber threats continue to evolve and increase in complexity, organizations need to adopt proactive, robust, and comprehensive cybersecurity strategies. One such strategy that stands out is behavior-based malware analysis and detection. This approach, which focuses on understanding and analyzing the behavior of software rather than its code structure, has emerged as a powerful tool for detecting, preventing, and mitigating cyber threats. However, the successful implementation of such a strategy demands more than the mere introduction of new processes or technologies.

An essential aspect of effectively integrating and leveraging behavior-based malware detection lies in the broader process maturity of the organization, as modeled by frameworks such as the CMMI. Transitioning an organization from a CMMI Level 1 to Level 3 is an undertaking of significant magnitude that calls for extensive planning, process improvements, training, and a fundamental shift in organizational culture. The focus here is not just on introducing new processes but on embedding or institutionalizing these processes throughout the organization.

This journey toward maturity and the integration of behavior-based detection techniques involves numerous challenges, from resistance to change and resource constraints to data security concerns and establishing effective performance metrics. Despite these challenges, with robust planning, communication, and leadership, organizations can successfully navigate this transition, enhancing their operational resilience, cybersecurity capabilities, and readiness to address evolving threats.

In conclusion, the integration of behavior-based malware analysis and detection into an organization's operations, guided by the principles of process maturity as captured by the CMMI, represents a critical pathway for organizations to bolster their cybersecurity posture. It's a journey that demands commitment, adaptability, and continuous improvement, but one that ultimately paves the way for a safer and more resilient digital future.

Summary

In today's complex digital ecosystem, the escalating sophistication of cyber threats demands innovative solutions. Behavior-based malware data analysis stands out as a cutting-edge method, emphasizing the dynamic actions of software over static code signatures. This shift in perspective empowers organizations to detect and tackle not just known threats but also emerging, elusive ones that conventional methods might overlook. Yet, the integration of this modern approach requires more than just adopting new tools or technologies – it necessitates embedding these methods into an organization's larger operational and strategic framework. One such framework is the CMMI, which guides organizations from basic process maturity to a higher, more optimized state. Marrying behavior-based detection techniques with the journey toward higher CMMI levels ensures not just technological advancement but also a cultural evolution. As organizations transition, they face challenges ranging from resource allocation to change management, but the payoff is a fortified, agile cybersecurity posture, primed for current threats and adaptable to future challenges.

As we have delved deeply into the intricacies and advancements of behavior-based malware data analysis and detection, it is evident that our current strategies and tools are evolving at an unprecedented rate. But what does the horizon hold for malware data analysis and detection? In the next chapter, *Chapter 6, The Future State of Malware Data Analysis and Detection*, we'll turn our attention to the future and explore the emerging technologies, methodologies, and potential challenges that await.

Part 3 – The Future State of AI's Use for Malware Science

In this part, we will answer the questions *What are the expectations regarding how AI will be used for malware detection and analysis?* and *What are the downstream impacts on businesses worldwide?*

This part has the following chapters:

- *Chapter 6, The Future State of Malware Data Analysis and Detection*
- *Chapter 7, The Future State of Key International Compliance Requirements*
- *Chapter 8, Epilogue – A Harmonious Overture to the Future of Malware Date Science and Cybersecurity*

6

The Future State of Malware Data Analysis and Detection

The rapidly evolving landscape of cyber threats and defenses is a testament to the dynamic nature of the digital age. As the sophistication and frequency of cyberattacks have intensified, so have the countermeasures and strategies employed by cybersecurity professionals. Central to these discussions has been the exploration of the future state of various cyber defense mechanisms.

From integrating advanced **machine learning** (**ML**) and **artificial intelligence** (**AI**) into detection systems to the promising prospects of next-generation sandbox environments, we will delve into the transformative potential of these mechanisms and the challenges and implications that they carry. With the stakes higher than ever in our interconnected digital ecosystem, understanding these future trajectories is crucial for ensuring a safer cyber landscape for all.

As we gaze into the future, several trends and developments promise to reshape the field of malware data analysis and detection that we will be covering in this chapter:

- **Advanced ML and AI integration**: Traditional signature-based detection systems have been rendered increasingly ineffective against novel malware, primarily due to the ease with which attackers can modify or generate new malware signatures. The future belongs to behavior-based detection, where AI and ML algorithms are trained to recognize abnormal patterns and behaviors in networked systems. These systems do not rely on pre-defined signatures but on understanding the "normal" functioning of a system and detecting anomalies.

- **Automated malware analysis**: With the sheer volume of new malware samples discovered daily, manual analysis has become a bottleneck. In the future, we can expect automated analysis systems to be more mainstream, capable of dissecting, categorizing, and understanding malware's functionalities in real time. This will significantly decrease the time taken to develop countermeasures.

- **Cloud-based threat intelligence platforms (TIPs)**: TIPs are already instrumental in today's cybersecurity ecosystems. In the future, cloud-driven, collaborative platforms will allow for real-time sharing of TI across various organizations and systems. This shared intelligence will enhance collective security postures by leveraging data from multiple sources.

- **Integration of big data analytics**: The sheer volume of data that modern networks generate can be overwhelming. However, buried within this data are patterns that can be pivotal in detecting sophisticated malware campaigns. Big data analytics, combined with AI, can sift through vast amounts of data, identifying subtle **indicators of compromise (IoCs)** that might be missed by traditional systems.

- **Deeper operating system (OS)-level integrations**: Future malware detection systems might be more deeply integrated at the OS level, offering a granular view of processes, file accesses, and network communications. This deep-level insight, when combined with advanced detection algorithms, can offer unprecedented detection capabilities.

- **Post-quantum cryptography**: The onset of quantum computing poses a threat to classical encryption systems. Malware that can exploit quantum vulnerabilities may become a reality. As a countermeasure, the cybersecurity industry will need to adopt post-quantum cryptographic solutions to safeguard data and enhance detection mechanisms.

- **Proactive defense mechanisms**: Instead of waiting for an attack to take place, the future might see more proactive defense mechanisms. These systems would actively hunt for vulnerabilities within a network, patching them before they can be exploited, and even potentially identifying and neutralizing threats before they become active.

- **Enhanced sandbox environments**: Modern malware often has sandbox detection capabilities, allowing it to remain dormant if it detects that it's being analyzed in a sandbox. The future will likely see the development of more sophisticated sandbox environments that can emulate real-world scenarios more effectively, tricking malware into revealing its true intentions.

The future of malware data analysis and detection is poised at the intersection of cutting-edge technology and innovative strategies. As threats evolve, so too will our defense mechanisms. Collaboration, machine intelligence, and a proactive approach will likely define the next frontier in our perpetual struggle against malicious cyber threats. While challenges abound, the integration of advanced technologies into our cybersecurity toolkits promises a more robust defense against ever-shifting threats of the digital realm.

Reading this chapter will equip you with invaluable insights into the future trajectory of malware data analysis and detection, preparing you to adapt and thrive in a constantly changing cyber landscape. You will gain a deep understanding of how emerging technologies such as advanced ML, AI, and post-quantum cryptography are reshaping traditional paradigms, enabling you to stay ahead of evolving cyber threats. Additionally, the chapter's exploration of proactive defense mechanisms and enhanced sandbox environments will empower you with practical knowledge and strategies, ensuring that you are well equipped to fortify your organization's cybersecurity posture for the challenges ahead.

The future state of advanced ML and AI integration in malware detection

In the dynamic realm of cybersecurity, envisioning the future means grasping the ever-evolving nature of threats and the continual adaptation of defensive measures. The inefficacy of traditional signature-based detection systems against the tide of novel malware variations signals an urgent need for change. As we look ahead, the spotlight turns to advanced ML and AI as primary tools for countering these threats.

Beyond signature-based detection

To appreciate where we are heading, it's vital to understand the constraints of the past. Traditional signature-based systems have rested heavily on a library of identified malware footprints. Yet, the era of static threats is behind us. The ability for malicious actors to effortlessly modify or generate new malware signatures leaves such systems in the dust.

Enter the world of behavior-based detection.

Behavioral analysis – the AI and ML revolution

The coming years will witness an increasing dependency on **behavior-based detection**, where AI and ML become central figures. This approach emphasizes understanding a system's "normal" operational blueprint and swiftly pinpointing anomalies or deviations from this norm. Let's look at this more closely:

- **Deep learning neural networks (DL NNs)**: DL, a subset of ML, relies on NNs that can be trained on massive datasets. The future likely holds systems that will use DL to discern intricate patterns of malware behavior that would be undetectable by human analysts.

- **Real-time anomaly detection**: As the quantity of data flowing within networked systems multiplies, real-time analysis becomes crucial. AI algorithms will be designed for instantaneous analysis, scanning vast streams of data on the fly to detect any aberrant behavior.

- **Auto-adaptive systems**: While the initial phases of AI and ML integration will rely on manual fine-tuning, future systems will be self-adaptive. They'll learn from every interaction, refining their detection mechanisms and minimizing both false negatives and false positives.

- **Integration with quantum computing**: With quantum computing's potential on the horizon, AI and ML algorithms will likely be enhanced by quantum processes, leading to unparalleled speed and accuracy in malware detection.

The new landscape of TI

Beyond revolutionary strides in AI and ML for behavioral analysis and detection, the horizon of cybersecurity is expanding to proactively anticipate and understand threats, forging a new frontier in TI. The future state will not be limited to the mere detection of threats but will also encompass a predictive dimension:

- **Predictive threat modeling**: Using historical data and continuously updated information from global sources, AI will help in generating predictive models, anticipating potential attack vectors, and hardening defenses proactively.

- **Unified global TI**: Imagine a decentralized yet interconnected TIP powered by AI, where every breach, attempt, or novel threat detected anywhere in the world contributes to a unified knowledge base. This platform will be self-evolving, ensuring defenses are always a step ahead of potential threats.

Challenges in the AI-driven future

The road to this AI and ML-driven utopia is fraught with its own set of challenges:

- **Training data integrity**: The effectiveness of ML models is dependent on the integrity of the training data. There will be an increased emphasis on ensuring that this data is both comprehensive and uncompromised.

- **Ethical use of AI**: As AI systems gain autonomy, ethical considerations around their use, especially concerning privacy, will take center stage. The cybersecurity community will need to strike a balance between proactive defense mechanisms and individual rights.

- **Countering AI-powered malware**: As defenders leverage AI, so will attackers. The future might see malware equipped with AI capabilities, designed to outsmart AI-driven defense systems. This would lead to a computational arms race, demanding continuous innovation.

As we stand on the cusp of a transformative phase in malware detection and defense, the promise of AI and ML shines bright. The future state is one of dynamic, interconnected, and intelligent systems that don't just react but anticipate. While the journey ahead is complex, the convergence of technology and intent signals hope. The cybersecurity realm is poised to transition from playing catch-up to setting the pace, driving innovation, and shaping a secure digital ecosystem for generations to come.

The future state of automated malware analysis

In the continuously mutating landscape of cybersecurity, the surge of new malware poses daunting challenges. Each day heralds the arrival of numerous malware samples, each with potentially unique functionalities, signatures, and attack vectors. Manual malware analysis, with its time-consuming and intricate processes, struggles to keep pace. The future, therefore, appears to rest on the pillars of automation.

Why manual processes are no longer viable

Traditional manual malware analysis entailed a meticulous dissection of malicious software. Analysts would study its behavior, ascertain its functionalities, and investigate the underlying code to comprehend its mechanisms. But the exponential rise in malware, buoyed by automated malware generation tools, means that manual methods are akin to using a bucket to empty an overflowing river. Let's look at why manual processes are no longer viable:

- **Volume overload**: Every day, thousands of new malware samples are detected. It's practically impossible for human analysts to scrutinize each one in depth.

- **Dynamic evolution**: Modern malware is not stagnant. It evolves, sometimes within hours, leveraging polymorphic and metamorphic techniques, further complicating manual analysis.

- **Increased complexity**: Malware today isn't just about simple viruses. We have **advanced persistent threats** (**APTs**), ransomware, rootkits, and more. Each demands a multifaceted approach to analysis.

The dawn of automated malware analysis

In recognizing these challenges, the cybersecurity industry is rapidly moving toward automated solutions. As we project into the future, several developments in automated malware analysis emerge as game-changers:

- **Real-time analysis systems**: The future promises tools that will instantly dissect and evaluate malware as it's detected. Instead of storing samples for later analysis, systems will assess them in real time, offering immediate insights into their functionalities.

- **DL integration**: DL models, trained on vast datasets of malware samples, will be instrumental in these systems. They'll predict malware behavior, categorize samples into families, and even propose preliminary countermeasures.

- **Cloud-powered analysis**: Leveraging the power of cloud computing, malware analysis will become more scalable. Massive datasets can be processed in parallel, ensuring that even the largest influx of malware doesn't overwhelm the system.

- **Interactive sandboxes**: Sandboxing, a technique wherein malware is executed in an isolated environment to observe its behavior, will evolve. Future sandboxes will be more interactive, capable of mimicking a variety of system conditions and deceiving malware that tries to stay dormant to avoid detection.

- **Automated reverse engineering**: Instead of manually examining malware code, advanced algorithms will automatically reverse engineer it. They'll break down the code, study its structure, and elucidate its functionalities without human intervention.

With these advancements on the horizon, the dawn of automated malware analysis signifies a paradigm shift in cybersecurity. As these technologies mature, they will not only streamline the detection and understanding of malware but also empower professionals to preemptively counteract threats, fortifying our digital landscapes like never before.

Benefits and potential of automation

The pivot to automation is more than just about keeping pace; it's about radically enhancing our malware analysis capabilities. Automation has the following benefits:

- **Rapid countermeasure development**: By understanding malware instantly, cybersecurity professionals can swiftly develop and deploy countermeasures, drastically reducing the potential damage a new malware can cause.

- **Comprehensive analysis**: Automated systems can provide a 360-degree view of malware, studying it from multiple angles simultaneously. This holistic approach ensures that no aspect of the malware remains unexamined.

- **Continuous learning**: Each new malware sample becomes a learning point. Automated systems will continuously refine their detection and analysis algorithms based on every new sample they encounter.

Challenges in the era of automation

While automation brings myriad advantages, the journey is not devoid of hurdles:

- **Dependence on quality data**: Automated systems are only as good as the data they're trained on. Ensuring the integrity and comprehensiveness of this data is crucial.

- **Evasion techniques**: Just as defenses evolve, so do attack methodologies. Malware developers will undoubtedly devise methods to evade automated analysis tools, leading to a perpetual game of cat and mouse.

- **Over-reliance on automation**: While automation will play a central role, human expertise should not be sidelined. Complex cases might still require human intuition and insights, and striking the right balance is vital.

- **False positives and negatives**: As with all systems, there's a risk of false alarms or missed detections. Minimizing these, while maintaining the speed of analysis, is a challenge.

The future state of malware analysis is one characterized by automation, speed, and adaptability. In a world where threats are continuously evolving, static and slow responses are untenable. Automated malware analysis systems, armed with advanced algorithms and vast computing power, will be the vanguard against these threats.

By transforming the way we approach malware, these systems will redefine the battleground. They promise a world where malware, no matter how novel or complex, is swiftly understood and countered, ensuring a safer digital realm for all. As we traverse this path, the synergy of technology, data, and human expertise will be pivotal in crafting a future where security is not just reactive but preemptive and profound.

Building on the advancements in malware analysis, the next evolution in cybersecurity is harnessing the power of the cloud for TI. Just as automation is revolutionizing malware detection and understanding, the vastness and flexibility of cloud platforms are set to reshape how we aggregate, analyze, and deploy TI.

The future state of cloud-based TI

In the expansive arena of cybersecurity, knowledge has always been one of the most potent weapons. The ability to predict, understand, and counteract threats is amplified manifold when underpinned by comprehensive, up-to-date intelligence. As we venture into the future of digital security, cloud-based TI emerges as a keystone, promising a more interconnected, responsive, and fortified defense mechanism against cyber threats.

The current landscape of TIPs

To gaze into the future, it's instructive to grasp the present. TIPs today collate, analyze, and disseminate information regarding potential and active cyber threats. They gather data from numerous sources, be it from internal systems, external feeds, or shared community insights. These platforms assist organizations in understanding the threat landscape, pre-emptively mitigating risks, and swiftly responding to incidents.

The advent of cloud-driven TI

As we delineate the future trajectory of TIPs, several transformative changes emerge:

- **Universal accessibility**: With cloud infrastructure at the helm, TI will be universally accessible. Organizations, regardless of size or geographical disposition, can tap into global intelligence feeds, ensuring that even the smallest entity is fortified with global knowledge.

- **Real-time data streams**: The cloud, with its vast computing and storage capabilities, facilitates real-time data processing. TI will no longer be periodic; it will flow in live streams, ensuring that every participant is continuously updated with the most recent developments.

- **Collaborative defense frameworks**: The future of cloud-based TIPs is inherently collaborative. Instead of isolated intelligence repositories, envision a vast, interconnected web where data from one endpoint can instantaneously benefit countless others. When one entity encounters a new threat, the collective immediately becomes aware and prepares.

- **Advanced analytical capabilities**: The convergence of cloud computing with ML and AI will supercharge analytical processes. Automated algorithms will sift through petabytes of data, extracting patterns, predicting threats, and providing actionable insights with unprecedented accuracy.

- **Customized threat feeds**: While the shared intelligence pool will be vast, not all data is relevant to every participant. Cloud-based platforms will use advanced filtering and categorization algorithms, ensuring that each organization receives intelligence tailored to its unique profile and threat landscape.

As the landscape of cyber threats continues to expand and evolve, the advent of cloud-driven TI marks a monumental shift in defense strategies. By amalgamating global accessibility, real-time updates, collaborative frameworks, and unparalleled analytical prowess, we are ushering in an era where defenses are not only robust but also dynamic and personalized. The promise of cloud-based TIPs is clear: a world where every digital entity, irrespective of its scale, stands shielded by the collective wisdom and strength of a connected cybersecurity community.

Benefits and potential of a cloud-centric model

This cloud-driven paradigm offers several transformative advantages:

- **Democratization of intelligence**: Historically, comprehensive TI was the domain of large enterprises with significant resources. The cloud democratizes access, ensuring that even start-ups or non-profits have access to world-class intelligence.

- **Enhanced proactivity**: With real-time data flows and advanced analytics, organizations can transition from reactive stances to proactive ones. Instead of merely responding to breaches, they can preemptively bolster defenses, sometimes even before a new threat becomes widespread.

- **Cost efficiency**: Leveraging shared cloud resources for TI is cost-effective. The economies of scale and shared infrastructure mean that organizations get maximum value without exorbitant capital expenditure.

- **Resilient systems**: An interconnected, cloud-based framework inherently possesses resilience. Even if one node or data center faces issues, the collective remains operational, ensuring uninterrupted intelligence flow.

Challenges in the cloud-based TI horizon

No evolution is without its set of challenges, and the shift to cloud-centric TIPs is no exception:

- **Data security and privacy**: Centralizing TI in the cloud raises concerns about data security. Ensuring that sensitive information remains confidential, while still contributing to the collective, is paramount.

- **Interoperability**: As various organizations collaborate, ensuring that their disparate systems can seamlessly communicate and share data becomes a challenge.

- **Quality control**: The veracity of shared intelligence is crucial. Mechanisms need to be in place to verify and validate data, ensuring that false or misleading intelligence doesn't compromise the collective.

- **Potential for centralized targets**: While cloud platforms offer numerous advantages, they could also become high-value targets for adversaries. Robust security measures are essential to protect these centralized repositories.

The future state of TI is both promising and challenging. As we embark on this journey toward a more cloud-centric, collaborative approach, the vision is clear: a digital world where knowledge is not just power but also shared, where every entity, big or small, benefits from the collective's experiences.

As cloud-based TIPs mature, they promise a seismic shift in how we perceive cybersecurity. From isolated fortresses, we evolve into interconnected sentinels, standing guard over the vast digital realm. This shared, united front against cyber adversaries not only enhances individual security postures but also solidifies the collective digital fabric against ever-evolving threats.

The future state of integration of big data analytics in cybersecurity

In the intricate chess game of cybersecurity, data is both a boon and a bane. On one hand, modern networks, devices, and applications generate immense volumes of data. This treasure trove, while overwhelming, harbors invaluable insights, patterns, and signals. When harnessed correctly, these can transform the very essence of digital defense. On the other hand, the sheer volume can obfuscate these crucial details, making them needles in vast digital haystacks. The future, thus, seems unequivocally anchored in big data analytics, especially when married to the potent capabilities of AI.

Understanding the magnitude of modern data

Before delving deep into solutions, it's essential to grasp the enormity of the challenge. Consider the following:

- Every minute, individuals and businesses send nearly 200 million emails

- Internet users conduct approximately 8.5 billion searches on Google daily

- IoT devices, projected to cross 50 billion by 2030, incessantly communicate, sending and receiving data

These are but a drop in the vast ocean of data produced daily. Within this digital deluge, malicious actors conduct their operations, often leaving faint, easily missed traces.

The imperative for big data analytics

Traditional cybersecurity systems, such as signature-based malware detectors, are ill equipped to handle this magnitude of data. Their linear, rule-based approaches falter amid the noise. Big data analytics emerges as the answer for several reasons:

- **Scalability**: Unlike traditional systems, big data solutions are designed to handle vast datasets efficiently. They can store, process, and analyze data without being overwhelmed.

- **Complex pattern recognition**: Cyber adversaries often employ sophisticated tactics that don't trigger typical security alarms. Big data analytics can identify complex patterns, correlations, and sequences that hint at a potential compromise.

- **Predictive capabilities**: Rather than just identifying current threats, big data analytics can forecast future ones. By understanding patterns and trends, these systems can predict potential vulnerabilities or areas of concern.

In the face of the modern digital age, where data grows exponentially and threats hide in its vastness, the significance of big data analytics cannot be overstated. It not only equips us with tools to decipher this vast ocean of information but also revolutionizes our ability to detect, understand, and predict cybersecurity challenges. In essence, the power of big data analytics transcends traditional boundaries, providing a proactive shield against the evolving cyber landscape and highlighting its paramount role in shaping a secure digital future.

Integration of AI – the game-changer

While big data provides the foundation, the real transformative potential is unlocked when combined with AI. Here's how AI elevates big data analytics in cybersecurity:

- **Automated analysis**: AI algorithms can automatically sift through petabytes of data, extracting relevant insights without human intervention. This not only speeds up analysis but also ensures 24/7 surveillance.

- **DL for deep insights**: DL, a subset of AI, can recognize and learn from intricate patterns in data. When a new type of threat emerges, DL models can quickly adapt, ensuring that similar threats are detected in the future.

- **Anomaly detection**: AI excels at understanding "normal" patterns and identifying deviations. In cybersecurity, this translates to pinpointing unusual behaviors or activities that might indicate a breach or malware activity.

- **Data fusion**: AI can integrate and analyze data from diverse sources, ensuring a holistic understanding of the threat landscape. This means correlating data from network logs, user activities, application behaviors, and external threat feeds to draw comprehensive conclusions.

Incorporating AI into big data analytics heralds a paradigm shift in cybersecurity, bringing forth unparalleled benefits in threat detection, understanding, and prediction. Yet, as with any transformative technology, it presents both opportunities and challenges. The benefits are clear – heightened security vigilance, predictive capabilities, and adaptive learning that keeps pace with evolving threats. On the flip side, the complexity and sophistication of AI-driven tools necessitate ongoing education, ethical considerations, and the need for robust countermeasures against AI-powered threats. In essence, while AI undoubtedly amplifies our cybersecurity capabilities, it also underscores the need for a balanced and comprehensive approach, ensuring that its immense potential is harnessed responsibly and effectively.

Transformative benefits for cybersecurity

The fusion of big data analytics with AI promises several transformative benefits:

- **Proactive defense**: Instead of being mere reactive entities, cybersecurity systems can become proactive sentinels. They can identify and counteract threats even before they fully manifest.

- **Reduced false positives**: One of the significant challenges in cybersecurity is the deluge of false alarms. By understanding intricate patterns and behaviors, AI-driven big data systems can significantly reduce these, ensuring that human analysts focus only on genuine threats.

- **Tailored security postures**: Organizations can customize their security strategies based on insights. If big data analytics reveals frequent attempts to exploit a particular vulnerability, organizations can prioritize its mitigation.

- **Enhanced IR**: When breaches occur, swift response is crucial. Big data analytics can provide comprehensive insights into the breach – its origin, affected systems, the nature of malware, and so on – ensuring that IR teams have all the information they need.

Challenges and considerations

While promising, this future state is not devoid of hurdles:

- **Data privacy and governance**: As organizations collect and analyze vast amounts of data, ensuring user privacy and adhering to regulations becomes paramount.

- **Infrastructure and resource requirements**: Implementing big data solutions necessitates robust infrastructure. Organizations need to invest in systems that can handle storage, processing, and analysis demands.

- **Skill gaps**: The niche domain of big data analytics combined with cybersecurity requires specialized skills. Addressing this talent gap is essential for the effective implementation of these systems.

- **Evolving threat landscape**: As defenses evolve, so do attack strategies. Malicious actors might devise ways to confuse AI algorithms or flood systems with misleading data. Constant evolution and learning are, therefore, essential.

The future state of cybersecurity seems set to be defined by the confluence of big data analytics and AI. As digital realms expand and threats become more nuanced, the traditional paradigms of defense are no longer sufficient. The next frontier involves harnessing vast streams of data, extracting nuanced insights, and crafting defenses that are not just reactive but predictive.

In this evolving landscape, organizations will no longer be mere passive entities bracing for the next attack. Instead, they will be proactive guardians of their digital domains, equipped with the foresight and knowledge to thwart adversaries even before they strike.

The future state of deeper OS-level integrations in malware detection

The cybersecurity landscape is in a perpetual state of flux. As technology becomes more ingrained in our daily lives, the avenues for malicious cyberattacks expand in tandem. At the core of almost every device we use is the OS, a critical piece of software that manages hardware resources and provides services for computer programs. With the evolving threat matrix, the need to bolster defenses at the very nucleus of our devices – the OS – becomes even more pressing. The future of malware detection, thus, seems inevitably tied to deeper OS-level integrations.

The current state of malware detection

Traditional malware detection methods have revolved around signature-based techniques. These rely on known patterns or "signatures" of malware. When a piece of software or a file matches this signature, it's flagged as malicious. While effective against known threats, this method struggles with novel or modified malware. Given the rapid proliferation of new malware variants, relying solely on signatures is increasingly untenable.

The rationale behind OS-level integrations

As we delve deeper into the intricate world of cybersecurity, one approach stands out in its promise to enhance threat detection and response: integration at the OS level. Understanding the rationale behind such integrations is crucial, as the OS serves as the bedrock upon which all digital processes and activities stand. Let's look at this more closely:

- **Granular visibility**: At the OS level, every process, application, and service runs under the OS's supervision. Deep integration provides a granular, detailed view of what's happening within the system – every file accessed, every network request, every system call.

- **Proactive defense**: Instead of waiting for malware to exhibit malicious behavior, OS-level integrations can identify and halt suspicious activities before they can inflict significant damage.

- **Holistic perspective**: Rather than examining isolated incidents or files, the OS has a holistic view of system behavior. This allows for a more contextual understanding, where seemingly benign activities, when viewed in conjunction, might reveal a threat.

Potential avenues for deeper OS-level integrations

Diving further into the intricacies of cybersecurity, a pivotal area of exploration emerges – the potential for deeper integrations within the OS. This realm, often overlooked, offers a myriad of avenues to fortify our digital infrastructures and provide an unprecedented level of threat surveillance:

- **Kernel-level monitoring**: The kernel is the heart of the OS, managing core functionalities. By embedding detection mechanisms directly into the kernel, systems can achieve real-time monitoring and swift response times.

- **Advanced process introspection**: Every application on a device runs as a process supervised by the OS. Deep OS integration would mean exhaustive monitoring of each process, ensuring its behavior aligns with its intended function.

- **File access controls**: Integrating malware detection at the OS level can introduce stricter, more dynamic file access controls. For example, if a typically read-heavy application suddenly starts writing data extensively, it can be flagged.

- **Network communication oversight**: Malware often communicates with external servers, either to exfiltrate data or receive instructions. By monitoring all network requests at the OS level, anomalous communications can be detected and halted.

Benefits of deeper OS-level integrations

Let us have a look at the benefits:

- **Swift detection and response**: Given the intimate integration, the time between detecting a threat and responding to it can be drastically reduced.

- **Reduced dependence on signatures**: While signatures remain essential, the emphasis shifts toward behavior. This is pivotal in detecting zero-day threats or novel malware variants.

- **Contextual analysis**: With a comprehensive view of the system, OS-level defenses can analyze threats in context, reducing false positives and offering a nuanced understanding of potential risks.

- **Resource efficiency**: Instead of running as a separate entity, the malware detection system, when integrated into the OS, can be more resource-efficient, reducing overheads and system lags.

Challenges and considerations

While the allure of deeper OS-level integrations is evident in their potential to redefine cybersecurity frameworks, it's imperative to navigate this path with a balanced perspective. Alongside the myriad benefits, some significant challenges and considerations come into play, warranting meticulous attention and foresight:

- **Complex implementation**: OS-level integration is technologically challenging. Ensuring stability, performance, and security while embedding additional functionalities is a tall order.

- **Potential vulnerabilities**: While deep integration offers enhanced protection, it also means that if compromised, the potential damage can be extensive. Ensuring the integrated detection mechanisms themselves are impervious to attacks becomes crucial.

- **Compatibility concerns**: As updates or changes are made to the OS, ensuring that integrated malware detection systems remain compatible and effective is essential.

- **User privacy**: With deeper oversight comes the responsibility of safeguarding user data and ensuring that privacy isn't compromised.

The future state of malware detection paints a picture of intertwined destinies – of operating systems and detection mechanisms evolving as a singular, unified entity. As threats become more sophisticated, the lines between an OS and protective layers will blur, converging into an ecosystem where defense isn't just an added layer but an intrinsic part.

This paradigm shift is more than just a technological evolution; it's a reimagining of how we perceive digital security. It's not about guarding the gates but about ensuring the very fabric of our digital realm is resilient. As we move toward this future, challenges will emerge but so will opportunities – to create digital spaces where security is as fundamental as the code that powers it.

The future state of post-quantum cryptography in countering quantum-vulnerable malware

The quantum revolution is on the horizon. Quantum computers, leveraging the principles of quantum mechanics, promise computational capabilities that classical computers, bound by bits, cannot hope to achieve in a lifetime. With these newfound capabilities come unprecedented challenges, especially in the realm of cybersecurity. Classical encryption systems, the bedrock of modern digital security, are suddenly at risk of becoming obsolete, and the potential for malware exploiting quantum vulnerabilities lurks ominously.

Understanding the quantum threat

The imminent threat from quantum computers primarily centers on their potential to break widely used encryption algorithms. Specifically, quantum computers can efficiently run algorithms such as Shor's algorithm, which can factor large numbers exponentially faster than the best-known algorithms on classical computers. This poses a direct threat to public-key cryptographic systems, such as **Rivest-Shamir-Adleman** (**RSA**) and **elliptic-curve cryptography** (**ECC**), which rely on the difficulty of factoring large numbers or computing discrete logarithms.

In the wrong hands, a sufficiently powerful quantum computer could decrypt sensitive data, intercept secure communications, and even facilitate advanced malware that leverages quantum vulnerabilities to evade detection or compromise systems.

Post-quantum cryptography – the new frontier

Post-quantum cryptography, often referred to as quantum-safe or quantum-resistant cryptography, is the study of cryptographic algorithms that are secure against potential threats posed by quantum computers. The goal isn't to *replace* quantum mechanics but to *develop methods* that remain secure even in its face. Here's a look at the promise it holds:

- **Lattice-based cryptography**: Based on the hardness of certain problems in lattice theory (such as the shortest vector problem), this approach is versatile and can be used to build a wide range of cryptographic primitives and protocols.

- **Hash-based cryptography**: Relying on the properties of cryptographic hash functions, hash-based signatures are considered a promising and mature approach for creating secure digital signatures in a post-quantum world.

- **Multivariate quadratic (MQ) equations**: Building public-key schemes based on the problem of finding solutions to systems of multivariate quadratic equations. While there are challenges in ensuring efficiency, research in this area is ongoing.

- **Code-based cryptography**: Originating from coding theory, this approach leans into the difficulty of decoding randomly generated linear codes. McEliece is one of the oldest encryption systems in this category, which has withstood decades of cryptanalysis.

- **Isogeny-based cryptography**: A relatively newer field, it involves the study of isogenies between elliptic curves. Promisingly, no sub-exponential-time quantum algorithms are known against this as of the last update.

Integration in malware detection and defense

Beyond just securing data, post-quantum cryptographic solutions can be pivotal in advancing malware detection and defenses:

- **Quantum-resistant authentication**: With post-quantum solutions, systems can ensure that software updates, patches, or commands are genuinely from trusted sources, mitigating the risk of quantum-powered **man-in-the-middle (MitM)** attacks.

- **Secure data analysis**: Malware detection often involves analyzing vast amounts of data, some of it sensitive. Post-quantum encryption ensures that this data remains secure even when analyzed, preventing potential quantum breaches.

- **Enhanced digital signatures**: Digital signatures verify the integrity of data. Quantum-resistant digital signatures will ensure that malware can't tamper with or falsify data without detection.

Challenges ahead

As we look forward to innovations that promise to revolutionize malware data analysis and detection, it's crucial to also recognize the challenges that lie ahead. From the need for global standardization in post-quantum cryptography to the complexities of transitioning systems and managing performance, each obstacle presents its own unique set of difficulties that demand our attention and strategic planning:

- **Standardization**: There's an urgent need for global standards around post-quantum cryptography. Organizations such as the **National Institute of Standards and Technology (NIST)** are actively working on this, but it's a complex, time-consuming process.

- **Transition**: Transitioning from classical to post-quantum systems will be resource intensive and fraught with potential vulnerabilities. Smooth transition strategies need development.

- **Performance**: Some post-quantum algorithms can be less efficient or require larger key sizes than their classical counterparts, which could have implications for system performance and storage.

The future state

As we hurtle toward the quantum era, the lines between classical and quantum realms will blur. The cybersecurity landscape will see a symbiotic integration of classical practices bolstered by quantum-resistant measures. The key lies in anticipation. While fully functional and threatening quantum computers may still be a few years away, the groundwork for defense needs to be laid now.

Malware, in its ever-evolving nature, will undoubtedly seek to exploit the quantum leap. However, with a proactive approach centered on post-quantum cryptography, the future state can be one of robust defense, where the marvels of quantum mechanics are celebrated without the looming shadow of its potential cybersecurity threats.

In essence, the post-quantum future is not just about coexistence but about forging a new path where innovation and security march hand in hand, creating a digital realm that's as secure as it is revolutionary.

The future state of proactive defense mechanisms in cybersecurity

In the realm of cybersecurity, the adage *the best defense is a good offense* is gaining traction. Historically, the approach to defending digital assets has been largely reactive: a threat emerges, and systems respond. But as cyber threats grow in sophistication, volume, and potential impact, this reactive model increasingly reveals its limitations. The future of cybersecurity beckons a shift from merely reacting to threats to proactively hunting and neutralizing them, reframing the very paradigm of defense.

Why proactive defense?

The reactive model, while having served us reasonably well in the past, now contends with a rapidly evolving threat landscape:

- **Volume and velocity of threats**: With malware variants proliferating at an unprecedented rate and cyberattacks becoming more frequent, waiting for an attack is no longer tenable.

- **APTs**: Some threats are designed to remain dormant or move stealthily within networks for extended periods, making reactive measures insufficient.

- **Zero-day vulnerabilities**: These are vulnerabilities unknown to the software vendor and, by extension, the users. Since there's no known fix at the time of exploitation, reactive defenses are often too late.

Given these challenges, proactive defense mechanisms emerge not as a luxury but as a necessity.

The cornerstones of proactive defense

In our evolving digital landscape, merely reacting to cyber threats is no longer sufficient. To truly fortify our cyber defenses, we must anticipate and preemptively counter potential threats. Enter the cornerstones of proactive defense – a set of advanced strategies and tools designed not just to respond but to actively seek out, understand, and neutralize threats. Let's delve into these foundational elements and the advantages they offer, while also acknowledging the challenges they present in real-world implementation:

- **Vulnerability assessment and management**: Instead of waiting to be informed about potential vulnerabilities, proactive systems continuously scan and assess networks and systems, identifying weak spots that might be exploited. This constant vigilance ensures that vulnerabilities are patched or mitigated before they can be weaponized.

- **Threat hunting**: Rather than waiting for automated systems to flag anomalies, dedicated cybersecurity teams actively "hunt" for signs of compromise or infiltration within an environment. Leveraging both technology and expertise, these hunters seek out subtle indicators of a threat, often catching what traditional systems might miss.

- **Endpoint detection and response (EDR)**: This is a security solution that goes beyond traditional antivirus. EDR tools continuously monitor and gather data from endpoints, looking for signs of threats. When detected, they can respond in real time, either alerting administrators or taking automated actions.

- **Deceptive defense techniques**: Involving tactics such as honeypots or decoy systems, these are designed to divert, confuse, or entrap attackers. By studying interactions with these decoys, defenders can gain insight into attack methodologies and potentially identify the culprits.

- **Automated TI**: Leveraging AI and ML, these systems can process vast amounts of data from various sources, predicting potential threat vectors and informing defenses accordingly.

Advantages of a proactive stance

Taking a proactive stance in cybersecurity offers a plethora of advantages that extend well beyond simple threat mitigation. From early detection to operational resilience, this section explores the key benefits of an anticipatory approach and how it can substantially fortify an organization's cybersecurity posture:

- **Early detection**: By continuously seeking out threats, organizations can often detect and neutralize them before any substantial damage occurs

- **Reduced attack surface**: Regular vulnerability assessments mean fewer weak spots for attackers to exploit

- **Operational resilience**: With threats addressed in their nascent stages, there's less likelihood of significant disruptions to operations

- **Insight and learning**: Active defense measures, such as deceptive techniques, offer valuable insights into attack methodologies, helping refine future defenses

Challenges in implementation

While the advantages of a proactive stance in cybersecurity are compelling, it's essential to also recognize the challenges that come with its implementation. This section delves into the complexities, from resource requirements to ethical considerations, that organizations must navigate to effectively employ a proactive defense strategy:

- **Resource intensive**: Proactive defense often requires significant investments in tools, technology, and skilled personnel.

- **Potential for false positives**: As systems actively hunt for threats, there's an increased likelihood of benign activities being flagged as malicious.

- **Evolution of threats**: Just as defenses evolve, so do attack methodologies. An active defense stance necessitates a commitment to ongoing learning and adaptation.

- **Regulatory and ethical considerations**: Some proactive measures, especially those that might involve interacting with attackers or potential counterattacks, can raise legal and ethical questions.

The road ahead – a dynamic defense ecosystem

The cybersecurity environment of the future may resemble a dynamic ecosystem more than a fortified castle. Instead of high walls and deep moats aimed at keeping threats out, imagine a responsive environment. In this paradigm, the system is aware, constantly adapting, learning, and – most importantly – actively seeking out potential threats.

Such a proactive defense mechanism isn't about aggression but about vigilance. It represents a cybersecurity model where the onus isn't just on repelling attacks but understanding, anticipating, and mitigating them before they can gain a foothold.

In this envisioned future state, the distinction between offense and defense in cybersecurity becomes blurred. It's not about launching counterattacks but about adopting an active stance – one of vigilance, adaptability, and resilience.

And so, the call for a proactive defense approach resonates with the evolving nature of the digital realm. As boundaries expand and the digital becomes even more intertwined with the physical, the stakes rise. In this complex tapestry, proactive, dynamic defense isn't just a strategy; it's a survival imperative. The future of cybersecurity lies not in awaiting the storm but in predicting and preparing for it.

The future state of enhanced sandbox environments in cybersecurity

In the world of cybersecurity, a sandbox typically refers to an isolated computing environment where suspicious programs can be executed to observe their behavior without risking harm to the actual system. This technique is invaluable for analyzing potential malware and understanding its operations and objectives.

Modern challenges – evolving malware tactics

As sandboxes became prevalent tools for threat analysis, malware developers adapted. Modern strains of malware are equipped with sandbox detection techniques, allowing them to identify when they're being run in an artificial environment. If detected, these malicious programs can alter their behavior, hide their true intentions, or even remain dormant, effectively evading analysis.

This cat-and-mouse game has presented significant challenges:

- **Limitations in emulation**: Many sandboxes emulate user activities (for example, mouse movements and keystrokes) to simulate real-world environments. However, certain malware can detect these simulated patterns, distinguishing them from genuine user behavior.

- **Environment checks**: Malware can check for signs of virtualized environments, looking for specific artifacts or configurations typical of sandboxes.

- **Timed responses**: Some malware is programmed to stay dormant for a specific period, only activating after it believes it is outside of a typical sandbox examination duration.

The vision – next-generation sandboxes

The cybersecurity industry is acutely aware of the limitations of current sandboxing technologies, and the future promises a paradigm shift in how these environments function and deceive advanced malware:

- **High-fidelity emulation**: Future sandboxes will likely offer high-fidelity emulation that mimics real-world systems with unparalleled accuracy. This goes beyond simple user-activity simulations. Instead, these sandboxes would replicate the intricacies of genuine system environments, making it challenging for malware to differentiate between the sandbox and a real target.

- **Adaptive behavior**: Leveraging AI and ML, next-gen sandboxes could adapt in real time, changing their characteristics and behaviors based on the malware being analyzed. This adaptability could help in tricking malware into believing it's operating in its intended environment.

- **Hybrid analysis**: By combining both static and dynamic analysis methods within the sandbox environment, analysts can glean a more comprehensive understanding of malware. While dynamic analysis observes the malware's behavior when executed, static analysis examines the code without running it. Together, they offer a holistic view of potential threats.

- **Extended duration analysis**: Recognizing that some malware activates only after prolonged periods, enhanced sandboxes might operate over more extended periods, weeks, or even months, patiently waiting to catch delayed activations.

- **Cloud integration**: As cloud computing becomes the norm, future sandboxes will seamlessly integrate with cloud environments. This allows for scalable analysis, where numerous samples can be examined simultaneously in isolated cloud instances.

- **Real-world interaction**: To truly deceive advanced malware, sandboxes of the future might interact with the internet or other systems in controlled ways, further convincing the malware of its successful infiltration.

- **Continuous learning**: Powered by AI, these environments will continuously learn from every interaction, refining their emulation techniques and staying a step ahead of evolving malware tactics.

Implications and benefits

The development of enhanced sandbox environments holds immense potential for cybersecurity:

- **Better TI**: With a deeper understanding of malware operations, cybersecurity professionals can develop more effective countermeasures and defensive strategies

- **Reduced false positives**: Enhanced detection accuracy ensures that benign software is not mistakenly flagged, reducing the operational overhead associated with false alarms

- **Faster response times**: Quick and accurate malware analysis means that threats can be neutralized more rapidly, reducing potential damages

- **Threat evolution insights**: By studying malware in these advanced environments, analysts can gain insights into the evolving **tactics, techniques, and procedures** (**TTPs**) of adversaries

Challenges ahead

While the future of sandboxing seems promising, it's not without challenges:

- **Increased complexity**: The advanced features of next-gen sandboxes make them more complex, requiring specialized skills for operation and interpretation.

- **Resource intensity**: High-fidelity emulation and extended analysis durations can be resource intensive, potentially straining organizational resources.

- **Adversarial AI**: Just as defenders leverage AI, attackers do too. The future may see malware equipped with AI capabilities designed to detect even the most sophisticated sandbox environments.

In the ceaseless tug-of-war between cyber defenders and attackers, the sandbox has been a pivotal tool, providing invaluable insights into the inner workings of malware. As malware grows in sophistication, the traditional sandbox environment's shortcomings have come into sharp focus. However, the horizon holds promise, with visions of next-generation sandboxes equipped to deceive, analyze, and understand the most advanced threats. These futuristic environments represent a crucial frontier in the ongoing battle to secure digital realms, reaffirming the industry's commitment to innovation and adaptability.

Summary

The journey through the future state of malware data analysis and detection has provided a comprehensive glimpse into the frontiers of cybersecurity. As we've observed, the integration of technologies such as ML, AI, big data analytics, and enhanced sandbox environments marks a seismic shift in our approach to cyber threats. While challenges persist, the potential benefits – from more accurate threat detection to proactive defense strategies – offer hope for a more resilient digital future. As cyber adversaries continue to adapt and innovate, a commitment to foresight, innovation, and collaboration will remain our strongest asset in safeguarding digital realms. The quest for a safer cyberspace is ongoing, and the insights gleaned from this exploration will undoubtedly inform and inspire the next generation of cyber defense strategies.

As we conclude this chapter, it's clear that the future trajectory of malware data analysis and detection is both intriguing and vital for our digital security. We've delved into how groundbreaking technologies, from advanced ML and AI to post-quantum cryptography, are transforming our defense mechanisms against evolving cyber threats. With an understanding of proactive defense mechanisms and advancements in sandbox environments, you're now better positioned to bolster your organization's cybersecurity posture in anticipation of the challenges that lie ahead. Moving forward, it's our collective responsibility to stay informed, adaptive, and vigilant in an ever-changing cyber landscape.

Having explored the intricacies of malware data analysis and the technological advancements that promise to redefine our cyber defenses, it's essential to understand another crucial aspect of the digital landscape: compliance. As our tools and strategies evolve, so too do the legal and regulatory frameworks that guide and govern our actions. In our next chapter, *The Future State of Key International Compliance Requirements*, we will dive deep into the evolving international regulatory environment, ensuring that while we fortify our defenses, we also remain compliant and in line with global best practices.

7

The Future State of Key International Compliance Requirements

The intricate relationship between technology, regulations, and global dynamics has paved the way for an evolving landscape of international compliance requirements. As the world becomes increasingly interconnected and technology-driven, businesses must navigate a complex tapestry of regulations that transcend borders. This chapter delves into the multifaceted realm of international compliance in the context of **artificial intelligence (AI)** and its pivotal role in cyber threat management. We will explore the historical evolution of AI's influence on compliance practices, its intersection with cybersecurity, and the potential scenarios that may shape the future of compliance on a global scale.

In a world where digital innovation is reshaping industries and economies, the management of cyber threats has emerged as a critical concern. Governments and organizations grapple with the challenge of safeguarding digital ecosystems against malicious activities while upholding ethical standards. The integration of AI into compliance practices has the potential to revolutionize threat detection, risk assessment, and mitigation strategies. However, this transformation is not devoid of challenges, as ethical considerations, regulatory frameworks, and the dynamic nature of cyber threats constantly reshape the compliance landscape.

As AI's influence on compliance grows, it intertwines with key international trends, shaping the future state of compliance requirements. This article delves into the anticipated trajectories of global data privacy regulations, AI ethics, cybersecurity, supply chain transparency, financial crime prevention, cross-border data flows, climate change regulations, blockchain and digital identity, **regulatory technology (RegTech)**, and the impact of geopolitical dynamics. By delving into each of these trends, we aim to provide a comprehensive understanding of the forces that will mold the compliance landscape in the years to come.

By reading this chapter, you will gain a holistic understanding of the ever-changing landscape of international compliance requirements in the context of advanced technologies such as AI. You will discover how key trends in global data privacy, AI ethics, cybersecurity, and more are shaping the future of compliance across industries. This will enable you to anticipate, adapt to, and navigate complex regulations, thereby strengthening your organization's risk management and ethical standards. Beyond this, you will deepen your understanding of how emerging trends such as supply chain transparency, financial crime prevention, cross-border data flows, climate change regulations, and geopolitical dynamics are interconnected in the larger compliance puzzle. Whether you are a business leader, policy maker, or technology aficionado, this chapter will equip you with the strategic foresight needed to stay ahead of compliance challenges in a rapidly evolving, technology-driven world.

In this chapter, we will delve into the following crucial areas:

- Global data privacy regulations
- AI ethics and governance standards
- Cybersecurity and risk management
- Supply chain transparency
- Financial crime prevention
- Cross-border data flow regulations
- Climate change regulations
- Blockchain and digital identity
- Regulatory technology
- Geopolitical dynamics

The future state of global data privacy regulations

The trend of increased data privacy regulations, as exemplified by the **European Union's General Data Protection Regulation (GDPR)** and the **California Consumer Privacy Act (CCPA)**, is likely to continue. More countries and regions might adopt similar regulations to ensure the protection of individuals' data. The future may see efforts to harmonize these regulations to facilitate cross-border data flows.

As the global economy becomes increasingly digital, data privacy has emerged as a fundamental concern. The proliferation of digital services, online transactions, and data-driven technologies has led to the generation and exchange of vast amounts of personal data. This data encompasses individuals' personal information, behavior patterns, preferences, and interactions across various platforms.

Governments and regulatory bodies around the world are recognizing the importance of safeguarding individuals' data and are enacting regulations to ensure its proper use and protection. The GDPR, implemented in the European Union in 2018, set a groundbreaking precedent by granting individuals greater control over their data and imposing strict requirements on organizations that collect, process, and store such data. Similarly, the CCPA in California aimed to empower consumers with rights over their personal information and the ability to opt out of data sharing.

This trend is expected to persist, with more countries and regions adopting comprehensive data privacy laws similar to GDPR and CCPA:

- The trend of countries adopting comprehensive data privacy laws is being driven by several factors, including the following:

  - The increasing value of personal data, which is being collected and used by businesses, governments, and other organizations in a variety of ways

  - The growing concerns about the misuse of personal data, such as for targeted advertising, discrimination, and identity theft

  - The rising awareness of individual privacy rights, as people become more comfortable asserting their right to control their data

  - The increasing interconnectedness of the world, which makes it easier for businesses and governments to collect and use personal data from people in other countries

- The success of the GDPR and CCPA has shown that it is possible to enact strong privacy laws that protect individuals' rights without stifling innovation. These laws have also helped raise awareness of the importance of data privacy and have encouraged other countries to consider similar measures.

- As more countries and regions adopt comprehensive data privacy laws, we can expect to see several benefits, including the following:

  - Increased confidence among consumers, who will be more likely to trust businesses with their data

  - A more level playing field for businesses, as they will all be subject to the same rules

  - Reduced risks of data breaches and other privacy violations

  - Increased innovation in the field of privacy-enhancing technologies

These regulations will not only enhance individuals' privacy rights but also impact how businesses collect, store, and process data on a global scale. Organizations will need to assess their data practices, implement stringent data protection measures, and provide clear and transparent information to individuals about how their data is being used. This entails obtaining explicit consent for data collection, ensuring data accuracy, and enabling individuals to access and control their data.

To navigate this evolving landscape, businesses will need to adopt robust data protection strategies, implement stringent security measures, and stay informed about changing regulations. Compliance with data privacy regulations will require businesses to assess their data flows, conduct data impact assessments, and establish data breach notification processes. Implementing technical and organizational measures to safeguard data, such as encryption and access controls, will be essential to prevent unauthorized access and breaches.

The future of data privacy compliance will likely involve efforts to harmonize regulations to facilitate cross-border data flows. As data is increasingly shared across international boundaries, inconsistent data privacy regulations can create obstacles for businesses operating globally. International collaboration and harmonization of data protection laws could enable seamless data transfers while maintaining high standards of privacy and security.

The trajectory of global data privacy regulations is toward stricter enforcement and broader adoption. As individuals' awareness of their data rights grows and digital interactions become more prevalent, businesses must adapt by prioritizing data protection, fostering transparency, and embracing a proactive approach to compliance. By aligning with evolving regulations and embracing best practices, organizations can navigate the complex landscape of data privacy while fostering trust and accountability in their digital operations.

The future state of AI ethics and governance standards

As AI becomes more integrated into various aspects of society, including compliance management, there will likely be a push for international AI ethics and governance standards. These standards could address issues such as bias in AI algorithms, transparency, and accountability in AI decision-making, and mechanisms to ensure AI compliance with laws and regulations.

The rise of AI technologies presents both opportunities and challenges for compliance. AI has the potential to revolutionize how businesses manage compliance processes by automating tasks, analyzing complex data, and improving decision-making accuracy. However, alongside these benefits, the deployment of AI introduces ethical considerations and potential risks that need to be carefully managed.

While AI can enhance efficiency and accuracy in compliance processes, it also raises concerns about biases, accountability, and transparency. AI algorithms learn from historical data, and if that data contains bias, the AI models may perpetuate and amplify that bias. This can lead to unfair and discriminatory outcomes, which is a significant ethical concern. Ensuring that AI systems are fair and unbiased is crucial to maintaining the integrity of compliance operations.

Ethical considerations related to AI decision-making will be crucial, particularly in sectors where AI is used to assess risks, detect fraud, or make important compliance-related decisions. AI models often operate as black boxes, meaning that their decision-making processes are not easily explainable. In compliance, where transparency and accountability are paramount, understanding how AI arrives at decisions is essential.

International collaboration will play a significant role in establishing ethical guidelines and governance frameworks for AI in terms of compliance. The diversity of AI applications across industries and jurisdictions calls for unified standards that ensure responsible AI use. Collaborative efforts involving governments, regulatory bodies, industry associations, and ethical AI experts will contribute to the development of guidelines that address the unique challenges posed by AI in compliance.

Businesses will need to adopt AI solutions that align with these evolving standards while ensuring transparency and fairness in their operations. Companies integrating AI into compliance processes must prioritize fairness, accountability, and transparency. They should implement AI models that can be audited and validated, and that include mechanisms to detect and correct bias. Ethical AI frameworks should be woven into business practices, from data collection and model development to ongoing monitoring and improvement.

To address the ethical implications of AI in compliance, businesses can consider the following aspects:

- **Bias mitigation**: Implement strategies to detect and mitigate bias in AI algorithms. Regularly review training data for potential bias and adjust algorithms accordingly.

- **Explainable AI**: Prioritize AI models that provide interpretable explanations for their decisions. This will enhance transparency and enable compliance professionals to understand and validate AI outcomes.

- **Accountability mechanisms**: Design AI systems with mechanisms to identify who is responsible for the outcomes of AI-driven decisions. This ensures accountability in case of errors or unethical practices.

- **Data privacy**: Ensure that AI models adhere to data privacy regulations and that personal data used for training and decision-making is handled responsibly and securely.

- **Ethics committees**: Establish internal committees or advisory boards focused on AI ethics to guide the development and deployment of AI technologies in compliance.

- **Continuous monitoring and auditing**: Regularly monitor AI systems to identify potential bias or issues. Conduct audits to evaluate the performance and ethical implications of AI-driven compliance decisions.

As AI becomes increasingly prevalent in compliance management, it is crucial to establish ethical standards and governance frameworks that ensure its responsible use. Businesses must actively engage in international collaborations to develop guidelines that address AI's challenges while leveraging its benefits. By adopting transparent and accountable AI practices, organizations can navigate the ethical complexities of AI in compliance and contribute to building a trustworthy and responsible AI ecosystem.

The future state of cybersecurity and risk management

With the increasing frequency and sophistication of cyber threats, international compliance requirements related to cybersecurity and risk management will likely become more stringent. Organizations may need to follow standardized cybersecurity protocols and reporting mechanisms to ensure the protection of sensitive data and critical infrastructure.

The digital landscape is constantly evolving, presenting both new opportunities and new vulnerabilities. As businesses and individuals become more reliant on digital technologies, the attack surface for cyber threats continues to expand. The increasing interconnectivity of devices, networks, and systems creates a complex environment where cybercriminals can exploit vulnerabilities to gain unauthorized access, steal sensitive data, or disrupt operations.

Cybersecurity threats, ranging from data breaches to ransomware attacks, continue to pose significant risks to businesses and individuals alike. Cybercriminals are continually adapting their tactics to exploit weaknesses in cybersecurity defenses. High-profile data breaches and cyber incidents have highlighted the potentially devastating impacts of such attacks on organizations' finances, reputation, and customer trust.

To address these challenges, international compliance requirements related to cybersecurity will likely become more stringent. Regulatory bodies recognize the urgency of protecting sensitive information and critical infrastructure in the face of evolving cyber threats. Compliance mandates are expected to outline specific cybersecurity measures that organizations must implement to safeguard data and systems.

Organizations will need to implement robust cybersecurity measures, conduct regular risk assessments, and adhere to standardized protocols for detecting, mitigating, and reporting cyber incidents. A comprehensive cybersecurity strategy involves a combination of preventive measures, such as firewalls and encryption, as well as proactive monitoring and incident response plans. Compliance requirements may necessitate the establishment of cybersecurity frameworks that align with recognized standards, such as the NIST Cybersecurity Framework or ISO 27001.

International cooperation will be essential in sharing threat intelligence and best practices to stay ahead of emerging cyber threats. Cyber threats transcend national boundaries, making collaboration between countries, industries, and cybersecurity professionals crucial. Governments and organizations need to share threat intelligence, tactics, and mitigation strategies to collectively strengthen cybersecurity defenses. Initiatives to establish international cybersecurity standards and information-sharing frameworks will contribute to a more secure digital environment.

To effectively manage cybersecurity and comply with evolving requirements, organizations can consider the following aspects:

- **Risk assessments**: Conduct regular assessments to identify vulnerabilities, evaluate potential impacts, and prioritize cybersecurity investments based on risk levels.

- **Incident response planning**: Develop and test incident response plans to ensure a swift and effective response in the event of a cyber incident, minimizing damage and downtime.

- **Employee training**: Educate employees about cybersecurity best practices, the risks of phishing attacks, and the importance of adhering to security protocols.

- **Encryption and access controls**: Implement encryption to protect sensitive data both at rest and in transit. Use access controls to limit unauthorized access to critical systems.

- **Continuous monitoring**: Deploy monitoring tools that provide real-time visibility into network activities, enabling the detection of unusual behavior and potential threats.

- **Collaboration**: Engage in information-sharing partnerships with industry peers and government agencies to stay informed about emerging threats and effective mitigation strategies.

- **Compliance audits**: Regularly audit and assess compliance with cybersecurity regulations to ensure that security measures are aligned with evolving requirements.

As the cyber threat landscape continues to evolve, organizations must proactively address cybersecurity risks and align with international compliance requirements. By implementing robust cybersecurity measures, fostering a culture of security awareness, and engaging in collaborative efforts, businesses can navigate the complexities of the digital world while safeguarding sensitive information and critical infrastructure.

The future state of supply chain transparency

International regulations focusing on supply chain transparency and sustainability are expected to grow. Requirements related to **environmental, social, and governance** (ESG) factors could become more standardized, requiring companies to demonstrate responsible practices throughout their supply chains.

The global supply chain is undergoing a transformation driven by consumer demand for transparency and ethical sourcing. Modern consumers are increasingly conscious of the environmental and social impacts of their purchases. As a result, they expect businesses to uphold ethical standards, ensure responsible sourcing, and minimize negative environmental and social effects.

As environmental and social concerns gain prominence, international compliance requirements will likely focus on ensuring responsible business practices across the entire supply chain. Governments and regulatory bodies recognize the importance of addressing issues such as deforestation, child labor, forced labor, and other unethical practices that can occur within supply chains. Compliance mandates will likely require businesses to adopt measures that promote transparency, accountability, and sustainability.

Businesses will need to assess their suppliers' practices, trace the origins of raw materials, and ensure compliance with regulations related to sustainability and labor standards. Achieving supply chain transparency involves understanding every step of the supply chain, from raw material extraction to the final product's delivery. This requires mapping out suppliers, conducting audits, and ensuring that each entity in the supply chain adheres to ethical and regulatory standards.

Collaborative efforts between governments, businesses, and **non-governmental organizations** (NGOs) will play a pivotal role in establishing unified standards for supply chain transparency and driving positive social and environmental impacts. Effective supply chain transparency requires cooperation among various stakeholders. Governments can enact regulations that set baseline expectations for ethical sourcing and environmental responsibility. Businesses can engage with suppliers to improve practices, and NGOs can monitor and advocate for responsible supply chains.

To effectively manage supply chain transparency and comply with evolving requirements, organizations can consider the following aspects:

- **Supplier engagement**: Collaborate with suppliers to ensure they meet ethical and sustainability standards. This might involve training, audits, and sharing best practices.

- **Traceability**: Implement systems to trace the origin of raw materials, ensuring transparency and accountability throughout the supply chain.

- **ESG reporting**: Develop mechanisms to track and report environmental, social, and governance performance. This can demonstrate your commitment to responsible practices.

- **Third-party audits**: Engage third-party auditors to assess supply chain practices and verify compliance with ethical and regulatory standards.

- **Technology integration**: Leverage technology such as blockchain to create transparent, immutable records of transactions and supply chain activities.

- **Supplier diversity**: Embrace diversity in your supplier base to promote social and economic inclusivity.

- **Stakeholder engagement**: Collaborate with industry associations, NGOs, and other stakeholders to establish industry-wide standards for supply chain transparency.

The call for greater supply chain transparency and sustainability is reshaping international compliance requirements. By embracing responsible practices and collaborating with suppliers and stakeholders, businesses can navigate these evolving regulations while contributing to positive social and environmental impacts. Transforming supply chains into transparent and ethical networks is not only a compliance necessity but also a strategic opportunity for companies to align with consumer values and build a more sustainable future.

The future state of financial crime prevention

Compliance requirements related to **anti-money laundering (AML)**, **counter-terrorism financing (CTF)**, and other financial crimes are likely to evolve. Regulators might adopt more sophisticated approaches, leveraging AI and machine learning to detect and prevent illicit financial activities.

In this section, we will delve deeper into the practical implications and strategic considerations surrounding the integration of AI and machine learning in combating financial crimes. Exploring a series of actionable steps and insights, we aim to equip organizations in the financial industry with the knowledge and strategies needed to thrive in this ever-evolving landscape of compliance.

The financial sector has long been a target for criminal activities, necessitating robust compliance measures to combat money laundering, fraud, and other financial crimes. Criminal organizations often exploit the complexity of financial systems to launder money, fund illegal activities, and evade detection. To counter these threats, governments and regulatory bodies impose compliance obligations on financial institutions to monitor and report suspicious transactions.

As technology advances, regulators will likely adopt more sophisticated tools and methods to identify and prevent these illicit activities. Traditional rule-based systems for detecting financial crimes can be limited in their effectiveness as they may miss subtle patterns and evolving tactics used by criminals. Regulators are increasingly recognizing the potential of AI and machine learning to enhance the accuracy and efficiency of financial crime detection.

The integration of AI and machine learning into compliance processes can enhance the detection of unusual patterns and behaviors, enabling more accurate and timely risk assessments. AI algorithms can analyze large volumes of financial data, identify anomalies, and detect patterns that might otherwise go unnoticed. Machine learning models can learn from historical data to adapt to new and emerging financial crime strategies, making them more effective at staying ahead of criminals' tactics.

Businesses in the financial sector will need to keep pace with these advancements and ensure that their compliance strategies align with the evolving landscape of financial crime prevention. Staying compliant with **anti-money laundering (AML)/countering the financing of terrorism (CFT)** regulations requires a proactive approach. Financial institutions will need to continually invest in technology, training, and expertise to effectively implement AI-driven compliance measures. This may involve collaborating with tech partners, developing in-house AI capabilities, and ensuring that compliance professionals have the necessary skills to leverage AI tools effectively.

To effectively manage financial crime prevention and comply with evolving requirements, organizations can consider the following aspects:

- **AI integration**: Explore AI and machine learning solutions that can enhance the detection of financial crimes by analyzing large datasets and identifying unusual patterns.

- **Data quality**: Ensure that data used for AI-based compliance is accurate, relevant, and up to date. Clean data is essential for the success of machine learning models.

- **Human oversight**: While AI can automate many aspects of financial crime detection, human experts are still essential to review and interpret AI-generated insights.

- **Continuous learning**: Implement AI models that can continuously learn and adapt to new threats and tactics used by criminals.

- **Regulatory knowledge**: Stay informed about evolving AML and CTF regulations to ensure that compliance measures align with current requirements.

- **Collaboration**: Engage with industry groups, regulatory bodies, and technology providers to stay informed about best practices and emerging technologies in financial crime prevention.

- **Testing and validation**: Regularly test and validate the performance of AI models to ensure their accuracy and effectiveness in detecting financial crimes.

The use of AI and machine learning in financial crime prevention marks a significant advancement in the field of compliance. By leveraging these technologies, businesses can enhance their ability to detect and prevent illicit financial activities, ultimately contributing to a more secure and transparent financial ecosystem. Adapting compliance strategies to align with these technological advancements will be crucial for financial institutions to effectively combat financial crimes in an ever-evolving landscape.

The future state of cross-border data flow regulations

As digital services and data flows become increasingly global, there might be efforts to establish harmonized frameworks for cross-border data transfers. These frameworks could ensure the secure and compliant movement of data between countries while respecting privacy and security concerns.

The digital economy relies on the seamless flow of data across borders, enabling international trade, communication, and collaboration. In our interconnected world, data is a valuable resource that fuels innovation, drives business operations, and enhances the quality of services. Businesses of all sizes rely on the ability to transfer data across borders to reach customers, partners, and markets around the globe.

However, differing data protection regulations across jurisdictions can create challenges for businesses operating in multiple countries. Each jurisdiction has its own set of data protection laws and regulations that govern how personal and sensitive data is collected, processed, and transferred. This can lead to complexity and uncertainty for businesses as they must navigate a patchwork of regulations and compliance requirements.

To facilitate global data flows while upholding privacy and security standards, there may be initiatives to establish harmonized frameworks for cross-border data transfers. Recognizing the importance of data flows to international commerce, there is growing interest in finding common ground among nations to streamline the movement of data. These frameworks aim to strike a balance between enabling data transfers and safeguarding individuals' privacy rights.

These frameworks could provide a unified approach to data protection, enabling businesses to navigate compliance requirements more effectively and maintain trust among consumers and partners. A harmonized framework would establish consistent principles for data protection, minimizing the need for businesses to adapt to varying rules in different jurisdictions. This approach not only reduces compliance complexities but also promotes consumer trust by ensuring that data is handled responsibly and as per established standards.

The following are some key considerations for establishing cross-border data flow frameworks:

- **Data protection principles**: Frameworks should establish core data protection principles that ensure the privacy and security of individuals' data during cross-border transfers

- **Consent and transparency**: Mechanisms for obtaining informed consent and providing transparent information about data processing should be standardized across jurisdictions

- **Data localization**: Frameworks could address concerns related to data localization, ensuring that data can flow freely across borders without requiring storage in specific countries

- **Accountability**: Establishing clear lines of accountability for data transfers and data breaches can enhance trust and enable effective enforcement

- **Recourse mechanisms**: Cross-border frameworks should include mechanisms for individuals to seek redress and for businesses to resolve disputes related to data transfers

- **International cooperation**: Collaboration between governments, regulatory bodies, and industry stakeholders is essential to develop and implement effective cross-border data flow frameworks

While the concept of harmonized frameworks for cross-border data flows holds promise, there are several challenges and considerations to address:

- **Differing legal traditions**: Finding common ground among countries with different legal traditions, cultural norms, and regulatory priorities can be complex

- **Technological advancements**: Rapid technological advancements may outpace the development of regulatory frameworks, necessitating flexibility and adaptability

- **Data sovereignty**: Some nations may have concerns about data sovereignty and may seek to impose restrictions on data transfers to protect national interests

- **Enforcement**: Ensuring effective enforcement of cross-border data flow regulations requires collaboration and coordination among regulatory bodies across different jurisdictions

- **Balancing interests**: Striking a balance between enabling data flows for economic growth and protecting privacy and security rights requires careful consideration

Harmonized frameworks for cross-border data flows have the potential to simplify compliance for businesses and facilitate the global exchange of data. While challenges exist, the benefits of establishing unified standards for data protection and transfer are significant. Such frameworks can contribute to a more predictable regulatory environment, enabling businesses to innovate, expand, and maintain trust in an increasingly interconnected digital world. Collaboration among governments, businesses, and other stakeholders will be key to successfully navigating the complex landscape of cross-border data flow regulations.

As we contemplate the evolving tapestry of cross-border data flow regulations and their implications for global businesses, another pressing regulatory arena beckons our attention: the environment. Just as the digital realm grapples with harmonizing data transfer standards, the physical world confronts a monumental challenge – climate change. The seamless transition from digital data flows to tangible environmental considerations illustrates the multifaceted nature of the global regulatory landscape.

The future state of climate change regulations

In response to growing concerns about climate change, international compliance requirements related to environmental protection and carbon emissions reduction are expected to strengthen. Companies could face stricter reporting and mitigation obligations to contribute to global climate goals.

The urgency of addressing climate change has prompted governments, businesses, and civil society to prioritize environmental sustainability. The scientific consensus on the impact of human activities on the planet's climate has catalyzed a global call for action. Governments are setting ambitious targets to limit global warming, and businesses are being called upon to play their part in mitigating the adverse effects of climate change.

Compliance requirements related to carbon emissions, energy efficiency, and sustainable practices will likely become more stringent to align with international climate goals. Governments around the world are introducing regulations and policies aimed at reducing greenhouse gas emissions and promoting sustainable practices. This includes regulations on emissions reporting, carbon pricing mechanisms, renewable energy adoption, and energy efficiency improvements.

Companies will need to measure and report their environmental impacts accurately, implement strategies to reduce their carbon footprint, and contribute to global efforts to mitigate climate change. As climate-related compliance requirements evolve, businesses will be required to monitor, measure, and report their carbon emissions and environmental impacts accurately and transparently. This may involve conducting greenhouse gas inventories, tracking energy consumption, and reporting progress toward sustainability goals.

To comply with evolving climate regulations, businesses can consider the following aspects:

- **Carbon footprint assessment**: Conduct a comprehensive assessment of the company's carbon footprint, including direct and indirect emissions, to identify areas for reduction

- **Emissions reporting**: Implement accurate and transparent emissions reporting mechanisms in alignment with international reporting standards and regulatory requirements

- **Sustainability strategies**: Develop and implement strategies to reduce energy consumption, adopt renewable energy sources, and enhance resource efficiency

- **Supply chain engagement**: Collaborate with suppliers to promote sustainable practices across the supply chain, from sourcing raw materials to delivering products

- **Innovation**: Invest in research and development to innovate sustainable technologies, products, and processes that contribute to emissions reduction

- **Carbon offsetting**: Explore options for carbon offsetting and investment in projects that support emissions reduction or removal

While the transition to more sustainable practices is crucial, there are challenges associated with meeting evolving climate compliance requirements:

- **Complexity**: Navigating diverse and changing climate regulations across different jurisdictions can be complex, requiring businesses to stay informed and adaptable

- **Financial implications**: Meeting stricter emissions reduction targets and sustainability goals may require significant investments in technology, infrastructure, and process changes

- **Data accuracy**: Accurate measurement and reporting of emissions and sustainability efforts require robust data collection and reporting systems

- **Innovation**: Developing and implementing sustainable practices and technologies may require innovative solutions that align with business goals

- **Global cooperation**: International collaboration is essential to ensure that climate regulations are effective and consistent, despite differences in regional priorities and circumstances

Compliance requirements related to climate change are set to intensify as the world confronts the pressing need to address environmental challenges. Businesses have a pivotal role in contributing to global climate goals by adopting sustainable practices, reducing emissions, and embracing environmentally responsible operations. By integrating sustainability into their core strategies, companies can not only navigate evolving climate regulations but also drive positive change and help shape a more sustainable future for the planet.

The future state of blockchain and digital identity

The adoption of blockchain technology and digital identity solutions could impact compliance requirements. Decentralized and secure digital identities might become a cornerstone of compliance processes, enhancing authentication, authorization, and privacy.

Blockchain technology has the potential to revolutionize compliance by providing secure, transparent, and tamper-proof records of transactions and activities. The distributed and immutable nature of blockchain ensures that once information is recorded, it cannot be altered or deleted without leaving a trace. This characteristic is particularly relevant to compliance as it can create a trustworthy audit trail for regulatory reporting, ensuring data integrity and reducing the risk of fraud.

Additionally, digital identity solutions based on blockchain can enhance security and privacy in compliance processes. Digital identities are the digital representations of individuals or entities, often used for authentication and authorization purposes. Traditional identity management systems can be vulnerable to data breaches and identity theft. Blockchain-based digital identity solutions offer a higher level of security by enabling individuals to have control over their data and granting access to it on a need-to-know basis.

These solutions can enable individuals to control their data while facilitating secure authentication and authorization for regulatory purposes. With blockchain-based digital identity, individuals can manage their personal information in a self-sovereign manner. This means that they have control over who accesses their data and for what purpose, reducing the risk of unauthorized data sharing and ensuring compliance with data protection regulations.

Businesses will need to explore how blockchain and digital identity can be integrated into their compliance strategies to enhance transparency, security, and efficiency. The potential applications of blockchain in compliance are diverse, ranging from streamlining **Know Your Customer** (**KYC**) processes to enabling secure cross-border data transfers while maintaining data sovereignty.

The following are the key considerations for integrating blockchain and digital identity into compliance:

- **Privacy by design**: Design systems that prioritize privacy and data protection, ensuring that only necessary and authorized parties have access to personal data

- **Interoperability**: Consider the interoperability of different blockchain networks and digital identity solutions to ensure seamless integration across systems

- **Regulatory alignment**: Ensure that blockchain-based compliance solutions align with existing and emerging data protection and identity verification regulations

- **User experience**: Design user-friendly interfaces for managing digital identities, focusing on ease of use and consent management

- **Data security**: Implement robust security measures, including encryption and multi-factor authentication, to safeguard blockchain-based identity systems

- **Transparency**: Leverage the transparency of blockchain to enhance transparency and accountability in compliance processes

While blockchain-based digital identity solutions offer significant benefits, there are challenges and considerations to keep in mind:

- **Regulatory uncertainty**: The regulatory landscape for blockchain and digital identity is still evolving, requiring businesses to navigate potential uncertainties

- **Technical complexity**: Implementing blockchain solutions can be technically complex, requiring expertise in blockchain development and integration

- **Data portability**: Ensuring data portability and interoperability between different blockchain-based identity systems can be challenging
- **User adoption**: Overcoming user resistance and promoting the adoption of blockchain-based digital identity solutions requires user education and engagement

Blockchain technology and digital identity solutions have the potential to reshape compliance processes by enhancing security, privacy, and transparency. Businesses that embrace these technologies can strengthen their compliance strategies while empowering individuals to have greater control over their data. As blockchain adoption continues to grow, exploring innovative ways to integrate blockchain-based digital identity into compliance operations will be a key consideration for forward-looking businesses seeking to enhance their regulatory practices in the digital age.

The future state of RegTech

The adoption of RegTech solutions, powered by AI and automation, could streamline compliance processes. Regulators might encourage the use of standardized RegTech tools to ensure more efficient and effective compliance management.

The rapid advancement of technology has given rise to RegTech solutions that leverage AI, automation, and data analytics to streamline compliance processes. The traditionally labor-intensive nature of compliance tasks, such as data collection, analysis, and reporting, has led to the emergence of innovative RegTech solutions. These tools harness the power of AI algorithms and automation to efficiently manage complex compliance requirements.

These tools can enhance efficiency, accuracy, and cost-effectiveness in compliance management. RegTech solutions offer a range of benefits, including faster data processing, reduced human error, and enhanced data accuracy. Automated workflows can handle repetitive tasks, allowing compliance professionals to focus on higher-value activities, such as analyzing trends, making strategic decisions, and responding to emerging risks.

Regulators may encourage businesses to adopt standardized RegTech solutions that enable consistent and effective compliance practices across industries and jurisdictions. Standardization of compliance practices is a challenge, given the diverse regulatory landscape across different regions and industries. RegTech solutions that follow standardized frameworks can help bridge this gap by providing a common platform for compliance management. This can lead to greater transparency, ease of collaboration, and streamlined reporting, benefiting both businesses and regulatory bodies.

By embracing RegTech, businesses can optimize their compliance efforts and allocate resources to more strategic activities, such as risk assessment and decision-making. As compliance tasks become more automated, compliance professionals can shift their focus from manual data processing to analyzing data insights, identifying potential risks, and developing strategies to address them. This transition empowers compliance teams to contribute to the organization's overall risk management and strategic goals.

The key considerations for adopting RegTech solutions in compliance are as follows:

- **Risk assessment**: Identify the specific compliance processes that can benefit most from automation and AI-powered analytics

- **Vendor selection**: Choose RegTech vendors that offer solutions aligned with your organization's compliance requirements and goals

- **Data security**: Ensure that the RegTech solution adheres to robust data security and privacy standards, given the sensitive nature of compliance data

- **Integration**: Integrate RegTech tools seamlessly into existing compliance systems and workflows

- **Training and adoption**: Provide training for employees to effectively use and maximize the potential of RegTech tools

While the potential benefits of RegTech in compliance are significant, there are challenges to navigate:

- **Change management**: Adopting new technology requires a cultural shift within an organization and effective change management strategies

- **Regulatory approval**: Ensure that RegTech solutions meet regulatory requirements and gain necessary approvals before implementation

- **Data quality**: RegTech tools heavily rely on accurate data, so data integrity and quality are essential for successful implementation

- **Human oversight**: While automation enhances efficiency, human oversight is still crucial to ensure accuracy and address complex compliance issues

In conclusion, the adoption of RegTech solutions holds the promise of transforming compliance from a resource-intensive task into an efficient and strategic process. As technology continues to evolve, businesses that embrace RegTech can gain a competitive edge by effectively managing compliance requirements, reducing operational costs, and enabling compliance professionals to focus on higher-value activities. Regulators' encouragement of standardized RegTech tools further highlights the importance of innovation in compliance management in an era of technological advancement.

The future state of geopolitical dynamics

Geopolitical shifts and international relations will influence compliance requirements. Collaborative efforts among countries and regions might lead to the development of common compliance standards, while tensions could result in more fragmented regulatory landscapes.

The geopolitical landscape is marked by evolving alliances, trade agreements, and diplomatic relationships. The interactions between nations and international organizations are constantly changing, shaping the global political environment. These geopolitical dynamics can have a profound impact on regulatory and compliance frameworks as countries seek to protect their interests, promote economic growth, and maintain security.

These dynamics can impact the alignment of compliance requirements across borders. As countries form new partnerships or reevaluate existing relationships, their priorities and regulatory approaches may shift. This can lead to changes in compliance requirements, such as data protection, trade regulations, and financial reporting standards.

Collaborative efforts among countries and regions may lead to the development of common compliance standards and frameworks. Recognizing the benefits of consistency and cooperation, countries and regions might work together to harmonize regulatory approaches. This could lead to the creation of international agreements or standards that businesses can adhere to across multiple jurisdictions, reducing complexity and enhancing predictability.

On the other hand, geopolitical tensions and divergent interests could result in fragmented regulatory landscapes, necessitating businesses to navigate varying compliance requirements across jurisdictions. When geopolitical tensions arise, countries may adopt divergent regulatory approaches to assert their sovereignty or protect their economic interests. This can create challenges for businesses operating across borders as they must understand and adhere to a patchwork of regulations.

Staying informed about geopolitical developments will be essential for businesses to anticipate compliance challenges and opportunities in different regions. The ability to anticipate regulatory changes stemming from geopolitical shifts can provide a competitive advantage. Businesses that stay well-informed about evolving political dynamics can proactively adapt their compliance strategies and operations to align with changing requirements.

Here are some of the key considerations for navigating compliance within changing geopolitical dynamics:

- **Global awareness**: Stay up to date on international news, diplomatic negotiations, and trade agreements that could impact compliance requirements

- **Scenario planning**: Anticipate potential regulatory changes based on geopolitical shifts and develop contingency plans to address different compliance scenarios

- **Government relations**: Foster relationships with government officials and regulators to gain insights into potential regulatory changes and advocate for business interests

- **Regional expertise**: Engage with professionals or consultants who have expertise in the compliance landscape of specific regions to navigate diverse regulatory environments

- **Flexibility**: Develop compliance strategies that can adapt to changing geopolitical dynamics, enabling swift responses to new regulatory requirements

Navigating compliance within the context of changing geopolitical dynamics comes with several challenges:

- **Uncertainty**: Geopolitical changes can be unpredictable, making it challenging for businesses to plan for and respond to compliance requirements

- **Resource allocation**: Adapting to varying compliance requirements in different regions may require additional resources and expertise

- **Legal complexity**: Legal systems and regulatory frameworks can differ significantly across jurisdictions, adding complexity to compliance efforts

- **Risk management**: Geopolitical tensions can introduce new risks, such as sudden changes in trade policies or economic sanctions

The interplay between geopolitical dynamics and compliance requirements underscores the need for businesses to maintain a global perspective. By understanding how shifting alliances, trade agreements, and international relations influence regulatory frameworks, businesses can effectively anticipate and address compliance challenges. An agile approach to compliance that considers geopolitical factors can position businesses to navigate changing requirements while maintaining operational efficiency and global competitiveness.

Summary

To summarize, in the era of AI-driven cyber threats and rapidly evolving technology, the future of international compliance requirements remains a confluence of diverse factors. As nations grapple with the intricacies of data privacy, technological advancements, and geopolitical tensions, the shape of compliance is being reshaped. Businesses that seek to navigate this complex terrain must adopt a proactive approach that integrates innovation, transparency, and responsible practices.

The path forward requires collaboration among governments, industry leaders, and regulatory bodies to establish harmonized compliance frameworks that balance the imperatives of innovation, security, and ethics. While challenges lie ahead, the potential rewards are substantial. The adoption of AI can enhance compliance efficiency and accuracy, heighten threat detection capabilities, and enable sustainable practices that contribute to global goals.

As we embrace the possibilities of a digitally connected world, the journey of international compliance is both a formidable challenge and an opportunity for growth. Businesses that remain agile, informed, and forward-thinking will not only safeguard their operations but also contribute to a more secure, ethical, and resilient global digital landscape. In a future where compliance is not a constraint but a catalyst for progress, the interplay between AI, cybersecurity, and international regulations will continue to shape the destiny of businesses and societies alike.

Having navigated through this chapter, you've not only acquired a multifaceted understanding of the complex landscape of international compliance in the era of AI, but you should've also answered the crucial "so what?" question for yourself. This is more than just academic exploration. It's an actionable toolkit that equips you to anticipate and adapt to ever-changing regulations in areas such as global data privacy, AI ethics, and cybersecurity. You now possess the strategic foresight and the practical tools to enhance your organization's risk management and ethical practices. Moreover, you've learned how these elements intertwine with emerging global trends – supply chain transparency, financial crime prevention, cross-border data flows, and more. In a world where regulatory compliance is as dynamic as the technologies driving it, your newfound knowledge prepares you to lead responsibly, make informed decisions, and mitigate risks effectively. So, whether you're a business leader, policy maker, or technology enthusiast, you're now better positioned than ever to navigate the complexities and opportunities of a rapidly evolving, technology-driven compliance landscape.

## 8

Epilogue – A Harmonious Overture to the Future of Malware Science and Cybersecurity

In the vast expanse of the digital age, technology and connectivity have become woven into the very core of our daily lives. This intertwining of our existence with the digital realm has brought about a surge of groundbreaking innovations, propelling humanity into an era of unprecedented advancements. However, just as a piece of music thrives on its highs and lows, this technological renaissance is juxtaposed with a formidable adversary—the burgeoning realm of cybersecurity threats. These threats lurk in the shadows, ever vigilant, always evolving, and seeking to compromise the sanctity of our digital havens.

Amidst this digital soundscape, malware stands as a formidable phantom, an omnipresent specter that continues to haunt the corridors of our virtual domains. Its form and function are fluid, changing its contours with the changing times, finding new ways to penetrate our defenses, and threatening to destabilize the balance of our digital world. This is not just an ordinary adversary; it is a morphing, adapting, and relentless foe that never ceases to innovate in its malicious pursuits.

But every action has its reaction. As the digital landscape has come under increasing threat, it has also witnessed the rise of a formidable champion—malware science. This emerging discipline is not merely a reactionary measure; it is a proactive endeavor, a field that seeks to understand, analyze, and ultimately neutralize the myriad threats posed by malware. It represents the frontline of defense, a beacon of hope in an ongoing battle for digital supremacy.

Delving deeper into the narrative of malware science, one can draw parallels to the rich tapestry of a symphony. Just as a symphony is composed of various movements, each contributing to the overall masterpiece, the life cycle of malware science is an intricate dance of multiple stages, each essential to the whole.

The initial stage, data collection, sets the tone. It is here that vast swathes of information are gathered from the vast expanses of the digital realm. This data, drawn from diverse sources, forms the raw material, the unrefined ore from which insights will eventually be forged. But raw data, in its initial form, is chaotic, filled with discrepancies and redundancies.

This leads to the next movement: preprocessing. In the realm of music, preprocessing can be likened to the tuning of instruments before a grand performance. It's a phase where the raw data is sifted, refined, and polished. Any noise, any irrelevant fragments that could distort the ensuing analysis, are meticulously removed. It's a stage of harmonization, ensuring that the data is primed and ready for the next step.

And then comes the crescendo: feature extraction. In this pivotal phase, the essence of the data is distilled. Just as a maestro carefully selects which instruments will play which parts to convey the desired emotion, in feature extraction, the most significant attributes of the data are identified and chosen. These features are the linchpins, the key markers that will guide the subsequent analysis, helping to discern the benign from the malicious.

This journey through the life cycle of malware science is a testament to the meticulous and methodical approach needed to tackle the multifaceted challenge of cybersecurity. As the boundaries between the physical and digital worlds continue to blur, it becomes paramount to ensure that the sanctity of our virtual spaces remains uncompromised. And in this endeavor, malware science stands as a vanguard, a beacon leading the way in the ceaseless pursuit of a safer, more secure digital future.

In the grand tapestry of cybersecurity, the various stages that culminate into an effective defense strategy can be likened to the flowing movements of a symphony. And at the heart of this melodic defense lie the machine learning models—each one a unique instrumentalist, waiting in the wings, ready to lend its voice to the overarching narrative.

As the data gets processed and refined, it sets the stage for the next act, where the machine learning models step in. These models, each distinct and specialized, are akin to soloists in a grand orchestra. Just as every musician fine-tunes their instrument, practicing diligently to master their craft, each algorithm is carefully designed and sculpted using the features that were previously extracted. These algorithms are not mere mathematical constructs; they embody the culmination of human creativity and computational dexterity. Armed with meticulously annotated data, they undergo rigorous training, gradually learning to distinguish the intricate patterns that demarcate benign software from its malicious counterparts.

The process is not merely technical; it is an art form. The delicate interplay between human expertise and algorithmic precision melds into a harmonious duet, striving to uncover the concealed rhythms and melodies that form the essence of cybersecurity challenges.

But as with any masterpiece, validation is paramount. This phase offers a profound pause—a moment of introspection where the ensemble's performance is scrutinized for authenticity and accuracy. Techniques such as cross-validation step into the spotlight, ensuring that the model's performance isn't a fleeting brilliance but consistently strikes the right chords. The essence of this movement is about reflection and reassurance, ensuring that the symphonic defense built so far stands robust and unyielding against the relentless waves of adversarial challenges.

And then, with all the grandeur of a symphony's climax, comes deployment. This isn't just the culmination of a process; it's the magnum opus of the entire endeavor. The models, now trained and validated, are brought to the forefront, poised to defend digital realms against a myriad of cyber threats. As they get integrated into real-world systems, the insights they've gleaned become the protective shield, a melodious barrier that stands resolute against the dissonant threats that aim to disrupt the digital harmony.

In this ever-evolving realm of cybersecurity, the confluence of data science, machine learning, and human expertise creates a symphony of defense—a melodious counterpoint that rises, undeterred, against the chaotic crescendos of cyber threats. Through each movement, from feature extraction to deployment, this orchestral endeavor signifies hope, resilience, and an unwavering commitment to preserving the sanctity of our interconnected digital world.

The saga of malware science is not an isolated tale, but rather a chapter in the grander narrative of cyber threat management. This intricate narrative spans decades, embodying the triumphs and travails of a digital era perpetually on the brink of metamorphosis. Every twist and turn in the story of technology's rapid ascendancy is mirrored by an equivalent evolution in cyber threats and the measures devised to thwart them.

In the embryonic stages of digital technology, when computers were still finding their footing in the societal fabric, the world witnessed the emergence of primitive viruses and worms. These seemingly benign entities, while simplistic by today's standards, were harbingers of a new kind of warfare—a conflict not confined to geographical boundaries but spread across the vast expanses of the digital domain. Yet, even in those fledgling years, the seeds of resilience and adaptation were sown. Cybersecurity experts, albeit a niche group at the time, began devising countermeasures, initiating the age-old game of cat and mouse that characterizes the cyber landscape.

As technology burgeoned, becoming more sophisticated and integral to every facet of modern life, so too did the malicious entities that sought to exploit it. The appearance of ransomware, with its nefarious ability to hold data hostage and extort vast sums, marked a sinister evolution in the cyber threat landscape. These were no longer mere annoyances; they had the power to cripple infrastructures, disrupt lives, and shake the very foundations of trust upon which the digital realm was built.

Yet, amidst this escalating chaos, emerged a beacon of hope. Recognizing the magnitude of the threat, nations began reaching out, transcending political, cultural, and geographical divides. This marked the rise of international collaborations, where countries, erstwhile competitors, now found common ground in their shared determination to stem the tide of cybercrime. The formation of treaties, exemplified by the landmark Budapest Convention, heralded a new era of cooperation. This wasn't merely a piece of legislation but a testament to humanity's ability to unite in the face of adversity. It embodied the collective recognition of the vastness of the digital realm and the shared responsibility to protect it.

Such treaties serve as robust pillars in the ever-shifting sands of cyberspace. They underscore the realization that in this interconnected digital world, isolated efforts are inadequate. Only through unity, collaboration, and shared wisdom can the relentless specter of cyber threats be effectively countered.

In essence, the journey of malware science and cyber threat management is a poignant reflection of humanity's perpetual quest for equilibrium. It speaks of battles waged in the nebulous ether of the digital domain, of relentless innovation countered by an equally relentless defense, and above all, of the indomitable human spirit that refuses to be subdued, no matter how formidable the adversary.

Delving deeper into the application of topology data analysis, it is paramount to recognize this methodology as a linchpin in understanding the multifaceted and complex architectures inherent in communication networks. Here, the undercurrents of data flow and the interweaving of information pathways become the focus, unfolding the intricacies and patterns that define a network's structure.

Within this realm, graph theory and network flow analysis serve as the navigational compasses, guiding the exploration through the labyrinthine structures of digital interactions. They unravel the labyrinth, uncovering the threads that interlace to form the complex tapestries of connectivity. Each node and each interaction becomes a beacon, shedding light on the underlying currents and tides of digital communication.

In this intricate dance of data, botnets and command-and-control servers operate like shadows, their conversations whispered in secret, their orchestrations subtle and elusive. They maneuver through the veiled corridors of networks, choreographing their malicious operations with stealth and precision, seeking to remain unseen, their movements unheard in the vast arena of digital interactions.

It is the silent vigilance and discerning gaze of topology data analysis that unveils these clandestine operations, drawing back the curtain to reveal the hidden dialogues and concealed maneuvers of malicious entities. It brings clarity to the obscured, lending visibility to the invisible and providing insight into the unseen orchestrations that seek to compromise the sanctity of the digital realm.

The revelation of these covert operations equips the defenders of the cyber realm with critical knowledge and strategic advantage. It allows for a proactive stance, an anticipatory strategy to counteract the insidious advances of malicious entities, ensuring the sanctity and integrity of digital communications.

This exploration into uncharted territories of network analysis is not just a journey of detection and revelation but is a continuous odyssey of adaptation and evolution. It underscores the ever-evolving narrative of cyber resilience, highlighting the incessant need for innovative methodologies and advanced strategies to safeguard our interconnected digital existence against the continually morphing landscape of cyber threats.

The grand entrance of artificial intelligence into the grand hall of malware detection is nothing short of a conductor stepping up to the podium, ready to usher in a new movement in the symphony of cybersecurity. As AI integrates itself with the myriad of machine learning algorithms, the ensuing composition is a majestic interweaving of data strands and intelligent motifs, a seamless fusion generating harmonious tones and complex harmonics in the battle against digital malevolence.

AI, with its meticulous precision and adaptative grace, performs like a seasoned maestro, leading the ensemble through the varying tempos and dynamics of the cybersecurity landscape. It dances through the shifting rhythms of cyber threats, interpreting the subtle nuances and articulations, learning, absorbing, and adapting to every new phrase and every subtle variation in the malicious score. Its relentless pursuit of harmony and perfection in this turbulent and unrelenting concerto makes it an invaluable virtuoso in the continuous concert against cyber adversaries.

But this magnum opus is not a solo performance. The blend of AI's analytical acumen and the nuanced intuition of human analysts creates a resonant duet—a dynamic interplay and resounding counterpoint that enriches the symphonic experience. The echoes of innovation intertwine with the sonorous strains of tradition, a balancing act that reverberates through the cybersecurity sphere and transcends the limitations of singular approaches.

This opulent and intricate dance of intelligence and insight forms a comprehensive symphony, with each component—a note, a chord, a melody—contributing to the overarching composition, building layer upon layer toward a crescendo of security and resilience. The synergy between human discernment and AI-driven precision becomes the harmonious ensemble that strikes the chords of balance, insight, and foresight, navigating the intricate passages and hidden leitmotifs of the cyber world with unparalleled mastery.

Within this evolving symphonic landscape, the concert of cybersecurity is continually composed, with each musician, be it human or artificial, contributing their unique tone and timbre to the overall harmony, augmenting the collective capability to face the unseen and unheard threats lurking in the shadows of the digital world.

Within the elaborate concerto of cyber innovation, a subtle but transformative modulation in tempo ensues—an elegy to the art of behavior-based malware analysis. This modality understands that, within the boundless and symphonic digital spheres, behavior is the maestro that dictates the true intent, unmasking the hidden motives behind the coded notes. The movement to behavior-based analysis is like a conductor who, with precision and finesse, guides the malware through a series of harmonious yet controlled phrases within a meticulously constructed environment, a carefully orchestrated rehearsal space.

Here, the vigilant security analysts become the audience to an intricate ballet of binary sequences and digital pulses, unraveling the dance of algorithms to discern the concealed movements and silent whispers of malicious software. They study the sequences, the steps, and the rhythms to expose the underlying intentions and secret desires of the malware, stripping it of its shrouded cloak and revealing its true nature.

This dynamic and responsive approach acts like a seasoned choreographer, learning and adapting to the ever-evolving dance of malware, witnessing its moves, its shadows, and its silent footprints. It reveals the eloquent yet deceptive dance of malware, its twists, its leaps, its undulations, outsmarting the ever-morphing polymorphic disguises and illuminating the enigma of zero-day exploits. It peers into the veiled movements and covert positions to discern the underlying patterns and hidden choreography of malicious orchestrations, enabling the defenders to counteract with synchronized precision and strategic elegance.

The harmonious equilibrium between keen observation and proactive interaction within this analytical dance enables the discerning of the discreet and clandestine intentions of the malware—unraveling the sophisticated disguises, interpreting the silent gestures, and demystifying the obscured rhythms. This method goes beyond the mere reading of musical notes on a score; it delves into understanding the emotions, the motivations, and the unseen forces driving the composition.

In essence, behavior-based malware analysis transcends the realms of static observation and reactive response, evolving into a harmonious ballet of proactive exploration and discovery. It allows the virtuosos of cybersecurity to step ahead of the beat, to anticipate the next move, and to understand the underlying rhythm of the malware dance, and in doing so, to compose countermeasures that are as fluid, as intricate, and as sophisticated as the threats they seek to neutralize. In this evolving dance between shadow and light, the nuanced interplay between analysis and action composes a harmonious ballet of resilience and adaptation, a dynamic symphony of defense in the relentless and ever-evolving battle against the myriad of cyber threats.

As we traverse the grand symphony of technological innovation interwoven with multifaceted ethical harmonies, it is vital to bear in mind that although utilizing AI for malware analysis is akin to introducing a new and promising instrument within this symphony, it does not serve as the universal remedy. AI, while resonant with potential, is still an evolving composition within the technological ensemble, with its limitations and unique rhythms that necessitate acknowledgment and understanding.

The integration of AI should be a harmonious concert with diverse analytical techniques, such as static and dynamic analysis, each contributing to a finely tuned performance of detection and protection. The symphony of malware science is an elaborate orchestration, where diverse techniques contribute distinct, irreplaceable notes, each resonating within the vast concerto of cybersecurity.

Static analysis, the meticulous scrutiny of malware codes without their execution, represents the careful examination of every note and rest within a composition, ensuring clarity and coherence. Dynamic analysis, the observation and exploration of malware behavior within a secured environment, is like watching the symphony come to life, each note interacting with the others, revealing the true nature of the composition. The automation provided by machine learning is the conductor, guiding and training models to recognize the obscure signatures and clandestine patterns of malicious concordances, orchestrating a myriad of elements into a unified, coherent performance.

Yet, amidst this technological orchestra, the human analyst stands as the composer, the irreplaceable maestro, understanding the intricate relations, the unspoken nuances, and the contextual symphonies that the machines are yet to comprehend. They bring forth insights into the unseen emotions, the unwritten subtexts, and the unplayed tones that lie beneath the visible spectrum of analysis, providing depth and context that transcend the binary limitations.

This blend of diverse analytical compositions—static, dynamic, machine learning, and human analysis—creates a harmonious and multilayered orchestra of malware science. Each component, each note, adds a layer of depth to the melody of detection and prevention, weaving together to create a complex and intricate symphony of cybersecurity. This orchestrated convergence of varied methodologies and perspectives enables the crafting of nuanced and sophisticated defense harmonies in the continuously evolving dance between innovation and ethical discernment.

In this elaborate interplay of melodies and harmonies, the continuous exploration of and adaptation to the multifaceted landscapes of cyber threats, and the ongoing dance between tradition and innovation, the symphony of malware science evolves, each note resonating with the promise of a more secure and resilient digital future. The intricate dance between diverse analytical approaches and human insights composes a living, breathing symphony, constantly evolving, constantly adapting, and rendering each movement a unique expression of the relentless pursuit of cyber resilience and digital harmony.

In the intricate and elaborate orchestration of malware science, an array of complexities play their symphonies, echoing through the vast realm of analysis and detection. Within this multifaceted concert, there exists no singular technique, no lone melody that can universally address the myriad of malware samples, each weaving its clandestine dance. The approach to unraveling and understanding them must be a harmonious symphony, meticulously blending a variety of analytical movements to accommodate the unique tempo of each malware sample and the resources available in the concert hall of cybersecurity.

The application of AI in this grand composition of malware analysis is relatively nascent, the first notes of its melody just beginning to resonate within the vast auditorium of technological possibilities. However, the revolutionary potential it harbors to transform the methods of detection and fortification against malware composes a resonant and promising overture. It stands as a formidable symphonist within the grand orchestration of cybersecurity, promising a future where the harmonies of protection and detection are more nuanced, adaptive, and resilient.

When the intelligent rhythms of AI are synchronized with other analytical compositions, such as the meticulous scrutiny of static analysis and the behavioral observations of dynamic analysis, a powerful and harmonious concerto emerges. This synergistic blend empowers organizations to craft more nuanced and responsive defense harmonies, enabling them to resonate with heightened awareness and enhanced responsiveness to the sophisticated ballets of malware attacks.

Each component in this ensemble—be it AI's evolving symphony, the unyielding echoes of static analysis, or the dynamic rhythms of behavioral analysis—brings its unique sound to the composition, adding layers of depth, texture, and nuance to the overall symphony. This orchestra of varied techniques reverberates through the realms of cyberspace, painting intricate musical narratives of defense and resilience against the sinister symphonies of malware.

Moreover, the harmonious integration of AI with these methodologies signals a hopeful crescendo in the constant battle against cyber threats, enabling the cybersecurity maestros to orchestrate innovative and adaptive countermeasures. The mutual enhancement between the components of this multifaceted orchestra allows for the creation of a resilient and enduring symphony, a symphony that safeguards our digital realms against the ever-evolving dance of malware, resonating with the enduring echoes of innovation, adaptation, and vigilance.

This fusion of melodies, harmonies, and rhythms in malware science is not merely a convergence of techniques but a continuous evolution—a harmonious dance between tradition and innovation, an ever-adaptive symphony playing in response to the clandestine concertos of the cyber adversaries. The unfolding music sheet of malware science is being written and rewritten, with new notes of wisdom, new harmonies of insights, and new rhythms of resilience added to its timeless score, echoing the unyielding human spirit in the face of evolving digital adversities.

The horizon of malware science and cybersecurity is aglow with potential and promise, echoing the harmonious symphonies of advancements and discoveries. However, this radiant future is intertwined with the essential need to address the subtle and profound ethical symphonies and challenges resonating within the rhythm of technological progress. As we stand on the threshold of uncharted territories in cybersecurity, the orchestration of ethical considerations harmonizes with the melodies of innovation, composing a symphonic narrative of responsibility and integrity.

Through concerted and harmonious collaboration, there exists a resounding hope and unwavering belief that AI can be a maestro in this grand symphony, conducting the melodies of digital safety with precision and grace. When wielded with thoughtful intent and ethical consideration, AI holds the potential to be an instrument of unprecedented good, painting the digital world with the harmonies of safety and resilience.

As we venture further into composing the intricate symphony of innovation interlaced with ethical harmonies, the confluence of AI with other analytical techniques resonates with the promise of constructing a formidable bastion against the ceaseless and ever-morphing symphonies of cyber threats. The alliance of human intuition with the tireless efficiency of AI becomes the opulent symphony, traversing the musical scores of the digital realm, and defending and protecting against the sinister harmonies of cyber adversaries.

Through meticulous composition, thoughtful integration, and global collaboration, we continue to pen the musical notes of a safer, more secure digital future. The ongoing composition of these harmonies embodies the aspirations and relentless pursuits of a global community united in its endeavor to secure the digital universe against the shadowy orchestras of cyber threats.

The symphony of cybersecurity continues to unfold its movements, echoing through the vast realms of the digital world. Every note crafted, every melody composed, and every harmony orchestrated by both human maestros and AI maestros resonate together in a concert of protection, safeguarding the intricate web of our digital existence. These harmonious resonations are a testament to our united front against cyber threats, a melody of hope and resilience, enveloping the digital realm in a protective embrace.

The future holds a luminous symphony filled with the harmonious convergence of ethics, innovation, and collaborative endeavors. It's a dance between the shadows and lights of the digital age, a timeless composition that seeks to ensure that the crescendo of our progress is attuned to the melodies of ethical integrity and mutual protection, composing a future where the digital world is a harmonious and secure space for all.

This harmonious symphony of cybersecurity, resonating with the intricate notes of innovation, ethics, and collaboration, bears witness to the boundless realms of human ingenuity and unyielding resilience. As the domains of the digital world are in constant metamorphosis, the symphony destined to protect it weaves new musical notations, embracing groundbreaking techniques, evolving technologies, and transformative insights. It is a perpetual composition, a melody in constant transformation, meandering through the ever-shifting landscapes of cyber threats and adversarial challenges.

This symphony, forever incomplete, is an ever-evolving melody adapting to the continual flux in the panorama of cyber threats, epitomizing our unrelenting and collective dedication to fortifying the complex structures of the digital universe. It's an enduring symphony that reverberates through the realms of cyberspace, resonating with the hopes and promises of constructing a future woven with safety and burgeoning resilience.

As we embark on our journey toward the uncharted territories of the future, the symphony of cybersecurity is destined to reach unprecedented crescendos of complexity and extensive reach. The harmony composed of relentless innovation, profound ethical reflections, and encompassing collaboration intricately crafts the musical score that stands as the guardian of our ever-expanding digital realm. The world, perched on the threshold of revolutionary breakthroughs, observes AI and a myriad of emerging technologies poised to transmute our perceptions and methodologies in detecting and combating the enigma of malware threats.

This perpetually evolving symphony invokes a dance of continual learning, meticulous adaptation, and cooperation—a harmonious orchestra where the delicate interplay between human sagacity and technological mastery coalesce to form a symphonic unity, reverberating through the corridors of the digital world. The maestros of human intellect and the virtuosos of technological innovation unite their talents, crafting a symphony that is both adaptive and comprehensive, painting the future with harmonious notes of protection and resilience.

In the grand scheme, every note played in this unfolding symphony is a step toward an even more resilient and secure digital realm. It's an evolving concerto of collective wisdom and collaborative efforts, echoing through the vast expanses of cyberspace, where each chord struck is a testament to our shared vision and mutual dedication to erecting fortifications around our shared digital sanctuaries. The symphonic dance of lights and shadows advances, intertwining with the pulsating rhythms of innovation and the harmonious chords of ethical considerations, shaping a score that is an emblem of our shared hopes and unwavering commitment to ensuring a safer, more secure, and enlightened digital future.

As we fix our collective gaze past the known horizons of our digital realms, the intricate symphony of cybersecurity unveils a realm where the profound harmonies of machine learning algorithms, the analytical prowess of AI-driven methodologies, and the precision of predictive modeling synchronize to conduct a symphonic assembly of unparalleled harmony and resonance. These avant-garde technologies embody the promise of forecasting and interpreting the ethereal shadows of threats even before they take corporeal form, composing a seamless and elegant defense against even the most sophisticated and meticulously orchestrated compositions of malicious design and nefarious intent.

The innovative suite of these technologies has the potential to weave a protective tapestry around our digital existence, meticulously predicting and identifying the subtlest harmonies of potential threats, thereby allowing us to strategize and formulate defenses with unprecedented foresight and precision. The melody of predictive intelligence, entwined with analytical insights, shapes a future where anticipatory defense becomes the cornerstone of cybersecurity, guarding against the unseen and the unknown, and creating a sanctuary within the intricate labyrinths of the digital sphere.

However, as we tread this uncharted symphonic journey, the path ahead is brimming with enigmatic challenges and unforeseen tribulations. The evolving complexities of the digital world and the ceaseless innovation in the realm of cyber threats demand a relentless pursuit of knowledge, adaptability, and a profound understanding of the multifaceted nature of the cyber domain. The symphonic convergence of AI and predictive technologies must continuously harmonize with the ever-transforming landscape of cyber threats, adapting and evolving to compose melodic defenses against the cacophonies of the malevolent.

The multifaceted challenges that lie ahead in this symphonic journey include ethical quandaries related to the use of AI, concerns over privacy and data integrity, and the unceasing race against the rapid evolution of malware and cyber threats. Each movement in this cybersecurity symphony necessitates meticulous composition, careful orchestration, and harmonious synchronization between varying elements to ensure the creation of a resilient and robust defensive masterpiece.

Moreover, the evolutionary leap in AI-driven strategies demands profound reflections on ethical imperatives and normative frameworks, underscoring the critical importance of maintaining a harmonious balance between technological advancements and moral considerations. It necessitates a continuous dialogue and cooperative symphony between ethicists, technologists, and policymakers to craft a future where the ethical dimensions of AI are not only recognized but are integral components of its development and deployment.

In this continual symphonic composition of future cybersecurity, every note of innovation must resonate with ethical clarity, every chord of progress must be in harmonious alignment with moral values, and every crescendo of advancement must echo with the timeless values of humanity and an unswerving commitment to the collective good of the digital world and beyond. The seamless ballet of machine learning, AI, and predictive modeling must, therefore, dance in harmonious alignment with the enduring principles of ethics and humanity, forging a future that is not only secure but also equitable, just, and reflective of our shared human values.

The moral and ethical conundrums interlaced within the detailed tapestry of AI-assisted cybersecurity echo the complexities of a meticulously composed symphony, each presenting its array of intricate harmonies and delicate nuances. These ethical dialogues resonate with concerns surrounding the inherent biases within AI models, the ominous potential for malevolent utilization, and profound questions regarding responsibility and the transparency of algorithmic decisions, urging us to navigate this harmonious symphony with circumspection and ethical vigilance.

Just as a maestro meticulously balances each instrument's unique voice, harmonizing them into a coherent, symphonic whole, the incorporation of AI into the landscape of cybersecurity necessitates a rigorous calibration and ethical contemplation to ensure its resonance with society's moral compass and ethical dimensions. This harmonious fusion between technology and morality demands continuous reflection and meticulous consideration to craft a future where technological advancements synchronize seamlessly with the foundational ethical principles of our societies.

In this boundless arena of international harmonization, the symphonic dance of cybersecurity perpetually evolves, with nations and institutions intertwining their efforts, crafting harmonious melodies to counteract the inherently transnational temperament of cyber threats. Historical resonances have illustrated the unyielding strength of unity and cooperative harmonies in the face of multitudinous adversities, and the future holds the symphonic promise of a fortified architecture of global collaboration. International treaties, agreements, and accords will persist in sculpting the terrains of our collective future, fostering an environment conducive to intelligence sharing, resource pooling, and strategic harmonization, all aimed at orchestrating a digitally secure and ethically sound global landscape.

This global symphonic collaboration weaves a tapestry of mutual trust and shared responsibility, enabling nations to echo their collective symphonies against the multifarious and constantly evolving threats in the cybersphere. It is through this harmonious convergence of ethics, international collaboration, and technological innovation that the future symphony of cybersecurity will be orchestrated, where the harmonious balance of instruments—each representing distinct nations, organizations, and individuals—will render a united and resonant melody of security, ethical integrity, and shared commitment to preserving the sanctity of our interconnected digital existence.

The endeavor into the realm of topology data analysis parallels the unearthing of novel, intricate instruments, each contributing to broadening the symphonic range and tonal richness of the cybersecurity orchestration. Each network node and singular data point interwoven into this tapestry of analysis engenders a more nuanced and harmonically rich melody of insights. It's akin to the acquisition of new, uncharted symphonic movements, each one unraveling deeper layers of understanding about the multifarious orchestrations of cyber threats and their clandestine maneuvers within the digital concertos.

With every progression in this analytical symphony, each nuanced element reveals a fragment of the overarching melody, allowing for a more profound exploration into the labyrinthine compositions of cyber threats. These nuanced insights are comparable to the subtle harmonies and intricate rhythms that enrich a musical piece, offering a multifaceted perspective into the cybernetic dance of offense and defense, allowing us to perceive the delicate interplays and covert dialogues within the digital ether.

As our proficiency in deciphering these multifarious cyber compositions evolves and our understanding of this complex symphony matures, the defenders of the cyber realm find themselves armed with a more refined and diverse arsenal of analytical instruments. These newly acquired tools enable the meticulous dissection of the covert symphonies of malevolent intent, allowing for the pre-emptive disruption of cyberattacks and thereby safeguarding systems that stand vulnerable to the concealed harmonies of digital antagonists.

This advancement in our analytical capabilities, underscored by the enriched symphonic insights provided by topology data analysis, marks a significant leap in the ongoing symphonic battle within the digital realm. It amplifies the resonant melodies of protection and fortification, enabling the orchestrators of cyber defense to craft more refined and anticipatory measures, ensuring the harmonious integrity of our digital symphony remains undisturbed by the discordant echoes of cyber malfeasance.

In essence, the exploration of topology data analysis introduces a wealth of novel symphonic elements and harmonious nuances, each contributing to the elevation of our collective symphony of cybersecurity. It bestows upon us a more intricate and nuanced understanding of the silent compositions of cyber threats, allowing the defenders to play a more anticipatory, harmonious counterpoint to the hidden symphonies of the cyber assailants, fortifying the digital concert hall against the unseen orchestrations of the malicious maestros.

In envisioning the crescendo of this grand symphony, we witness a profound confluence of human insight and machine intelligence, harmonizing in a composition so breathtaking that it seems to transcend the boundaries of our digital cosmos. The inception of AI marks not just the inclusion of a new instrumental voice, but the advent of a revolutionary era in cybersecurity—a transformative period where the harmonious interplay between man and machine becomes the cornerstone of our digital fortifications.

The machine learning algorithms within this orchestral convergence serve as the tireless virtuosos, traversing the extensive terrains of data landscapes, extracting patterns and harmonies that are far too subtle and intricate for the human mind to perceive. Their unceasing scrutiny of sprawling datasets echoes the relentless pursuit of an instrumentalist mastering their craft, identifying subtle nuances and unprecedented patterns, and painting a complex melody of interconnected insights.

Yet, within this intricate symphony, the human expert remains the eminent conductor, wielding the baton that guides this multifaceted, AI-powered orchestra through the myriad movements of the cybersecurity symphony. It is the human maestro who infuses life into the orchestra, interpreting the voluminous outputs of AI, lending profound context and interpretative depth to the machine-generated melodies, and shaping the musical dialogue between the contrasting voices within the symphonic narrative.

This human element serves as the guiding beacon, deciphering the intricate symphonies rendered by AI and transforming the rhythmic patterns and harmonic sequences into coherent, actionable insights. The human conductor elucidates the enigmatic compositions of AI, rendering the often abstract symphonies into tangible harmonies of understanding and allowing the grand ensemble to resonate with unparalleled clarity and coherence.

Furthermore, the human maestro orchestrates the dynamic interplay between various AI instrumentalists, ensuring a balanced and harmonious execution of the symphonic piece and fine-tuning the ensemble to resonate with the overarching thematic essence of the cybersecurity narrative. It is this symphonic partnership, this harmonious confluence of human intuition and machine precision, that brings forth a crescendo so monumental that it reverberates through the annals of cyber defense, marking a pivotal moment in the evolution of our collective symphony.

As we reflect on this momentous climax within the symphony, the fusion of human sagacity and artificial prowess emerges as the magnum opus of our times, creating a harmonious tapestry of resilience and innovation. It represents a symphonic dialogue between tradition and transformation, echoing the eternal dance between human essence and technological transcendence, and crafting a resonant legacy for the future generations of the digital symphony.

Amidst the intricate symphonic dance of codes and encryptions, the profound technique of behavior-based malware analysis emerges into the limelight, orchestrating a pivotal movement within our evolving composition. Much like a meticulous choreographer deciphering the nuanced pirouettes within a labyrinth of ones and zeros, this sophisticated approach unravels the underlying narratives of malware, delving deep into its intrinsic movements and unveiling its stealthy choreography.

Understanding the balletic symphony of malicious intent and actions, this approach allows security maestros to not only decipher but also counterbalance the rhythm and flow of this malevolent dance. These experts choreograph an elaborate suite of countermeasures designed to seamlessly intercept and disrupt the advancing threats in the midst of their calculated performance, effectively rewriting their intended narratives and transforming their destructive harmonies into echoes of thwarted ambitions.

Through this detailed exploration of the unique dance of malware, security connoisseurs comprehend the sophisticated choreography of malicious software, meticulously crafting defenses that mirror the elegance and precision of balletic maneuvers, and ensuring the delicate balance within the cyber symphony remains undisturbed by the discordant notes of malicious entities.

And thus, as we draw the curtains on our journey through the resounding symphony of malware science and cybersecurity, the enduring melody—imbued with resilience, innovation, and harmony—continues to resonate through the infinite expanse of the digital cosmos. It echoes beyond the confines of these words into an ever-evolving universe where the malevolent dance of threats continually morphs and where our harmonious defenses adapt and transcend, painting the canvas of the digital world with intricate strokes of security and innovation.

This harmonious prelude to the future symphony of cybersecurity serves not only as a reflection of our relentless spirit of innovation and unwavering pursuit of knowledge, but also as a living embodiment of our collective resolve and commitment to safeguarding the vast terrains of the digital scape. It is a symphonic tapestry that weaves the essence of human resilience and collective vigilance, creating a resonant piece that echoes the promise of a future where the boundless realms of cyberspace are protected by a united front—a harmonious alliance between human intellect and technological prowess, ever-vigilant against the shadows lurking within the symphonic dance of the digital world.

As the harmonious echoes of the symphony resonate through the boundless expanses of the digital universe, it stands as an enduring reminder that, although the melodies evolve and the rhythms transform, the foundational principles reverberate with unyielding constancy—a steadfast commitment to fortifying the myriad corridors of the digital domain, a relentless quest for unveiling the unknown realms of knowledge, and a symphonic unity emerging from the intricate dance between human innovation and the relentless march of technological evolution.

Much akin to the revered composers and illustrious conductors who, with each stroke of the baton, refine and redefine their celestial compositions, shaping each note, each harmony to perfection, the realm of cybersecurity, too, is continually honing its myriad strategies, its diverse melodies, and its intricate harmonies, orchestrating a future where the harmonious strains of security echo through every corner of our increasingly interconnected digital world.

In this relentless pursuit of harmonic equilibrium, the field of cybersecurity diligently crafts and recrafts its approaches, adjusting the tempos, modulating the harmonies, and infusing innovative rhythms to create a magnum opus that endeavors to encapsulate the essence of safety and resilience within the echoing chambers of our digital existence. Each adaptation, each recalibration, is a conscientious step toward creating a symphonic masterpiece that resonates with the aspirations of a secure and enlightened digital future.

As the metaphorical curtains draw to a close and the light dims on our collective presence on this metaphysical stage, the echoing symphony persists—its multifaceted notes resonating through the vastness, and each harmonic vibration standing as a timeless testament to our unwavering resilience, our boundless creativity, and our indomitable spirit in navigating the ever-evolving labyrinth of challenges and mysteries.

The symphony, ever-evolving, becomes a living, breathing entity—its pulsating rhythms a reflection of our continual evolution, its resounding crescendos a depiction of our triumphant breakthroughs, and its soothing adagios a serene representation of our unbroken unity and collective resolve. In this grand dance of harmonies and melodies, the echoes of our shared endeavors and aspirations continue to resonate, painting the infinite canvas of the cosmos with the vibrant hues of our unwavering hope, relentless pursuit of excellence, and the eternal symphony of shared dreams and unified visions.

Appendix

1. Kaspersky, *A Brief History of Malware*

2. Accenture. (2017). *The Cost of Cybercrime Study*

3. Ahern, D. M., Clouse, A., & Turner, R. (2004). *CMMI distilled: A practical introduction to integrated process improvement (3rd ed.). Addison-Wesley.*

4. Argentina National Ministry of Security. (2019). *Informe de Ciberdelito*

5. Atlantic Council. (2020). *Breaking trust: Shades of crisis across an insecure software supply chain*

6. Bendich, P., Marron, J. S., Miller, E., Pieloch, A., & Skwerer, S. (2016). *Persistent homology analysis of brain artery trees. Annals of Applied Statistics, 10 (1).*

7. Brundage, et al. (2018). *The Malicious Use of Artificial Intelligence: Forecasting, Prevention, and Mitigation*

8. Buczak, Anna L. and Erhan Guven. (2016). *A Survey of Data Mining and Machine Learning Methods for Cyber Security Intrusion Detection, IEEE Communications Surveys & Tutorials*

9. Buczak, Anna L. and Erhan Guven. (2016). *A Survey of Data Mining and Machine Learning Methods for Cyber Security Intrusion Detection, IEEE Communications Surveys & Tutorials*

10. California Consumer Privacy Act (CCPA)

11. Carlsson, G. (2009). *Topology and data. Bulletin of the American Mathematical Society, 46(2), 255-308.*

12. Chazal, F., & Michel, B. (2017). *An introduction to Topological Data Analysis: fundamental and practical aspects for data scientists. arXiv preprint arXiv:1710.04019.*

13. Chesney, Robert and Danielle Citron. (2019). *Deep Fakes: A Looming Challenge for Privacy, Democracy, and National Security*, California Law Review

14. CMMI Institute.

15. CNN. (2020). *Las Vegas School District Hit by Ransomware Attack*

16. Coveware. (2021). *Q4 2020 Ransomware Marketplace Report*

17. CSO Magazine: *The 10 most powerful cybersecurity companies.*

18. Cybereason. (2020). *Ransomware Year-in-Review: 2020*

19. Cybersecurity Ventures. (2019). *2019 Official Annual Cybercrime Report*

20. Cybersecurity Ventures. (2019). *Global Ransomware Damage Costs Predicted To Reach $20 Billion (USD) By 2021*

21. Cybersecurity Ventures. (2021). *Cybersecurity Jobs Report*

22. Edelsbrunner, H., & Harer, J. (2008). *Persistent homology – a survey. Contemporary mathematics, 453, 257-282.*

23. Edelsbrunner, H., Letscher, D., & Zomorodian, A. (2002). *Topological persistence and simplification. Discrete and computational geometry, 28(4), 511-533.*

24. Emsisoft. (2020). *The Cost of Ransomware in 2021: A Country-by-Country Analysis*

25. Gartner. (2021). *Gartner Forecasts Worldwide Security and Risk Management Spending to Reach $150.4 Billion in 2022*

26. General Data Protection Regulation (GDPR)

27. Giusti, C., Ghrist, R., & Bassett, D. S. (2016). *Two's company, three (or more) is a simplex. Journal of computational neuroscience, 41(1), 1-14.*

28. Harary, F., & Palmer, E. M. (1973). *Graphical enumeration (Vol. 62). Elsevier.*

29. Hiscox. (2020). *Hiscox Cyber Readiness Report 2020*

30. IBM Security. (2020). *Cost of a Data Breach Report 2020*

31. IBM Security. (2020). *Cost of a Data Breach Report 2020*

32. Kaspersky. (2020), *Kaspersky Security Bulletin 2020. Statistics*

33. Kotter, J. P. (1996). *Leading Change. Harvard Business School Press.*

34. Maletic, J. I., & Marcus, A. (2000, May). *Data cleansing: Beyond integrity analysis. In Conference on Information Quality (pp. 200-209).*

35. McAfee & Center for Strategic and International Studies. (2018), *Economic Impact of Cybercrime – No Slowing Down*

36. Mitnick, Kevin. (2017). *The Art of Invisibility*, Little, Brown and Company

37. NPR. (2020). *Ransomware Attack Hits Universal Health Services*

38. OECD. (2014). *Risks and Returns: Managing Risk for Development*

39. OECD. (2014). *Risks and Returns: Managing Risk for Development*

40. Ponemon Institute. (2018). *2018 State of Cybersecurity in Small & Medium Size Businesses*

41. Proofpoint. (2021). *State of the Phish*

42. Protenus. (2017). *Breach Barometer*

43. Raff, et al. (2015) *Learning the PE Header, Malware Detection with Minimal Domain Knowledge, ACM Conference on Data and Application Security and Privacy*

44. Raff, et al. (2015). *Learning the PE Header, Malware Detection with Minimal Domain Knowledge, ACM Conference on Data and Application Security and Privacy*

45. Robert Half 2022 Salary Guide. `https://www.roberthalf.com/salary-guide`

46. San Francisco Examiner. (2016). *SF Muni hacker hit others by scanning for year-old Java vulnerability*

47. Seqrite. (2019). *Seqrite Quarterly Threat Report Q3 2019*

48. Serianu. (2018). *Africa Cyber Security Report*

49. SonicWall. (2021). *2021 SonicWall Cyber Threat Report*

50. Symantec. (2020). *Internet Security Threat Report*

51. Szor, Peter. *The Art of Computer Virus Research and Defense.* Addison-Wesley Professional, 2005

52. The Commission on the Theft of American Intellectual Property. (2017). *The Theft of American Intellectual Property: Reassessments of the Challenge and United States Policy*

53. The Hindu BusinessLine. (2019). *Ransomware Attacks Caused Indian Businesses Potential Loss of Over $4 Billion in H1 2019: Seqrite*

54. The IP Commission. (2017). *The Theft of American Intellectual Property: Reassessments of the Challenge and United States Policy*

55. The New York Times. (2017). *A Cyberattack the World Isn't Ready For*

56. The New York Times. (2020). *First Death Reported in a Cyberattack*

57. Training Magazine's 2021 Training Industry Report

58. U.S. Federal Trade Commission. (2020). *FTC Report Examines Cybersecurity Practices of Seven Internet Service Providers*

59. U.S. Small Business Administration Office of Advocacy. (2019). *Small Business GDP, 1998-2014*

60. World Economic Forum. (2020). *Understanding the Impact of a Cyberattack*

61. ZDNET. (2019). *Brazilian energy company suffers ransomware attack*

62. Zetter, Kim. *Countdown to Zero Day: Stuxnet and the Launch of the World's First Digital Weapon.* Crown, 2014

Index

Packtpub.com

Subscribe to our online digital library for full access to over 7,000 books and videos, as well as industry leading tools to help you plan your personal development and advance your career. For more information, please visit our website.

Why subscribe?

- Spend less time learning and more time coding with practical eBooks and Videos from over 4,000 industry professionals

- Improve your learning with Skill Plans built especially for you

- Get a free eBook or video every month

- Fully searchable for easy access to vital information

- Copy and paste, print, and bookmark content

Did you know that Packt offers eBook versions of every book published, with PDF and ePub files available? You can upgrade to the eBook version at packtpub.com and as a print book customer, you are entitled to a discount on the eBook copy. Get in touch with us at customercare@packtpub.com for more details.

At www.packtpub.com, you can also read a collection of free technical articles, sign up for a range of free newsletters, and receive exclusive discounts and offers on Packt books and eBooks.

Other Books You May Enjoy

If you enjoyed this book, you may be interested in these other books by Packt:

Linux for System Administrators

Viorel Rudareanu, Daniil Baturin

ISBN: 978-1-80324-794-6

- Master the use of the command line and adeptly manage software packages
- Manage users and groups locally or by using centralized authentication
- Set up, diagnose, and troubleshoot Linux networks
- Understand how to choose and manage storage devices and filesystems
- Implement enterprise features such as high availability and automation tools
- Pick up the skills to keep your Linux system secure

Cloud Penetration Testing

Kim Crawley

ISBN: 978-1-80324-848-6

- Familiarize yourself with the evolution of cloud networks
- Navigate and secure complex environments that use more than one cloud service
- Conduct vulnerability assessments to identify weak points in cloud configurations
- Secure your cloud infrastructure by learning about common cyber attack techniques
- Explore various strategies to successfully counter complex cloud attacks
- Delve into the most common AWS, Azure, and GCP services and their applications for businesses
- Understand the collaboration between red teamers, cloud administrators, and other stakeholders for cloud pentesting

Packt is searching for authors like you

If you're interested in becoming an author for Packt, please visit `authors.packtpub.com` and apply today. We have worked with thousands of developers and tech professionals, just like you, to help them share their insight with the global tech community. You can make a general application, apply for a specific hot topic that we are recruiting an author for, or submit your own idea.

Share Your Thoughts

Now you've finished *Data Science for Malware Analysis*, we'd love to hear your thoughts! Scan the QR code below to go straight to the Amazon review page for this book and share your feedback or leave a review on the site that you purchased it from.

https://packt.link/r/1804618640

Your review is important to us and the tech community and will help us make sure we're delivering excellent quality content.

Download a free PDF copy of this book

Thanks for purchasing this book!

Do you like to read on the go but are unable to carry your print books everywhere?

Is your eBook purchase not compatible with the device of your choice?

Don't worry, now with every Packt book you get a DRM-free PDF version of that book at no cost.

Read anywhere, any place, on any device. Search, copy, and paste code from your favorite technical books directly into your application.

The perks don't stop there, you can get exclusive access to discounts, newsletters, and great free content in your inbox daily

Follow these simple steps to get the benefits:

1. Scan the QR code or visit the link below

https://packt.link/free-ebook/9781804618646

2. Submit your proof of purchase
3. That's it! We'll send your free PDF and other benefits to your email directly

www.ingramcontent.com/pod-product-compliance
Lightning Source LLC
Chambersburg PA
CBHW080523060326
40690CB00022B/5007